Use of Co-operative Logos - Important Disclaimer Statement

All cover logos and logos found within serve to illustrate the diversity of co-operative organizations globally, but do not in any way constitute formal or otherwise any endorsement by the logo owners of the content provided within this publication. All logos used are readily found within the public domain.

CO-OPERATIVE ENTERPRISE
BUILDING A BETTER WORLD
Copyright ©2013 Global Co-operative Development Group, Inc.
ISBN 978-1622874-01-9 PRINT
ISBN 978-1622-874-00-2 EBOOK

LCCN 2013949638

September 2013

Published and Distributed by
First Edition Design Publishing, Inc.
P.O. Box 20217, Sarasota, FL 34276-3217
www.firsteditiondesignpublishing.com

ALL RIGHTS RESERVED. No part of this book publication may be reproduced, stored in a retrieval system, or transmitted in any form or by any means — electronic, mechanical, photo-copy, recording, or any other — except brief quotation in reviews, without the prior permission of the author or publisher.

Co-operative Enterprise

Building a Better World

© Global Co-operative Development Group Inc. 2013

Terry MacDonald

Gregory Wallace

Ian MacPherson

Contents

PART ONE - SETTING THE STAGE 1

Chapter One - The Nature of Co-operation: Competition, Conflict, and Co-operation 3

In The Beginning..3

Darwin and Spencer on Survival 3

Kropotkin Discovers Mutual Aid 4

Morris Looks at Monkey Business and Human Behavior..5

Craig's Take on Co-operation, Competition, and Conflict 7

Benkler's Boost - Co-operation Triumphs Over Self-Interest 11

Craig's Conditions for Contractual Co-operation 14

Take Aways 15

Chapter Two - From People's Movements to Co-operative Systems of Enterprise...............17

People's Movements 17

Co-operation as a Social Movement 19

Co-operatives as Systems of Enterprise..21

Movements and Systems as Opposite Sides of the Coin 23

Co-operative Movements and Systems around the World 25

Some Co-operative Systems of Enterprise..26

Take Aways 32

PART TWO – HOW CO-OPERATIVES ARE DIFFERENT 33

Chapter Three - The Co-operative Value Proposition 35

Making the Case..35

The Co-operative Enterprise Business Model...35

Co-operative Principles and Values 38

The Importance of Purpose in a Co-operative..40

How Co-operatives Create Value 42

Co-operatives and the Pursuit of Peace..45

United Nations Declares 2012 the International Year of Co-operatives 46

Not Going Away Anytime Soon...46

Tangible and Intangible Benefits and Contributions 47

    Take Aways 48

Chapter Four - The Public, Private, and Co-operative Sectors 49

    An Orange is not an Apple or a Pear 49

    Organizational Dynamics 49

    Some Early Illustrations and Comparisons 59

    Take Aways 63

Chapter Five - Leadership and Management Effectiveness in Co-operatives 65

    Managing the Co-operative Difference 65

    First Things First 66

    Mind the Gap 67

    Where and How Co-operatives Come In 68

    What Co-operative Leaders Must Do 70

    Co-operative Enterprise Sustainability 75

    Putting the Pieces Together 78

    Take Aways 81

PART THREE - CO-OPERATIVES TODAY 83

Chapter Six - National and International Co-operative Development 85

    Overview 85

    Types of Co-operatives 85

    Co-operative Structures 87

    Some Co-operative Statistical Highlights 93

    Co-operatives and the Global Economy 99

    Co-operatives Celebrate Financial Success 101

    Take Aways 102

Chapter Seven - Wealth Creation, Community Development, and Poverty Reduction 103

    Connecting the Dots 103

    Co-operatives and Wealth Creation 104

    Co-operative Ownership and Control of Financial Resources 109

    Co-operatives and Community Development 111

    Co-operatives Create and Maintain Employment 115

    Co-operatives and Poverty Reduction 116

    Co-operative Agents Support International Co-operative Development 117

Other Groups or Agencies Supporting Co-operative Development 120

Co-operatives are Not a Quick Fix 121

Take Aways 121

Chapter Eight - The Pivotal Role of Government in Enabling Co-operative Development 123

Creating Legislation 123

Co-operative Law - The World Over 124

Co-operative Law in Development Settings 126

Co-operatives in Western Settings 129

Alignment, Non-alignment, or Other 130

To Tax or Not to Tax - That is the Question! 132

How Governments Can Enable Co-operative Development 133

What Co-operatives Can and Should Do 134

The Next Decade 136

Take Aways 137

PART FOUR - BUILDING A BETTER WORLD 139

Chapter Nine - Some Strategies and Tactics for Success 141

Starting Co-operatives for the Right Reasons 141

Creating Communities of Support 142

Building Financial Strength 145

Successes Far Outweigh Failures 150

Beware Also Means Be Aware 151

A Good Idea Until Properly Planted Can Not Produce 152

Take Aways 152

Chapter Ten - Towards a World Vision for Co-operatives 155

The Battle of Ideas: Taking Ideology to the Next Level 155

So What Is A Muddle? 158

The Biggest Problem in the World 160

Building a Better World 163

Take Aways 164

Chapter Eleven - The Opportunities and Challenges Ahead 167

Moving Forward 167

Blueprint for a Co-operative Decade 167

    Three Key Questions 172

    Strategic Focus Areas 175

    Thinking Outside of the Box 176

    Some Next Steps 179

    Take Aways 180

PART FIVE – EVERYTHING ELSE CO-OPERATIVE 181

Chapter Twelve - Some Sources, Resources, and Postscripts 183

    Sources and Resources 183

        How to Start a Co-operative 183

        Popular Co-operative Magazines, Books, and e-Books 184

        Co-operative Games and Exercises 185

        More Links to Co-operative Sources and Resources 185

        Social Media and Co-operatives 186

        The Top Level Domain Name ".coop" 186

        Global Co-operative Development Group Inc. 187

        Co-operative Friends and Supporters 187

Post Script to Co-operative Enterprise 189

Biographies 191

Index 193

Notes 201

INTRODUCTION AND ACKNOWLEDGEMENTS

Introduction

Have you ever walked or driven past a business that included the word 'co-operative' in its signage? If you are like most people you are probably familiar with what the business does and so you never bother to give it a second thought. Maybe you have dealt at a credit union for most of your financial affairs, but didn't realize that it was also a co-operative. That fact is co-operative organizations can be found almost everywhere in the world - from artisan co-operatives, to fair trade producer and marketing co-operatives, to service utilities like electricity co-operatives, to housing co-operatives, to worker co-operatives where employees own their factories, to consumer co-operatives that sell groceries and fresh produce, to farmers' co-operatives that supply gasoline and agricultural products, even to health and funeral co-operatives. The list of types of co-operatives is almost endless. However, you may be surprised to learn that each of these organizations is structured quite differently from other forms of enterprise; that they operate democratically, are successful financially, and are concerned for the community or communities in which they exist. Each of them, whether they are large or small, young or older, share similar values and principles.

The purpose of this book is to introduce you in considerable detail to what we call the 'co-operative enterprise', and to explore with you the broader question of why co-operatives are important in today's world. This is not a "how to" book, in the normal sense. It is however (we hope) an excellent foundation upon which to broaden your understanding and appreciation of co-operative forms of enterprise, not only in your country - but around the globe. You will learn why co-operation works and also see why sometimes it may not work, and you will learn about best practices and success factors within co-operatives. If you are an employee, a manager, or an elected official within a co-operative, you will also learn about why and how leadership and management effectiveness are different in co-operative forms of enterprise.

The book is divided into five parts. The first part is called **"Setting the Stage"**, and contains two chapters. The first chapter introduces the reader to the nature of co-operation, while the second chapter looks at the evolution of co-operation all the way from social movements to business systems of enterprise. The second part is entitled **"How Co operatives Are Different"** and begins by presenting what we call the "co-operative value proposition". The third and fourth chapters provide details on the difference between the co-operative sector, the private sector, and the public sector. Chapter Five describes why and how leadership and management effectiveness are different in a co-operative. The third part is entitled **"Co-operatives Today"** and it includes three chapters. Chapter Six describes "National and International Co-operative Development", and Chapter Seven looks at the role co-operatives have played and are playing in "Wealth Creation, Community Development ,and Poverty Reduction" around the globe. The last chapter in this section describes the "Pivotal Role for Government in Enabling Development." Part Four is entitled **"Building a Better World"** and it includes three chapters. The first chapter, Chapter Nine is entitled "Some Strategies and Tactics for Success". Chapter Ten is entitled **"Towards a World Vision for Co-operatives"**. Chapter Eleven is **"The Challenges and Opportunities Ahead"**, and it invites and challenges readers - and all co-operators - to seriously imagine what the future might be for co-operative forms of enterprise. No small undertaking to be sure!

Just for fun we have included a final part called **"Everything Else Co-operative"** into which we cram additional co-operative website links and interesting content which we think you might like and which didn't exactly seem to fit anywhere else. You decide! We also include some of our parting after thoughts (post scripts) in this section.

You are also invited to use the internet to explore our website and to link into the big wide world of co-operative enterprise. You can click on www.co-operativeenterprise.coop . We are not expecting to be too overwhelmed, and so we will be pleased to respond to your comments and your inquiries.

Acknowledgements

This book was written by three members of the Global Co-operative Development Group Inc., together with the assistance and support of numerous other experienced co-operators, researchers, advocates, and educators from around the world. It is perhaps equally important to acknowledge that the initial inspiration to write this book came from many individuals who have thought long and taught much about co-operatives, co-operative movements and co-operation, but we want especially to recognize the contributions of a long time co-operator and educator named Jack Craig, also known as the author John G. Craig, formerly a professor from York University in Toronto Canada. He and other supporters and contributors like John Jordan are described in more detail in the "Co-operative Friends and Supporters" section in Chapter Twelve and at the end of this publication. We are especially appreciative of the general editing and other support provided by Joan MacDonald, and the professional editing and support provided by Joy Emmanuel. We also wish to acknowledge our graphics consultant David Yett.

Finally, it is important to acknowledge that co-operative organizations, which one can find all around the world today, only exist because of the one billion or so individual people who are their members and who see co-operative forms of enterprise as a better way of doing business than had existed previously.

Ian MacPherson, President
Greg Wallace, Director and Secretary-Treasurer
Terry MacDonald, Managing Director

Global Co-operative Development Group Inc.
Summer 2013

PART ONE - SETTING THE STAGE

Understanding Co-operation

Chapter One - The Nature of Co-operation: Competition, Conflict, and Co-operation

In The Beginning

We think there probably are as many definitions and examples of co-operation as there are versions of dictionaries. To start, we will simply use the definition that 'co-operation is working together to achieve an end".

Even using that simple definition there is a lot to be said about the notion of co-operation, and there is even a myth to be laid bare and a few surprises to be unearthed.

There are some people who assume 'competition' is simply the opposite of 'co-operation'. This is unfortunate and inaccurate. In part, this may be based upon the economic notion that capitalism somehow takes competition as its principal element, and socialism somehow takes co-operation as its principal element. In our experience, using rhetorical associations and misusing or mixing of the terms does little to explain the more important concept of co-operation and the various relationships co-operation has to both competition and conflict. In this section, we shall attempt to avoid overused clichés and political innuendos, and instead provide a more in-depth review of co-operation as well as competition and its angry cousin, conflict.

We will begin with Charles Darwin and Herbert Spencer and look at how the notion of 'survival of the fittest' came into use. We will continue by looking at co-operation amongst animals, and amongst people in the early 1900s, as did the famous writer and researcher Peter Kropotkin. Kropotkin was familiar with Darwin's work, but found it lacking when applied to human circumstance. We will then look at the findings of Desmond Morris, a world renowned zoologist / anthropologist of the late 1960s and 70s who considered how animals and humans co-operate and compete. Next we will look carefully at the findings of Jack Craig, a professor of sociology and a co-operative practitioner who, after years of study, published his findings concerning the nature of co-operation in the 1970s and 80s. We will conclude by sharing the findings and claims of contemporary Harvard University professor and researcher Yochai Benkler.

Darwin and Spencer on Survival

Most people alive today will have heard about Charles Darwin's Theory of Natural Selection,[1] which later he and Herbert Spencer referred to as the "survival of the fittest" theory.[2] Much of Darwin's work and writings took place between 1855 and 1865. Since then, the catchy but inaccurate phrase "survival of the fittest" has been repeated millions of times by people around the world. While the original expression referred specifically to the biological evolution of non-human species over time, it soon came into common use as a simple explanation for the wide variances in human prosperity and well-being. The notion at the time was that somehow the disparities in wealth were simply nature's way for organizing affairs within a competitive world. Darwin's primary thesis, which was that the adaptiveness of a species was a principle basis for its survival, was for the most part ignored.[3] Darwin's related point, that social organization and specifically social habits played an important role in the adaptiveness of a species, was not until later considered to be of any significance. As we shall illustrate, the adaptiveness and thus the survival of the human race is achieved not only through competition but also through collaboration and its more complex sister, co-operation.

Kropotkin Discovers Mutual Aid

Peter Kropotkin made extensive investigation into what he termed 'mutual aid', which involved people helping people to better themselves and their lives. However, Kropotkin did not just look around at how people were helping others and themselves. He carried out what was at that time (the end of the 19th century) the most extensive work ever undertaken on the topic. Although his research had taken place some few years earlier, Kropotkin first published a series of essays in the British monthly literary magazine *Nineteenth Century* between 1890-96.[4] His full book, entitled *Mutual Aid: A Factor of Evolution*, was published in 1902.[5]

Kropotkin describes at length how institutions in France, Russia, England, and throughout the world from Roman times until his time have acted to weaken or to eliminate people uniting or working together to help themselves. Nevertheless,

> **The mutual-aid tendency in man has so remote an origin, and is so deeply interwoven with all the past evolution of the human race, that it has been maintained by mankind up to the present time, notwithstanding all vicissitudes of history. It was chiefly evolved during periods of peace and prosperity, but became most important when even the greatest calamities befell humankind -- when whole countries were laid waste by wars, and whole populations were decimated by misery, or groaned under the yoke of tyranny -- the same tendency continued to live in the villages and among the poorer classes in the towns; it still kept them together, and in the long run it reacted even upon those ruling, fighting, and devastating minorities which dismissed it as sentimental nonsense. And whenever mankind had to work out a new social organization, adapted to a new phase of development, its constructive genius always drew the elements and the inspiration for the new departure from that same ever-living tendency.**[6]

Kropotkin's examples of co-operation and mutual aid at the turn of the century are extensive and varied, and begin in the animal world which includes the behavior of ducks and sparrow, land-crabs and bees, and ants and wolves, to name just a few. Using literally hundreds of detailed examples of human individuals and groups, he describes seamen helping those drowning; miners helping to rescue miners in distress; plus all manner of human organizations including guilds, unions, local societies, alliances, and clubs. All such groups are formed by people for their own benefit or for mutual benefit, but organized voluntarily with a common goal or goals in mind.

While a proponent of co-operative effort, Kropotkin also acknowledges that individual initiative plays an important role parallel to co-operative initiative.

> **It will probably be remarked that mutual aid, even though it may represent one of the factors of evolution, covers nevertheless one aspect only of human relations; that by the side of this current, powerful though it may be, there is, and always has been, the other current -- the self-assertion of the individual, not only in its efforts to attain personal or caste superiority, economic, political, and spiritual, but also in its much more important although less evident function of breaking through the bonds, always prone to become crystallized, which the tribe, the village community, the city, and the State impose upon the individual. In other words, there is the self-assertion of the individual taken as a progressive element.[7]**

Korpotkin's view was that in society individuals who are able to assert themselves and succeed should be recognized as being assertive and successful. It is clear that Kropotkin felt strongly that similar recognition should be accorded for instances of successful co-operative effort and mutual aid, since historically such efforts had often been condemned or ignored. His call for equal recognition for successful co-operative initiatives might still be made in many places in the world today. Kropotkin's research added ferment to the development of early co-operative thought not only in Russia, but also in Switzerland, France, England, and Canada.

Kropotkin's book, which to this day is available for purchase on Amazon.com and has a 5 star rating,[8] drew on his experiences gathered across Europe and his knowledge of the larger world to illustrate the phenomenon of co-operation. After examining the evidence of co-operation in animals, in pre-feudal societies, in medieval cities, and in modern times, he concluded that co-operation (working together) and mutual aid (the act of helping each other) were the most important factors in the evolution of any species and its ability to survive.[9] Further, it was Kropotkin's firm belief that besides what he referred to as the law of mutual struggle, there is in nature the law of mutual aid, which, for the progressive evolution of any species, is far more important than the law of mutual contest.[10] Although now more than 100 years hence, these are by no means small conclusions for us to contemplate considering the overall state of the world we are living in today.

Morris Looks at Monkey Business and Human Behavior

Desmond Morris, who refers to himself as a zoologist, indicates it is fair game for him to describe what he sees and knows about the naked ape. His book *The Naked Ape* was first published in 1967 and was translated into 23 different languages.[11] It too is still available for purchase today. Morris begins by stating that there are one hundred and ninety-three living species of monkeys and apes. One hundred and ninety-two of them are covered with hair. The exception is a naked ape self-named Homo sapiens. His entire analysis revolves around the way apes behave and the way humans behave. Morris looks in detail at ape and human behavior related to sex, rearing, exploration, fighting, feeding and comfort. Morris describes in some considerable detail how the 192 non-human species of apes and monkeys have adapted and succeeded by using co-operative behavior, whether it was in hunting and rearing their young or defending against attack.[12] Similar behavior was also evident throughout eons in human development. For example, hunting and gathering have always been done in groups for both security and for efficiency reasons.

What Morris illustrates in his comparisons of apes and human development is the importance of social and power relations in groups and tribes. Culture and norms can be important factors in group and tribe behavior. Knowing whether it was ok for the weaker apes to go hunting with the stronger ones is similar to knowing when to stay silent when a supervisor is chastising unsatisfactory behavior.[13]

Morris goes on to point out:

> **The co-operative spirit that is present in such pack hunters as wolves is largely absent from the world of the primate. Competitiveness and dominance is the order of his day. Competition in the social hierarchy is, of course, present in both groups, but it is less tempered by co-operative action in the case of monkeys and apes.[14]**

For Morris, co-operation involved learning and applying behaviors that produced mutually satisfactory outcomes within social settings. Conflict on the other hand typically occurs when there are unresolved competitive differences over things like territory, resources, or relationships. This Morris argued was equally true for humans and for apes. Unresolved differences that we notice are typically amongst those in positions of leadership in a group or tribe are only resolved through fighting physically until a winner is obvious, or through some other form of confrontation in which one participant eventually backs down. We see this as win–lose relationships. Co-operation on the other hand tends to involve relationships where mutual goals are implied (such as in hunting) and where the power dynamics in a group (such as who gets to share in the rewards of the hunt first) are already reasonably well understood or defined. Desmond Morris' claims that mankind's behavior mimics that of apes, which while highly controversial to some readers, also provides valuable insight into man's individual and social behavior.

Although he never cites Korpotkin, Morris uses similar examples to describe another form of co-operation, such as when one family member is aiding another, or a friend is aiding a friend. He cites an interesting case of a female chimpanzee with a small cinder in her left eye.[15] Whimpering and obviously in distress, she approached a male. The male sat down and examined her intently, and then proceeded to remove the cinder with great care and precision, gently using the tips of one finger from each hand. "This is more than simple grooming. It is the first sign of true co-operative medical care,"[16] stated Morris.

Morris best sums up his critique of human behavior by stating, "This unusual and highly successful species spends a great deal of time examining his higher motives and an equal amount of time studiously ignoring his fundamental ones."[17] We feel this is particularly the case when it comes to our understanding of co-operation and our use of co-operative behaviors in governance and problem solving.

We have included reference to Morris's work to illustrate that we are looking at the broad sweep of history and not just at the early stages of evolution.

Craig's Take on Co-operation, Competition, and Conflict

John G. Craig, also known as John (Jack) Craig,[18] a former university professor and author of various papers and books on co-operation and co-operatives, introduces us to the notion of co-operation from both a sociological and an organizational perspective. Craig, who has throughout his lifetime studied co-operation and co-operative organizations in Canada and internationally, is able to give us a more in-depth look at what co-operation actually involves.

Craig begins by reaffirming and elaborating on what Kropotkin had said some 120 years earlier. In short, those species that co-operate the most survive and flourish. In terms of the human species man has been living in clans and tribes since the dawn of the early Stone Age and from that time until the present, people have continued to build co-operative relations based on mutual aid.

Co-operation, as more formally and perhaps more broadly defined by Craig, can include almost all of those forms of human interaction which sociologists refer to as social organization. Co-operation as a concept can be broken down into a variety of types, with more specific and precise meanings. The different types which Craig identifies are as follows:[19]

> **Automatic co-operation** refers to those co-ordinated activities or joint efforts of an impersonal nature which take place between individuals in physical proximity to each other. It is unplanned and often unnoticed by its participants. It may occur as a group response to a common threat or simply as a response to an ordinary situation in which individuals have learned to co-operate. Examples of automatic co-operation are queuing at bus stops and supermarket check-out counters, and the movement of people in and out of crowded elevators.

> **Spontaneous co-operation** is perhaps the oldest and most natural form of co-operation in human interaction. It is also the most widespread in everyday life. Its basis is the friendly relationships that often exits between individuals, and it is un-prescribed by tradition, contract, or command. This type of co-operation takes place within the family, in neighbourhood groups and play groups, and through other close personal forms of association. Small group research, family studies and research into friendship groups have provided considerable information on the occurrence of spontaneous co-operation

in a variety of settings. In these settings, when common action is required, individuals are generally quick to co-operate because of the strength of the social ties between them.

Traditional co-operation is regulated, not by instinct, volition nor circumstance, but rather by the traditional social norms of the participants. It is often part of the moral fabric of the community and is described in community traditions. Examples of traditional co-operation include the sharing of food in hunting and gathering cultures, community barn-raisings, and volunteer fire brigades, as well as the organization of much of communal life. In these cases, co-operative behaviour may be regarded as simply the moral and correct way of living.

Directed co-operation is based on demand. There is a clear and well-accepted goal, and individuals are directed to co-operate in order to achieve that goal. An important example of directed co-operation is found in a military organization whose goal is to win a battle. Soldiers are commanded to co-operate, in accordance with specific orders as to how they should organize and conduct themselves in the course of the battle. This type of co-operation is very prevalent in modern society, and is facilitated by an organizational hierarchy. The hierarchy provides a means of co-ordinating highly specialized work carried out by many individuals so that it is directed towards the achievement of organizational goals. Co-operation is thus the result of formal structural arrangements with which the individual is expected to comply, by reason of his or her participation in the organization. Football, basketball, hockey, and other organized team sports employ this form of directed co-operation.

Contractual co-operation is prevalent in modern industrialized society. In this case, co-operation is both voluntary and formalized, based upon an explicit agreement between individuals to work together towards the achievement of a common goal. Often a separate organization is established in which membership is required, and legal sanctions are set out regarding the duration of the co-operative contract and the specific conditions of membership. Contractual co-operation is not confined to voluntary organizations. It is also evident in many work-related situations. For example, in applying for and accepting a job, the individual in effect undertakes a voluntary commitment to co-operate in working towards the employer's goals and objectives. He/she also accepts certain terms and conditions of employment (the equivalent of membership in a voluntary organization). Incidentally, the remainder of this book deals primarily with contractual co-operation.

Appreciating the varying dynamics involved in different types of co-operation helps us to understand why in some circumstances people or groups co-operate and in other circumstances they do not.

Craig points out two particular behaviors,[20] namely 'competition' and 'conflict' are as much a part of human history as co-operation behavior.

Competition often implies a win-lose situation. In economic terms, it is argued that competition between providers can lower prices to the consumer and improve the quality of goods and services available. In theory, one or more providers must lose to a better provider and as a consequence consumers reap the benefits. While competition can provide consumer benefits as well as shareholder returns to top performers, it is also true that in today's world of multinational "too big to fail corporations", business competition tends to be more of an implied ideal than a practical reality.

When two people interact, the interaction will be either co-operative, meaning that both participants can win if the goal is achieved, or competitive, in which the fact that one wins means that the other necessarily loses. In such a situation, it appears that competition and co-operation are opposites. This is true for dyads or very small groups; but in situations involving many individuals, the two concepts are independent and related in a much more complex way. A sports team may use a high degree of co-operation in order to develop effective plays against another team. The process within the team is co-operative, and the process between the teams is competitive. There must also be co-operation between the competing teams during events. There may also be an element of competition among the players in the co-operating unit, where they are vying with each other for personal gains (such as gaining prestige, playing a specific position or earning salary increases). Competition of this kind does not need to detract from the team's co-operative effort, and it may in fact, increase its chances of winning. Similarly, people in organizations may compete for high status roles, yet maintain a high degree of co-operation to achieve the goals of the organization. The competition of ideas is a very important aspect of participation and co-operation, though it is also true that people can effectively – sometimes very effectively – think through problems or develop different ways of thinking about a subject by thinking in groups. University students often compete for the best marks in their studies, although some of their best experiences might come from projects in which they worked with other students. Competition for the best ideas raises the quality of the output from the lowest common denominator to the group achieving excellence. To view these two concepts as opposites may therefore be useful for groups of two, but it can be misleading in larger human groups. On the other hand, discovering the best ideas may take place through group discussions and collaboration. For example, there are cases in which co-operative organizations, such as credit unions, actively compete with each other for business volume based on services provided, yet they co-operate in matters such as marketing, risk management, member and employee education, information technology, and government relations.[21]

If human behaviour is viewed through the overly simplistic lens of individual competition, it seems only natural for people to consider competition as the opposite of co-operation. This flawed analysis has been often mistakenly and implicitly associated with the thought of Adam Smith and his book *An Inquiry Into the Nature and Causes of the Wealth of Nations*, published in 1776. In passing comments, he referred to the concept of the 'invisible hand',[22] whereby *each person, by looking out for himself or herself*, inadvertently helps to create the best outcome for all.[23] This metaphor, often not associated with the underlying moral imperatives and social views that Smith fundamentally championed, can be interpreted as putting 'selfishness of the individual, indeed the selfishness of mankind' above all else. Even though there have been many dissenters and objectors to this distortion of Smith's views, it has become widely supported by a great many of the world's most powerful leaders and wealthy families.

It is very important to note that Adam Smith, in his earlier work, *The Theory of Moral Sentiments*,[24] and Peter Kropotkin in his work, *Mutual Aid: A Factor of Evolution*,[25] both saw human beings as capable of empathy and possessing sentiments compelling them to act morally and co-operatively and not only in their own self-interest.

Competition, while not the opposite of co-operation, depending on how it is structured or how it is perceived, can have both positive and negative consequences. Often negative consequences can be expected in a competitive situation when conflict becomes a part of the game.

Conflict, in the simplest of terms, usually manifests itself when there are unresolved differences in circumstance or in perceived outcomes such that one or more of the parties involved are threatened, maligned, or attacked. This can be the case when gangs battle over turf, when sports teams momentarily dispense with rules of the game and instead use fists, or when nations lock horns with other nations.

Conflict may be defined as a struggle over values or claims to status, power,[26] and scarce resources, in which the aims of the conflicting parties are not only to gain the desired values but also to neutralize, injure, or eliminate their rivals. Conflict may take place between individuals, between groups, or between individuals and groups. While conflict may be and often is physical, it does not necessarily need to be. Craig describes four main types of conflict:[27]

1) Person versus Self (internal struggle between competing needs and wants).

2) Person versus Person (one person struggling with another person).

3) Person(s) versus Society/World (one person or group struggling with another group).

4) Person(s) versus Nature (one person or group struggling with nature).

Conflict is a concept that is independent of co-operation. Usually there are different values, motivations and behaviors involved. In certain circumstances, conflict may be an integral part of inducing and sustaining co-operative behaviour, and the two may co-exist in various social settings. Sometimes a low level of conflict is matched by a low level of co-operation. In type two above, two individuals may agree to co-operate and take their dispute outside to settle it, rather than creating a common brawl. However and more importantly, sometimes in type three and type four conflicts a high level of conflict can induce a successful and sustained co-operative response from groups or communities. This was the case in the 1930s and 1940s in western Canada, where whole communities formed savings and credit unions (financial co-operatives) because they were in conflict with banks from eastern Canada. The same co-operative response to a threatening situation is demonstrated when communities work together to battle an approaching forest fire or control spring flood waters.

Craig's assertions are based on his firsthand experience with co-operatives and with co-operation. He emphasizes that co-operation can be a shrewd and highly successful strategy — a pragmatic choice that gets things done at work and at school even more effectively than competition does. The past three or four decades have brought forth this realization in many North American organizations. Those organizations that have maintained competitive individualism within the work setting have had a hard time competing with organizations that build a co-operative environment in the work setting and between stakeholders or sets of organizations. The adversarial or win-lose models of labour management relations in North America has put many industries at a disadvantage when compared to countries like Germany, Japan and Sweden that tend to have a co-operative approach to labour management relations. Perhaps one could compare the relative team development of the Mozilla's FireFox internet browser (with thousands of independently developed add-ins) to its older cousin – Internet Explorer.

Craig's views and experience help us to understand much about what has been learned over the past several hundred years concerning co-operation, competition, and conflict, but how does the world see co-operation today? For answers to this question we turn to the respected Harvard University professor Yochai Benkler and his recent book, *The Penguin and the Leviathan: How Co-operation Triumphs Over Self-Interest*.[28]

Benkler's Boost - Co-operation Triumphs Over Self-Interest

Yochai Benkler has decided it is time to ask openly why self-interest has historically seemed to triumph over co-operation. Benkler begins by claiming that it shouldn't be necessary to claim that co-operation is more relevant than self-interest since there are all kinds of co-operative and collaborative examples all around us. He cites South West Airlines, Toyota, one of Chicago's community programs, Linux, and Wikipedia as examples of co-operative initiatives that have all succeeded. Most of Benkler's research focuses on the past decade or so, even though he does build his case based on research and findings of people like Peter Kropotkin. Benkler acknowledges that in society there are some people who are selfish, but most are not.

In fact, in hundreds of studies in numerous disciplines, a basic pattern emerges. In any given experiment, a large minority of people (about 30 percent) behave as though they really were selfish, as the mainstream commonly assumes. But here is the rub: fully half of all people systematically, significantly, and predictably behave co-operatively.[29]

Instead of beginning by championing co-operation, Benkler begins by asking "Why has the myth of self-interest persisted?" He looks at four inter-related reasons:[30]

- **First**, it is partially correct that some people some of the time do act selfishly.
- **Second**, in the decades after WWII, it was assumed within many organizations that most human behavior was rooted in incentives and punishments; and it was a part of the western culture, particularly the American culture, to deny any behavior not explained by free market or capitalist approaches.
- **Third**, it was simpler and therefore easier to go with the ideas in good currency at the time.
- **Fourth**, by now almost two generations have been educated and socialized to think in terms of universal selfishness.

It is the fourth reason that we vote for as the most important in understanding why selfishness has weighed in so heavily in people's minds until this last decade. It is difficult for us to decide whether in the age of persuasion it was corporate media's sales pitch to the *"me generation"* or the business schools dogma of *"You must learn to compete if you want to succeed"* which had the greater sway over people's hearts and minds. We expect that to Benkler, it would have been both.

Benkler explains that in spite of what the corporate world would have us believe people everywhere are not robots and selfish brutes, but rather follow a moral compass and do not hesitate to save a drowning baby or bestow acts of kindness on others when it is needed.

In today's culture, are there other reasons why people still co-operate? One reason, which includes aspects of self-interest, is based on the notion that if you scratch my back, I'll scratch yours. So some people may co-operate with others when they believe there is a chance that they may receive something back in return. This is direct reciprocity. Benkler suggests that people may actively co-operate over time in the belief that at some point they will receive help or support from others in return. This is indirect reciprocity. Benkler concludes by saying that there are early indications to support a theory that some people may have inherited a 'co-operative gene' making such persons more co-operative more so than self-interested.[31]

From experience, it is evident that there are factors which contribute to, and factors which detract from, people co-operating. We will consider some of the principal factors that contribute to co-operation.

'Communications' can greatly assist individuals and groups in co-operating. In looking at successful co-operative systems, we begin to see why it is that communication is vitally important. Benkler emphasizes that factors such as 'empathy and solidarity, moral norms, fairness, trust, and leadership' all help contribute to co-operation, and all rest on there being effective communication. Benkler describes 'fairness' in some detail.[32] What we consider to be fair isn't always easy to ascertain since what is considered fair to one may not be fair to another. Fairness can be described in terms of outcomes, intentions, and processes. If, for example, there were various but different prizes to be distributed, most people would co-operate and agree to accept whatever they were given, provided recipient names were drawn randomly. Many times people will not co-operate if they believe another person or persons in the group do not intend to co-operate, and conversely many times people will co-operate if they believe others are intending to co-operate. The process of queuing for services at airports or at checkouts in a grocery store works best because of the accepted belief that 'first come – first served' is fair. Someone who jumps the queue or who tries to slide in the middle or even at the front of the line is, in most cultures, chastised by others in the line and asked to return to the end of the line because their actions are unfair. However, in some countries the process can be more complicated. In countries in Africa and Asia where there may be wide differences in economic standing, an obviously important and apparently wealthy individual may be permitted to go to the head of the line because those already waiting may feel that respecting wealth and power is more important than ensuring fairness.

Benkler closes his argument concerning how co-operation triumphs over competition when he presents two different but compelling cases.[33] In the first case, we learn how Japanese automobile production and productivity in the US far surpassed that of traditional US manufacturers, principally by introducing measures that facilitated greater co-operation. The reason this case is significant is because it demonstrated that it was not something particular to Japanese culture that made the important difference, but instead it was the co-operative work organization and management styles that made the difference. Most businesses around the world today consider group leadership skills and teamwork as desirable attributes in building their workforce.

In Benkler's second case, a large number of people co-operate and contribute their knowledge and expertise freely and collaboratively in the development of open source software. They do so for pleasure, to give something back, and to learn by doing. Often, their motivations are non-monetary. Wikipedia, Firefox, and Linux are some of the examples you may already be familiar with. The fact that there are thousands and thousands of people contributing their time and energy to community organizations and groups like Volunteer Services Overseas and Rotary International is proves that services, whether paid or unpaid, can and are being delivered co-operatively.

While Benkler's broad- brush look at co-operation and how it triumphs over competition provides useful insights, he goes on to identify worthwhile ingredients for fostering increased co-operation within businesses and across society as a whole in future. The ingredients of what he calls 'designing for co-operation'[34] are summarized below.

- Communication (the most important requirement within a co-operative system);
- Framing, fit and authenticity (words must match reality as in the meal should equal the menu);
- Looking beyond ourselves (empathy and solidarity can help us discover our common interests);
- Constructing moral systems (clearly defined values are crucial to co-operation);
- Rewards and punishment (controls can be helpful when carefully designed and applied);

- Reputation, transparency and reciprocity (knowing who we are can dispel corruption) ; and
- Building for diversity (frameworks that allow us to co-operate also have to be somewhat flexible).

While Benkler's arguments that co-operation triumphs over competition may certainly be open to further debate, we will contend, based upon our experience, that in today's world co-operation is every bit as important to individual, organizational, and societal well-being as is competition.

In the next and final section in this introductory chapter, we will look much more precisely at what it takes for conscious deliberate co-operation to develop and to be sustained within groups and organizations.

Craig's Conditions for Contractual Co-operation

After studying, and working with and in, hundreds of co-operative organizations for most of a lifetime, John (Jack) Craig describes for us more discrete factors which must exist if conscious deliberate co-operation (contractual co-operation) is to become manifest. [35] If you are considering creating a co-operative, or if your co-operative seems to be struggling, you may be able to use this checklist of factors to help as you move forward:

- Superordinate goal (Is there a broad goal clearly articulated and collectively support?)
- Commitment to non-exploitation of others (Are the risks and the rewards fair to all concerned?)
- Commitment to democratic decision-making (Are everyone's interests being fairly represented?)
- Commitment to mutual self-help (Is there an appreciation that we benefit by helping each other?)
- Voluntarism (Is there a willingness on the part of members to contribute their time and energy?)
- Organizational skills and economic factors (Is the enterprise sustainable and does it have the necessary leadership and managerial skills to grow and develop co-operatively?)
- External environment (Are the market, social, regulatory, and other environments supportive?)

Over the years we have seen how the presence of all of these factors can contribute to the success of co-operative organizations. Likewise we have seen that the absence of even one factor, if left unattended or unconsidered, can over time result in the failure of the organization. While we appreciate that there are other elements which influence the success or failure of an organization, we've taken the liberty of calling Craig's conditions for contractual co-operation *co-operative critical success factors,* and encourage those in positions of leadership to consider each of them and the questions implied within them carefully. You will discover in Chapter 5 why each of these factors can play an important role in creating 'communities of support' for a co-operative enterprise.

In the following chapters, we shall expand upon what we have touched upon to this point, and delve more deeply into co-operative movements and the design of large and complex co-operative systems.

Take Aways

1. History has shown us that co-operation is a long standing human attribute, as is human competition and conflict.

2. Co-operation can involve helping and caring for each other, although it may simply involve working together to achieve a common goal or purpose.

3. The value of co-operative behaviour among people does not mean the end of competition, but serves to illustrate the diverse ways in which human beings are able to relate to each other.

4. Co-operation and competition should not be seen as opposites. They are both important, and like conflict, they are aspects of our nature that need to be considered and better understood.

5. There are various types of co-operation. Some types of co-operation can be very simple and easy to understand, while others can be more complex and may be more difficult to create and to sustain.

6. Co-operation can be expected to grow best when circumstances are favourable.

7. The most formal form of co-operation is called contractual co-operation. The remainder of this book deals with this form of co-operation.

Chapter Two - From People's Movements to Co-operative Systems of Enterprise

People's Movements

Perhaps you have heard the phrases "Human Rights Movement", "Civil Rights Movement," "Occupy Wall Street Movement," or maybe "the Co-operative Movement". At the same time some of you may also have heard expressions such as "the credit union system" or "the co-operative system", "the banking system", "the free market system", or even "the welfare system". Do movement and system mean the same thing? What exactly are the differences between a movement and a system? More specifically, is the co-operative reality in the world today a movement or a system? We will answer all of these questions. We will also illustrate how the co-operative movement and the co-operative system are distinct but complementary dimensions of the co-operative sector.

For some the two words "movement" and "system" seem to be synonyms; they mean the same thing. However, for others each term has adherents and detractors. To some, the term "movement," with its overtones of protest and populism, seems inappropriate in an era when many co-operatives have achieved hard-won recognition as large, well-managed enterprises. The term "system," on the other hand, is often perceived as further diminishing the notion of co-operation as a social movement. As a result, references to the co-operative "system" are not well received in parts of the world where the sense of a "peoples' movement" is still very strong.

In a great many countries, co-operators have traditionally referred to themselves as part of a movement, "the Co-operative Movement." The co-operators involved have served as advocates and promoters for their particular co-operative and have in many instances championed co-operatives over arguably perhaps other less enviable forms of enterprise. For many, seeing their co-operatives prosper and grow has been a good part of their reward. In the past three decades, however, other co-operators, particularly those in the west, have increasingly used the phrase, "the Co-operative System" to describe what has in many cases has become a complex set of business entities working together to satisfy member needs.

In Canada, for example, credit union leaders speak of the credit union financial system. Canada's largest retail co-operative (Federated Co-operatives) refers to itself and its 250 locations as "the Co-operative Retailing System".[1] Nevertheless, the terms movement and system are often used interchangeably by co-operators from around the world.

We will make a quick start by explaining some differences between a movement and a system.

Movements are organized to bring about social change. Wikipedia lists 80 different movements, including those mentioned above.[2] Movements are driven by visions of a better world; but to realize those visions, movements create organizations which often become business enterprises. Very often, visionary leaders give way to professional managers. Thus systems are born.

Systems are more structured than movements. The organizational structures and processes within systems also tend to be more precisely defined and controlled. The parts of a larger system are often autonomous or semi-autonomous but interdependent, and are guided by shared ideals. For example, local consumer co-operatives often organize to establish a regional or a national co-operative (sometimes referred to as a second-tier co-operative or federation) to help provide business services in various areas such as branding and marketing support, supply and logistics support, as well as educational and financial services.

In a historical sense, it has been suggested by John Jordan that a system is subordinated to a movement.[3] In practice, however, Jordan finds the resources and momentum inherent in organizations tend over time to subordinate the movement to the system. Within co-operative forms of enterprise, for example, this tension between movements and systems stems from the following aspects:

1. As co-operatives grow and develop, the strong sense of ownership usually felt by volunteers in the formative stages gradually gives way to professional management. The emphasis on the system usually comes from managers who are struggling to keep control of business activities and to maintain a clear focus of the organisation -- and to build their careers.
2. The growth of institutional loyalties that tend to see the organisation as being the complete embodiment of the "movement".
3. The impact of legislative frameworks.
4. The decline of member engagement.
5. Weak or declining support for what had been movement issues, goals and ideology.

Jordan explains the differences this way. "It is true that the movement and the system display different but complementary tendencies. Movements typically are unencumbered by formal alliances, although they may be supported by other movements such as the labor movement, the environmental movement, or the agrarian movement. Movements generally address themselves to a more complete concept of humanity. Movements attempt to stake out what they would like the future to be and so they are future oriented. Systems often have a large investment in the present, and an interest in dealing with specific needs. Systems generally are more forward-oriented than future oriented. Both tendencies are essential to our co-operative reality."

Management and planning processes in co-operatives must accommodate both dimensions; otherwise, the organization will tend to be short-sighted and focused only on its existing functions. The last part of this publication puts forward various key initiatives which we feel may aid both co-operative movements and systems to create a shared vision for co-operatives and their member owners around the world.

John Jordan suggests we can profitably understand the terms *movement* and *system* as referring to distinct but related dimensions of the co-operative reality. Understanding the distinctive attributes and characteristics of each can assist us in imagining a co-operative vision of a better world, as we will touch on in the last section of this publication.

Co-operation as a Social Movement

History provides an appropriate entry into a discussion of social movements. The initial stages of the co-operative movements in England and elsewhere were marked by considerable analysis of the state of society, the source of its challenges, and the nature of the co-operative alternative as a response. These are characteristic activities of a social movement in the process of formation, and generally result in a statement of the movement's ideology. We might loosely define an ideology as a verbal image of the good society and the means of achieving it, together with an identification of the forces hostile to that vision. Ideology is that body of ideas and beliefs which can also include stated values or principles which taken together as a whole serve to reflect the interests of a particular group or groups.

On occasion, movement leaders also advocate long and hard against an aspect of the current condition. In the process of a movement forming, advocates within the movement often assume very damning attitudes to what they perceive themselves to be contesting or arguing against. Claims of usurious interest rates, of sweat shop labor practices, of racial and gender discrimination, and of the dumping of hazardous waste in developing countries, are illustrative of different types of injustice which movement leaders might voice as requiring remedy by taking action.

The future component of an ideology has two parts. In one, the goals of the movement are stated. The goals are some specific changes in the social structure, the environment, or the institution that the movement is working towards implementing. In the other part, the utopian vision is proclaimed - the circumstance through which the accomplishment of the movement's goals can be realized. In the same way as each ideology has an image of the past and the present so it has an image of the future – and it is the dream of what might be that primarily drives its supporter to embrace change.

This has been true of co-operative movements. We should not forget that the Rochdale Pioneers who commenced business with the purpose of pioneering the way to a new and better social order. Without that ideal, their co-operative enterprises would never have been begun, and we might not have today's co-operative movements and systems. Utopian co-operators, including Robert Owen, George Keen, and Alex Laidlaw, were primarily responsible for keeping alive the dreams of a better, more co-operative world.

Jordan goes on to explain that three characteristics of social movements are important in the co-operative setting:[4] **first**, the significance of a movement's vision as a motivator and guide to decisions; **second**, the broad and inclusive quality of a movement and its vision; and **third**, the tendency of movements to create institutions. Let us look briefly at each characteristic as Jordan explains.

First, ideology or visions of the future are extremely important in guiding the pattern of co-operative development. This is because ideals are powerful motivators to action, and because the content of a vision provides concrete guidance in making particular decisions. For example, the analysis by early co-operators that the annual surplus was generated by the users led to the recognition that it should be returned as a dividend on patronage, while capital was rewarded on a limited and fixed basis.[5] Similar thinking (for example - what do we deem is fair and just) created the notion of 'one member – one vote'.

It is clear in reading statements by early leaders of co-operative movements that their visions were not empty rhetoric. Movements are driven by *vision*—impelled by its urgency and guided by its content. Visions were thought to be the only realistic response to the human condition. Here is one quotation from 1910:

> **There can be no question that the world's economic future depends upon co-operative effort of some kind. The old, wasteful, competitive system has had its day. Hardly a month goes by without some merger of trade interests being affected to exploit the many in the interests of the few. The tendency to effect economics in production and distribution by a merger of interests is sound in principle, but vicious in the prevailing method of operation. The only alternatives are either the socialization of the interests, of the whole people, of the production and distribution of wealth, a demand for which the combines and trusts are feeding, or the voluntary organization of the peoples' labour and resources under the well-tried and well-proven principles of the Co-operative Movement.**[6]

Second, movements are holistic;[7] they concern man and society as a whole. The vision concerns the person as a complete being in a social setting. In theory, social movements are open to a broad cross section of society, not limited to an exclusive group. This is important, as both of these dimensions distinguish genuine social movements from mere interest groups formed to promote a particular narrow interest of their members. Some might suggest that agricultural co-operatives or worker co-operatives represent the narrow interest of members and thus lack movement characteristics. To this we would counter by saying both farmers and workers indeed do make up broad cross sections of society and there are numerous examples where the two groups have embraced a broad vision of society and their roles within it.

Third, social movements give rise to institutions.[8] Historically successful social movements extend beyond issuing a statement of ideology or a proclamation of a utopian vision; they mobilize and act. They establish organizations, and in the case of the co-operative movement, enterprises that pursue both social and economic goals. But as a movement develops, institutions and organizations often shift focus away from the vision of the ideal future and towards administering its increasing investments in the present. This usually introduces a period of modification of the vision as leaders become preoccupied with managing the realities of the present.

Conventional wisdom tells us that visions are mystical and utopian, and utopia does not exist. This view argues that we should expect the declining importance of vision to be regularly observed in social movements and organizations. Often in periods of growth and continuity this is allowed to occur.

Charismatic leaders give way to professional managers – often an apparent prerequisite for institutional survival. Nevertheless in co-operative organizations, at particular points in time, visionaries and at times courageous movement leaders are needed to renew the visions that provide ongoing guidance to the development of institutions and organizations which serve specific purposes.

At some point, we come to realize that there are those who see co-operatives and perhaps themselves as part of a movement, and there are those who see co-operatives and perhaps themselves as part of a system, regardless of the particular organizations or institutions involved. A crucial aspect of this condition however is that the institutions that have been created are more highly organized and more deeply concerned with the present than is the case with those who are part of a movement.

Co-operatives as Systems of Enterprise

The fact that in many parts of the world today it is now common place for co-operators to refer to "the credit union system," "the co-operative retailing system," or simply "the co-operative system," suggests an awareness that the 'set of organizations' created by the movement share certain relationships with it. It also suggests that it is useful to think of these organizations as being distinct from the movement, even though created by it. A report of the United States Credit Union National Association's (CUNA) planning committee is explicit on this notion of system:[9]

> **Looking ahead, the committee envisioned our national credit union movement truly reflecting the kind of co-operation we see within a credit union...The answer which developed and which made the most sense to the committee is to build a framework which can take the maximum advantage of our philosophical and organizational strengths while joining or pooling our efforts in ways that are mutually beneficial and supportive of efforts at every level. The concept and organizational form that best seems to embody this intent is the SYSTEM. So, the need to think of ourselves and to act as one, while maintaining our special differences and varieties, came to translate itself for the committee into the vision of a future where credit unions really function as one system in certain important areas.**

Similar examples exist elsewhere. For example, we can identify a milk products co-operative system in France,[10] a co-operative marketing system for cotton and coffee in Uganda,[11] and a dairy co-operative system in India.[12]

Thus, the term "system" draws attention to organizations which are interdependent to some extent, and yet identify with one another as part of a larger entity. The idea of the co-operative system is narrower than the concept of the co-operative movement. We can for example distinguish between two global co-operative systems, one representing various types of co-operatives and known as the International Co-operative Alliance, and a second representing financial co-operatives and known as the World Council of Credit Unions. Both are parts of what is the larger, purpose-driven co-operative movement.

Two specific dimensions of purposeful systems require mention here: first, that the parts of a system are interdependent; and second, that systems are also guided by ideals.[13]

First, co-operative systems are composed of interdependent parts.[14] Interdependence encourages us to recognize that the relationships between co-operatives in the system are not ones of master and servant, but of entities which are formally autonomous but recognize that they are creations of a common movement and that their futures are linked. Therefore each is, in a variety of ways, dependent on the other.

Jordan has developed a useful set of preliminary indicators of the extent of interdependence in a co-operative system:[15]

1. Linkages through overlapping directors on boards;
2. Co-operatives encouraging their members to join other co-operatives;
3. Extent of contact and consultation between management of different co-operatives;
4. Extent of joint ventures among co-operatives;
5. Extent to which co-operatives share buildings, technology, or other facilities;
6. Use of common personnel and benefit policies for co-operative employees;
7. Extent to which there are transactions between co-operatives;
8. Extent of shared training or management development programs;
9. Extent to which co-operatives invest in and support each other or their central organizations;
10. Extent to which co-operatives assist a co-operative in difficulty;
11. Extent of common activity to promote public understanding and acceptance of co-operation; and
12. Extent to which co-operatives join together through second and third-tier organizations (also known as Federations or Centrals) to represent themselves to government.

One can use these indicators to assess the extent of interdependence among co-operatives in a given sector, such as financial co-operatives or agricultural products marketing co-operatives; or within a given region, or nationally. Co-operatives in a given sector or geographic system can be ranked as being highly interdependent, moderately interdependent, or displaying little interdependence.

Second, systems, like movements, are guided by ideals.[16] If we explore the literature on social systems, we find that social scientists use the concepts of idealization and ideal-seeking behaviour to explain the performance of effective social systems. This is because it is impossible for one to act strictly on the basis of experience to date, to "live a day at a time." Our actions always take place under the horizon or image of an expected future. We act to bring about the state of affairs we desire. As individuals or organized groups, we exhibit ideal-seeking behaviour.

In an organization, those ideals may be quite realistic or they may be fantasies. The important point is that they represent concepts or visions of a state of affairs beyond the present. As such, they represent an imaginative leap into the future, and the harnessing energies and resources to bring about a state of affairs beyond anything already experienced. Co-operative leaders have often pursued ideals that they accept may not be attainable - but that can be continuously approached. Thus to them the formulation of ideals and the design of idealized futures are not empty exercises in utopianism, but necessary steps in setting long-range directions for continuous development. They treat ideals as ultimate objectives whose formulation depends on our current knowledge and understanding of ourselves and our environment. Therefore, they require reformulation over time based upon what we have learned in attempts to achieve them.

Movements and Systems as Opposite Sides of the Coin

The answer to our question is that although movements and systems are driven by visions and ideals, they display quite different, but complementary tendencies. Each has distinct attributes which complete and balance those of the other.

To illustrate this we shall introduce a number of distinctions, and elaborate somewhat on points introduced previously. The first relates to the relative orientation of movement and system. Please See Figure 2.1.[17]

The movement is driven primarily although not always exclusively by vision, which includes an idealized picture of a future state. This represents an imaginative leap, a statement of what we would like to see, and it is thus an expression of our values. From a movement perspective, we can think of planning as proceeding backward from the vision to the present. Movements are capable of doing this because they are less encumbered by commitments to the present state of affairs. Movements thus represent a futures orientation.

Systems, on the other hand, represent significant investments in the present and in the short-term future. Their planning processes tend to reflect modest improvements to existing organizational programs. The system tendency, then, is to begin with the current condition and to assume a modest forward orientation. We can represent these two tendencies in a simple diagram.

Figure 2.1

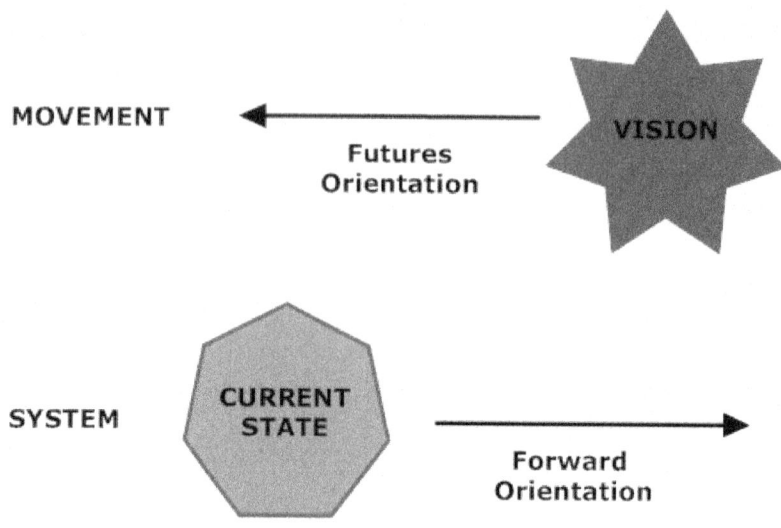

The relative orientation of movement and system

Jordan explains[18] that his approach is not to suggest that co-operative systems are not capable of entertaining visions of desired future situations, or that movements do not get bogged down in considerations of present reality and institutional developments. All it suggests is the relative tendency of movements to concentrate more on visions and of systems to concentrate more on the projection forward of current conditions. By recognizing these tendencies, we are able to allocate to both movement and system supporters those particular dimensions that they can each best undertake. The objective is to bring together the forward and the future orientations so that we can connect where we are now (the system's current condition) with where we would like to go (the movement's vision).

Another relevant distinction can be made between the nature of human needs as they are represented both in the movement and the system.

The movement is rooted in the individual and in each person's needs. The movement also exists on a collective level, but it focuses on the integration of shared human needs. For example, think of the Civil Rights, Anti-nuclear and Environmental movements – they are concerned with the individual and the larger society at the same time. As for the co-operative movement, it envisions a society in which people have cultivated co-operative ways to enhance their lives and how they live with one another and in which co-operative organisations are the most important institutional forms – for both economic and social purposes.

Co-operative organizations, on the other hand, often are designed to address a particular aspect or segment of needs, such as the need for financial services or marketing of agricultural products. Each organization represents the differentiation or specialization of a particular human need.

Figure 2.2 summarizes these two tendencies: [19]

Figure 2.2

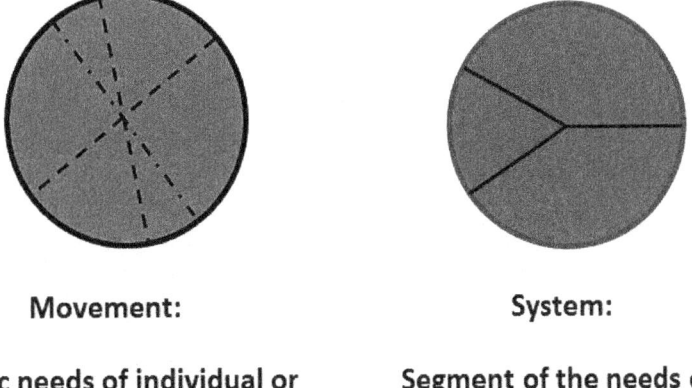

Movement:

Holistic needs of individual or groups

System:

Segment of the needs of individual or group

Holistic and segmented needs

Thus, the co-operative movement is better designed to deal with holistic needs or with reintegrating needs which are being met by specific co-operative organizations. The co-operative system, on the other hand, is composed of co-operatives meeting particular types of needs. It represents the organizational dimension of co-operative activity, while the movement represents the individual and collective dimension of co-operative activity. This perhaps help us to understand why co-operative systems prefer to focus more on their particular functions (i.e., retailing, marketing, banking) instead of actively co-operating to address longer-term, collective challenges.

In summary, the concepts of movement and system capture different dimensions of reality. Unless both are recognized, planning and future processes are likely one-sided and focused on the existing functions and activities of the organization, rather than on broader purposes or on the interests of the members, and the community. Indeed, many co-operators in certain mature co-operative systems are now suggesting that their system is producing good operational or business results but is not addressing the question of their ultimate purpose or vision. We see this condition as both a challenge and an opportunity; one which we will address in the final section of this publication.

Co-operative Movements and Systems around the World

From a 'movement – system' perspective it is not surprising to see that the pattern of co-operative development varies greatly around the world. In some countries co-operatives have become what development practitioners describe as 'part of the mainstream' and operate within very elaborate business structures as interdependent systems of enterprise. In other places co-operatives are being reborn. In some African countries, older co-operative systems have collapsed. In most instances these organizations were called co-operatives but were in reality systems established by government decree back in the early 1900s as part of colonial supply chains for coffee and tea production. The new co-operatives that have re-emerged, after earlier ones have collapsed or fallen out of favour, are now rediscovering what being a co-operative in today's world really means. As such, their leaders and officials often exhibit the enthusiasm and commitment more commonly found in movement driven co-operatives. This has proven to be inspiring to visiting co-operators from other co-operative systems. In Europe and Asia a great many co-operatives have multi-tier structures and operate as highly integrated systems of enterprise. The United Kingdom, India and Japan have a number of such systems. The same can be said for Argentina and Brazil. In Argentina, worker co-operatives are flourishing, [20]albeit with state support; and since there are many that are new, they are still in the process of building themselves up as systems of enterprise. In other instances and in other countries, new co-operatives are being created. For example, in Canada and the US we are seeing the creation of multi-stakeholder co-operatives.[21]

Clearly, the pattern of development varies from one circumstance to another, from one country to another, from one region to another, and from one continent to another. Governments always play important roles in a co-operative movement's transition to a formal system. You may wish to refer to Chapter 8 to learn more about the pivotal role governments play in co-operative development. In each case one can say, while co-operatives may only be just beginning, or already have been long established, they are all by their nature, constituents in a larger global co-operative movement; a movement that is being celebrated by co-operatives around the world, and one which was recognized in 2012 by the United Nations as the International Year of Co-operatives.

Some Co-operative Systems of Enterprise

It seems appropriate that we should include in this chapter some real life examples of successful co-operative systems of enterprise to give you a sense of how large and complex some co-operatives systems of enterprise have become. At the same time, we have included a small co-operative from Brazil that appears to be rapidly making its way from being a local movement- driven organization to becoming a part of a larger co-operative system of enterprise.

The RaboBank Group (Netherlands)[22]

The Coöperatieve Centrale Raiffeisen-Boerenleenbank B.A. is a financial services provider with offices worldwide. Their main location is in the Netherlands. It is a global leader in Food and Agri financing and in sustainability-oriented banking. The group comprises 141 independent local Dutch Rabobanks, a central organization (Rabobank Nederland), and a large number of specialized international offices and subsidiaries. Food & Agribusiness is the prime international focus of the Rabobank Group. The Rabobank Group currently consists of the following divisions:

1. Rabobank Nederland - the facility and staff organisation that serves the local banks. It currently performs the following core activities: i) Market support for the domestic retail banking business; ii) Group functions, i.e. ICT, legal, and other specialty departments, iii) Wholesale banking and international rural and retail banking.
2. Local Banks - Approximately 141 independent and co-operative local banks in the Netherlands.
3. Rabo International - Rabobank's investment banking wing.
4. Rabo Vastgoed Groep - Project developer, real estate.
5. Robeco - Investment management.
6. De Lage Landen - Vendor finance, leasing and trade finance.
7. Schretlen & Co - Asset management, private banking sector.
8. Obvion - mortgage intermediary.
9. FGH Bank - Dutch real estate bank.
10. ACCBank - Agricultural Credit Corporation, Ireland.
11. Bank BGZ - Retail bank, Poland.
12. Rabobank N.A. - California-based financial services corporation, formerly VIB corp.
13. Rabo Mobiel, a mobile virtual network operator in the Netherlands.
14. Rabo Development, with advisory services and minority participation in various international markets, including: Tanzania, Zambia, Rwanda, Mozambique, China, Brazil, and Paraguay.

Rabobank Re-invents Itself - *In the late 1990s Rabobank Group undertook a serious and extensive multi-year self-examination debate exercise to consider their core reason for being and whether they could be more effectively organized. The exercise resulted in a clear re-dedication to the co-operative structure and to their continued operation as a co-operatively owned and controlled financial institution. While it may be impractical for a system to attempt to turn itself into a movement, Rabobank demonstrated through this exercise that it is possible for a co-operative system to reconnect itself with its roots, as well as to look beyond itself and to the future, and to the larger world for challenges and opportunities which were waiting to be addressed. We are aware of other such initiatives, and believe that the Rabobank's exercise is an important example which other established co-operative systems should consider from time to time as a part of their planning for the future.*

Desjardins Group (Canada)[23]

The Desjardins Group (or *Mouvement des caisses Desjardins* in French) is the largest association of credit unions in North America. Located mostly in Quebec as well as in Ontario, Manitoba, and New Brunswick, it is composed of 536 local caisses populaires. The entire system is grouped into 11 regional federations. The Desjardins Group has over 20 subsidiaries offering products and services related to insurance (Desjardins Financial Security, Desjardins General Insurance), real estate (Place Desjardins), venture capital funds (Desjardins Venture Capital) and brokerage (Desjardins Securities). The Desjardins Group, through its subsidiary Développement International Desjardins, is active in over 50 developing countries through technical assistance programs and various investments. Desjardins Group is also active in the United States via the Desjardins Bank and in Western Canada via Western Financial.

The Co-operative Group (England)[24]

The corporate members include 22 large independent consumer co-operatives. These co-operatives are represented alongside the regional boards at annual meetings and in the board of directors, and are entitled to dividends based on the amount of their purchases from the group. There are over 6,000,000 members in the British consumer movement.

The Co-operative Group operates Co-operative Food, Co-operative Travel, Co-operative Funeralcare, and Co-operative Pharmacy Divisions, plus the Co-operative Banking Group, Co-operative Legal Services, Co-operative Farms, Co-operative Electrical and the Co-operative Motor Group.

Land O' Lakes (United States)[25]

Land O'Lakes is a member-owned agricultural cooperative based in Arden Hills, Minnesota, focusing on the dairy industry. The co-operative states that it has about 3200 producer-members, 1000 member-cooperatives, and about 9000 employees who process and distribute products for about 300,000 agricultural producers. The co-operative is one of the largest producers of butter and cheese in the United States. The co-operative does business in more than 50 countries.

Cooperative Bank of Kenya (Kenya)[26]

The Cooperative Bank is a large financial services institution. As of December 2011, it was the third-largest financial services provider in Kenya by asset value. The bank has four subsidiary companies: Kingdom Securities Limited - Nairobi, Kenya - 60% share ownership; Co-op Trust Investment Services Limited - Nairobi, Kenya - 100% share ownership; Co-operative Consultancy Services (K) Limited - 100% share ownership; and CIC Insurance Company Limited - 25% share ownership. The bank provides services from 90 branch locations.

The bank's stock is owned by Coop Holdings Co-operative Society Limited, a holding company owned by the co-operative societies within Kenya (64.56 %), and by over 111,700 other individual and institutional investors through the Nairobi Stock Exchange (35.44 %).

Amul (India)[27]

Amul is a dairy co-operative in India. Formed in 1946, it is a brand name managed by an Indian co-operative organisation, Gujarat Co-operative Milk Marketing Federation Ltd. (GCMMF), which today is jointly owned by 3.03 million milk producers in Gujarat, India. Amul is the largest food brand in India and the world's largest pouched milk brand. Currently co-operative unions making up GCMMF have 3.1 million producer members. Besides India, Amul has entered overseas markets such as Mauritius, UAE, USA, Oman, Bangladesh, Australia, China, Singapore, Hong Kong, and a few southern African countries.

Mondragon Corporation (Spain)[28]

At the end of 2011, the Mondragon Corporation was providing employment for 83,869 people in 256 companies in four areas of activity: Finance, Industry, Retail, and Knowledge.

- **The Finance area includes the banking business of Caja Laboral, the insurance company Seguros Lagun Aro, and the Voluntary Social Welfare Body, Lagun Aro.**
- **The Industry area includes companies which manufacture consumer goods, capital goods, industrial components, products and systems for construction, and provide services to business.**
- **The Retail area includes Eroski, one of the leading retail groups of Spain. The worker-owners and consumer-members are involved in the management of Eroski, with both groups participating in the Co-operative's decision-making bodies. At the end of 2009, Eroski was operating an extensive chain of almost 2,400 stores made up of 113 EROSKI hypermarkets; 1,063 EROSKI/centers, Caprabo and EROSKI/city supermarkets; 224 branches of the EROSKI/viajes travel agency; 58 petrol stations; 40 Forum Sport stores; 289 IF perfume stores; 7 Abac leisure and culture outlets; and 40 goods depots. In addition to this chain, there are 481 self-service franchise outlets. Moreover, Eroski has 4 hypermarkets, 16 supermarkets and 17 petrol stations in the south of France, and it has 4 perfume stores in Andorra.**

The Retail area is also home to the food group Erkop, which operates in the catering, cleaning, stock-breeding, horticulture and services sectors and has as its leading provider Auzo Lagun, a co-operative engaged in group catering, and the cleaning of buildings and premises, and also offers an integrated service in the health sector.

- **The Knowledge area has a dual focus: education-training and innovation, which have both been key elements in the development of the Corporation. The University of Mondragon is a university of a co-operative nature. It combines the development of knowledge, skills, and value and maintains close relations with business, especially the Co-operatives. Technological innovation is generated through the Co-operatives' own R&D departments, the Corporate Science and Technology Plan, the work of the Corporation's 12 technology centres and the Garaia Innovation Park.**

Crédit Agricole (France)[29]

Crédit Agricole S.A. (CASA) is the largest retail banking group in France, second largest in Europe, and the eighth largest in the world by Tier 1 capital according to The Banker magazine. Crédit Agricole S.A. is majority owned by 39 French co-operative retail banks, Caisses Régionales de Crédit Agricole Mutuel.

Its subsidiaries include: Credit Agricole CIB, the investment banking division of Crédit Agricole ; Newedge, global futures and options brokerage serving institutional investors (50-50 joint venture with Société Générale) ; CACEIS Investor Services, Asset servicing entity, joint venture with Natixis Cheuvreux, the European and American securities brokerage division; CLSA, the Asian securities brokerage division ; Predica and Pacifica, the insurance divisions; Amundi, its asset management subsidiary, jointly owned with Société Générale ; Uni-Éditions, a French magazine publisher;ACBA Crédit Agricole, an Armenian bank ; Cariparma FriulAdria, an Italian bank ; Crédit Agricole Egypt, an Egyptian bank; Crédit Agricole Srbija, a Serbian bank; Crédit du Maroc, a Moroccan bank; Emporiki Bank, a Greek bank 91% owned by CA; LCL (Previously Crédit Lyonnais), a French bank ; Credit Agricole Bank Polska S. A. (previously LUKAS Bank S. A.), a Polish bank ; Credit Agricole Bank (previously Index Bank); a Ukrainian bank; and CA Grands Crus, a French vineyard owner.

Through its subsidiaries, Crédit Agricole SA is involved in the following services: French retail banking, international retail banking, specialised financial services, asset management, insurance and private banking, and corporate and investment banking.

Credit Agricole's structure (system) is rather extensive. The following diagram (see Figure 2.3) following from their 2011 annual report illustrates the various ownership and subsidiaries structures in the co-operative bank.

Given the exceedingly large and complex organizational structure some observers suggesting Crédit Agricole SA operates as much as a private sector institution as it does a co-operative. Given its scale this appears to be a necessity. In our view, because of its ownership structure, we would perhaps best choose to describe it as a co-operative system of enterprise.

Figure 2.3

Organisation of Crédit Agricole Group and Crédit Agricole S.A. as of Dec 31, 2011[30]

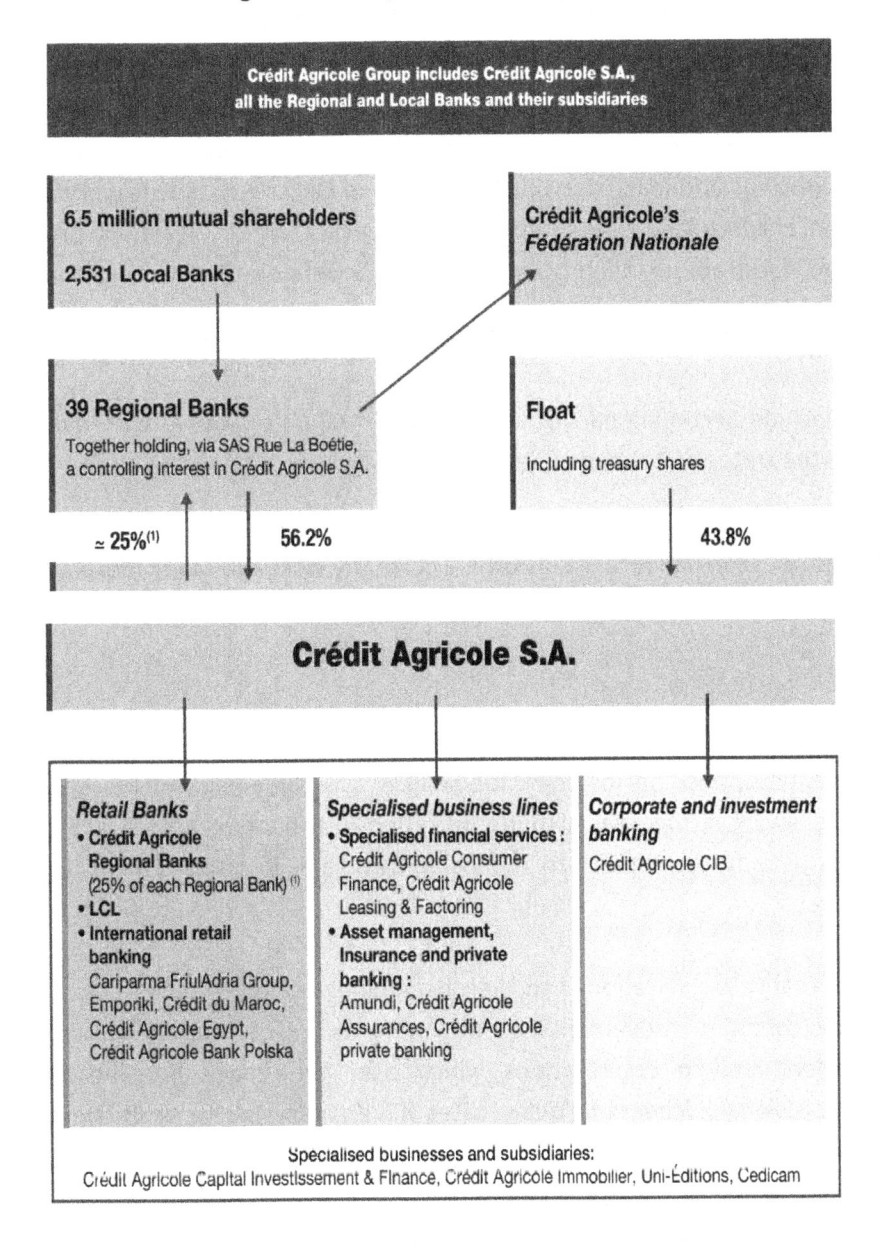

ZEN-NOH (Japan)[31]

ZEN-NOH is the largest trade co-operative enterprise in the world. In English ZEN-NOH translates to National Federation of Agricultural Co-operative Associations. It is a federation of agricultural cooperatives in Japan. ZEN-NOH consists of 1,173 agricultural cooperatives and federations. ZEN-NOH is involved in the marketing, tracking, and quality assurance of the products of its cooperatives. ZEN-NOH is also largely involved in the production of farming equipment, primarily tractors.

COMAPI (Brazil)[32]

COMAPI is a relatively new (1994) co-operative venture in North East Brazil. It has been assisted with support from NATERRA Worldwide, and is involved in high quality honey production. COMAPI benefits 1100 rural families in 32 communities in 10 counties of the state of Piaui. Each community has several beekeeping groups formed by 4 or 5 families and two coordinators. The two coordinators oversee all the beekeeping work in the community and meet monthly with the members to discuss issues, bring suggestions, raise concerns and make decisions. Everyone in the community is welcome to participate – beekeepers, women, children, and elders. With 20,000 hives, COMAPI sustainably produces and exports high-quality, organic, fair-trade certified honey. The beekeepers directly benefit from the sales. Honey revenues are reported to have increased family incomes by an average of 65% - in some cases doubling their previous income.

COMAPI plans include becoming part of a planned central co-operative with nine other beekeeper co-operatives from the states of Piaui and Ceara, Brazil.

Please appreciate that the above list of co-operatives are notable examples of co-operative systems of enterprise. This is not an exhaustive list, as others currently exist and many more are developing.

Take Aways

1. All movements espouse an ideology. Ideology is a verbal image of the good society and the means of achieving it, together with identification of the forces hostile to that vision. All social movements have future aspects to their ideologies and it is this dimension that makes them change-driven.

2. Many co-operative organizations had their beginnings as movements in reaction to some social or economic condition. Movements are driven by visions of a better world, but to realize that vision, leaders created organizations which over time have become successful business enterprises. Visionary leaders in many cases have given way to professional managers. Thus systems are born.

3. In many parts of the world it is now common place for co-operators to refer to "the credit union system," "the co-operative retailing system," or simply "the co-operative system." Co-operative systems are composed of interdependent parts and, like movements, are guided by ideals.

4. Co-operative systems of enterprise have grown very large and very complex. Movement and system capture different dimensions of reality. Unless both are recognized, planning and future processes are likely one-sided and focused on the existing functions and activities of the organization, rather than what might be broader purposes or interests of the members, and the community.

PART TWO – HOW CO-OPERATIVES ARE DIFFERENT

Appreciating the Distinctiveness

Chapter Three - The Co-operative Value Proposition

Making the Case

We will begin by looking at what we call we the "a co-operative business model", and the values and principles upon which it is based. We will look at the value a co-operative creates from a number of different perspectives. We will looking at the values or benefits which local co-operatives create for their members and their communities, as well as benefits created by second and third-tier co-operatives regionally and nationally. We will also touch on the *benefits* co-operatives contribute to society at large.

The Co-operative Enterprise Business Model

The co-operative business model logically is based on co-operation more than on competition. This is important because, as you will see, the co-operative model emphasizes values, motivations, and behaviours that are not as commonly found in the corporate world. A second difference between co-operatives and other corporations is the member - versus - investor orientation. Co-operatives focus on generating benefits (which may or may not be profits) and satisfying member's needs, while corporations typically focus on creating and maximizing wealth for their investors. In co-operatives, when there earn surpluses, they typically remain within the communities in which they were created. Given these differences, the operating philosophies between the two can differ greatly.

Co-operatives are established because people in communities identify common needs that they want met. They are often established in communities where important services are being lost or new services are required. The priority of the co-operative is to ensure the continued availability of the service it provides, with earning generation being a secondary concern. In producer or worker co-operatives sustainability of the enterprise or structure may be the top priority, with the priority of returns to members following closely behind.

Co-operatives are therefore driven by both social and economic concerns. They are often community-based enterprises that are established by their member/owners to meet their economic and social service needs. A priority for a co-operative is to improve the quality of life for its members, not simply to maximize profits for shareholders.

Co-operatives differ in a number of ways from other business models. The basic distinctions that make co-operatives unique can be summarized as follows: [1]

- **Different Purpose:** Whereas the primary purpose of a private sector enterprise is to maximize profit for its owners and/or shareholders, the primary purpose of a co-operative is to meet the common service needs of its members. Needless to say, a co-operative must always aim to maintain a level of earnings sufficient to support current operations and to provide for future growth.

- **Different Control Structure:** Whereas share ownership is the controlling factor in most private sector businesses, members are the controlling factor in a co-operative enterprise. In a co-operative, each member has one vote regardless of the number of shares held.
- **Different Allocation of Earnings:** Whereas investor-owned businesses must distribute profits in the form of dividends allocated based on number of shares held, co-operatives distribute profits to members in proportion to the business they conducted with the co-operative during its business year.

The table shown below Figure 3.1 provides a comparison of some of the various business factors involved.[2]

Figure 3.1

Comparisons of Business Factors

Factors	Co-operative Enterprise	Corporate Sector
PURPOSE		
Focus	Satisfy member as well as community needs.	Target market usually with growth opportunities.
Values	Democratic, equality, shared ownership and risk, self-help, member and community needs based, generally risk averse, acquisition and exploitation of resources to satisfy member needs.	Profit-focused, acquisition and exploitation of resources to maximize shareholders' wealth, often risk taking, to maximize compensation of executive management.
CONTROL STRUCTURE		
Ownership	Shareholders minimum of 3 - 5 people and unlimited based on a shared or common community bond, (in a few co-operatives some non-voting shares may be traded on the open market).	Shareholders (individual or many persons including other corporations), shares may be held privately or traded on the open market).
Decision-making	Democratic - consensual or one member one vote; in larger co-operatives executive management may play a significant role in co-operative decision-making based on the co-operative's values.	Majority rules - based on number of common shares held; in larger corporation executive management may play a significant role in corporate decision-making based on the corporation's values.
ALLOCATION OF EARNINGS		
Profit & Non-profit	Both are possible.	Both are possible.
Return on Investment	Depending on profitability, market rate of interest may be paid on shares, and a patronage rebate may be given based on utilization of services or service contribution made, and after making any allocation to reserves to meet other statutory or other requirements, and making necessary provision for any income tax; community donations and project participation common.	Unlimited return (dividend) on share investment, including capital gains or losses if shares are traded on the open market and after making any allocation to reserves to meet statutory or other requirements, and making necessary provision for any income tax; community donations and project participation selective.
Financial Liability	Limited to shareholder investment.	Limited to shareholder investment
Income Tax	Non-profit co-operatives are typically not taxable depending upon legislative jurisdiction. For profit co-operatives are generally required to pay tax based on the tax jurisdiction in which they operate.	Non-profit corporations are typically not taxable depending upon legislative jurisdiction. Other corporations are required to pay tax based on the tax jurisdiction in which they operate.

It is important to emphasize that in any form of co-operative enterprise established business functions and business activities must be diligently organized and managed. As one co-operative historian has been quoted as saying, contrary to what some might expect, "... running a co-operative requires a lot more than holding a love in or a group hug if you want it to be sustainable." In many instances, co-operatives must compete with other forms of business, and in some cases also actively compete amongst themselves. Business functions and metrics in areas such as business productivity, return on assets and on equity, period over period growth, customer/member satisfaction, sales and marketing, aging of receivables, human resource management, research and development, and risk management all require management's attention and must be kept within established parameters as appropriate for the particular type of enterprise.

Underpinning the business model as described above are the basic values and principles adopted by co-operatives around the world. These principles and values have evolved only slightly over the past century, although they continue to be refined as time goes on.

Co-operative Principles and Values

The co-operative principles are a set of basic standard guidelines that shape the operation of all co-operative enterprises. They are the way in which all co-operatives put their values into practice. They are what distinguish co-operatives from other enterprise models. Since providing its first list of Principles in 1937, the International Co-operative Alliance has revised and updated them twice. The most recent revisions have been undertaken because of the ever widening use of the co-operative model and in response to economic and social change. As a result, there is now a new generation of socially and environmentally conscious individuals who are using the co-operative business model because co-operative principles and values fit with their own values and life styles. For example, bicycle and car sharing co-operatives are being formed to conserve energy and harness wind energy, and biofuels co-operatives are being formed to produce "green" energy. Although the co-operative principles and values have been reframed, their original elements have been maintained and continue to be relevant in our contemporary world.

At its world conference in Manchester, England, in 1995, the International Co-operative Alliance adopted a new definition and set of principles and values for the 21st century. These ten values and the seven principles which arise from them are embodied in what the International Co-operative Alliance refers to as the *Statement of Co-operative Identity* as explained below.

Figure 3.2

Statement on the Co-operative Identity

Definition

A co-operative is an autonomous association of persons united voluntarily to meet their common economic, social, and cultural needs and aspirations through a jointly-owned and democratically-controlled enterprise.

Values

Co-operatives are based on the values of self-help, self-responsibility, democracy, equality, equity and solidarity. In the tradition of their founders, co-operative members believe in the ethical values of honesty, openness, social responsibility, and caring for others

Principles

The co-operative principles are guidelines by which co-operatives put their values into practice.

1st Principle: Voluntary and Open Membership

Co-operatives are voluntary organisations, open to all persons able to use their services and willing to accept the responsibilities of membership, without gender, social, racial, political or religious discrimination.

2nd Principle: Democratic Member Control

Co-operatives are democratic organisations controlled by their members, who actively participate in setting their policies and making decisions. Men and women serving as elected representatives are accountable to the membership. In primary co-operatives members have equal voting rights (one member, one vote) and co-operatives at other levels are also organised in a democratic manner.

3rd Principle: Member Economic Participation

Members contribute equitably to, and democratically control, the capital of their co-operative. At least part of that capital is usually the common property of the co-operative. Members usually receive limited compensation, if any, on capital subscribed as a condition of membership. Members allocate surpluses for any or all of the following purposes: developing their co-operative, possibly by setting up reserves, part of which at least would be indivisible; benefiting members in proportion to their transactions with the co-operative; and supporting other activities approved by the membership.

4th Principle: Autonomy and Independence

Co-operatives are autonomous, self-help organisations controlled by their members. If they enter into agreements with other organisations, including governments, or raise capital from external sources, they do so on terms that ensure democratic control by their members and maintain their co-operative autonomy.

5th Principle: Education, Training, and Information

Co-operatives provide education and training for their members, elected representatives, managers, and employees so they can contribute effectively to the development of their co-operatives. They inform the general public - particularly young people and opinion leaders - about the nature and benefits of co-operation.

6th Principle: Co-operation among Co-operatives

Co-operatives serve their members most effectively and strengthen the co-operative movement by working together through local, national, regional and international structures.

7th Principle: Concern for Community

Co-operatives work for the sustainable development of their communities through policies approved by their members.

The new definition of co-operative principles is intended to serve a wide and growing array of co-operative enterprises. It identifies the fundamental characteristics of any co-operatively run enterprise. They include: co-operative autonomy, association of persons, voluntary membership, member need, joint ownership, democratic control and business viability.

Set within the co-operative identity, these values and principles clearly distinguish co-operatives from all other forms of enterprise. As stated by Canadian co-operator Ian MacPherson, "Viewed as a totality, these Principles, linked to their sustaining values and summarized in the definition, indicate what is unique about co-operatives regardless of where they exist."

The Statement of Co-operative Identity as shown above is available from the International Co-operative Alliance in multiple languages from their website at: www.ica.coop/, using the search term "identity" as of June 2013.

The Importance of Purpose in a Co-operative

The founding members of a co-operative form their organisation with a purpose in mind. That purpose may have initially been expressed in discussions by proponents in small group meetings made to enlist new members, or in the newsletters or blogs of the organization, and later in the more formal articles of incorporation, in bylaws and in the business plan. This is similar to other forms of endeavour. What is unique about co-operatives is that in many cases the purpose has not been, or cannot be, satisfied by those in the private or public sectors.

Examples exist around the world.

- **Consider the formation of credit unions in North America and elsewhere.** The unwillingness of banks and others to provide financial services (mainly loans) to individuals and small business (for example, Canadian farmers in the prairie region during 1930s and 1940s) created the need for individuals and small groups to pool resources and form savings and credit unions, which today we simply call credit unions.
- **Many of the same Canadian farm members had already formed grain marketing co-operatives or *pools* to ensure better prices for their produce than they received from private grain buyers.**
- **Workers in Argentina realized the only way they could sustain their livelihood when the factories were closing during the last decade and no one was willing to purchase them, was to organize workers' co-operatives.**
- **Small traders in the Philippines and in Ecuador decided they could do better by forming their own saving and credit co-operatives, when banks didn't want their business.**
- **Individuals wanting insurance services in Kenya, Canada and in the Philippines realized that they could get better services if they used a co-operative business model.**

In some cases individuals had been refused services or had been overcharged by existing providers; in other cases no such service was locally available. For example, in Argentina workers came together to begin recycling waste products when no one else was interested.[3] Today, there are several hundred such co-operative enterprises. They employ thousands of workers and at the same time help provide a cleaner and safer environment for everyone.

Do co-operatives have a history of achieving the purpose or purposes for which they were created? The answer is a resounding YES! Co-operatives today make up by far the largest element of what is known in some quarters as the third sector.[4] The third sector typically includes volunteer organizations, non-profits, and other groups which can loosely be referred to as social enterprises (community run enterprises such as food banks and local employment centres). The very fact that co-operative organizations are continuing to thrive and grow rapidly in many fields around the globe suggests that the co-operative enterprise business model works and is sustainable across a wide variety of circumstances from India to Australia to the Netherlands to Argentina. While there are few global figures on the survival rates of co-operative forms of enterprise, reports from Canada show that the survival rates of co-operatives in that country were almost double when compared to private sector enterprises, with 64% of co-operatives and 36% of private enterprises surviving after five years, and 46% of co-operatives reaching the 10-year mark compared to only 20% of private enterprises.[5]

Of course, not all co-operatives succeed, and not all co-operatives survive over time. This is to be expected with any enterprise. Sometimes member-owners decide their organization has failed or is failing to achieve its purposes and that it is time to sell, merge, downsize, or wind up. A complex example from Canada involves what previously was known as the Saskatchewan Wheat Pool.[6] The Pool was a major grain handling, agri-food processing and marketing co-operative based in Saskatchewan, Canada. To many of the Pool's members, their co-operative had grown too large and had ceased acting like a co-operative. In March 1996, the Saskatchewan Wheat Pool with the approval of the majority of its member owners became a publicly traded company, thus breaking from its roots as a co-operative. Within a few years it had ceased to be a co-operative.

In other cases, a co-operative may cease to be sustainable because of unfavourable market conditions, and thus be unable to achieve its intended purpose. It may seek to merge with another co-operative or a series of co-operatives in order to remain viable, and thereby continue to serve its members, or it may be sold in part or in whole to interested investors. (Readers are urged to see the **"Beware Also Means Be Aware,"** section in Chapter 9 for further details on a process that is sometimes referred to the demutualization of a co-operatively owned enterprise.)

***Crowd Sourcing and Crowd Funding** - One of the latest developments made available to us via the web and social media is called crowd sourcing, which has an offshot called crowd funding. It is interesting to note that this new development is not unlike what co-operatives invented more than a century ago by bringing together many small owner investors, from across a defined community, with very limited risk or liability, to help achieve a desired or needed purpose.*

How Co-operatives Create Value

Simply stated, co-operatives allow people to pool their human, financial and technical resources, and to achieve results that otherwise would not be possible. Tangible benefits may be seen immediately in areas such as improved services, more product availability, and better prices. It is not uncommon for co-operatives to provide useful business skills and other types of education to members as part of their service offering.

Intangible or difficult to quantify benefits include leadership and problem-solving skills developed by and for members. The local ownership and governance of a co-operative means the business plan, the strategies and the policies adopted by the co-operative, reflect the situations within the community. Another intangible benefit is that, over time and based on experience, co-operative members and leaders come to rely on themselves to solve economic and social problems instead of on government or outside agencies. In some cases, co-operatives join together, or act through their federations or central organizations, to take action or advocate action by governments in order to address issues of concern.

This was the case in Canada when credit unions successfully pressed for cost of credit disclosure, for themselves and especially finance companies that were charging - but not disclosing - extremely high rates of interest. This eventually led to "cost of credit disclosure" regulations being enacted.

While there are always reasons for confidentiality respecting a particular member's dealings or an employees work performance, co-operatives operate on an open and a transparent basis. Openness and transparency are two avenues for avoiding corruption within any organization.

> *Co-operative Contributions Are Not Always Visible - While not always recognized locally, co-operatives (particularly second and third-tier co-operatives) in many countries also own sizable office, business and other productive assets. Such assets include office towers, electricity distribution networks, oil and gas refineries, wholesale food distribution facilities, information and communications networks, logistics and shipping facilities, and of course both small and large manufacturing facilities.*

When dealing with a co-operative member, concerns can easily be raised and issues or concerns addressed by approaching the co-operative manager or by contacting a member of the board of directors. Since members own the co-operative, they also have the right to attend and speak out during annual meetings of their local co-operative.

One member, one vote is an important principle in all co-operatives. The democratic dimension of co-operatives is an important educational and developmental element in co-operatives around the world. The members of a co-operative democratically elect their board of directors and in some cases committee members. The board and committee members frequently receive little and in some case no remuneration for their efforts. Elected officials that do receive a per diem or other form of remuneration, typically senior professionals from larger co-operatives, must do so within the co-operative's approved policies. In a co-operative, elected officials always know that they are accountable to the members who elected them. Often these same leaders are or go on to become successful leaders or business persons within their local community.

As well, different types of co-operatives can create particular benefits. Marketing co-operatives can help members increase their sales volume and obtain better selling prices. Producer co-operatives can add value to their members' raw products. Profits that usually go elsewhere can instead be passed on to co-operative members. Consumer co-operatives can help their members to buy in volume and at increased savings. Consumer co-operatives may also be able to provide increased access to goods and services not previously available to them (e.g., affordable home delivery of fresh vegetables and organically grown food). Savings and credit co-operatives (credit unions) help their members save money when borrowing for a house, a vehicle, or for education. They can provide competitive rates and services to assist savers. Co-operative insurance companies can help members reduce premiums as well as pay member claims in cases where private insurance companies could refuse. Finally, worker-owned cooperatives can create improved working conditions for workers, including job security, and of course, member owners share in a portion of the profits of the enterprise depending upon the labour they provide. Typically, worker co-operatives have lower employee turnover, higher productivity, and stronger profits when compared to other forms of enterprise.

Clearly, co-operatives have a significant positive impact on the communities in which they serve. They create and retain local jobs, pay various taxes, and typically have a long-term commitment to the community and its future success. Since co-operative surplus earnings are returned to local owner members, more money remains in the community, thereby strengthening the local economy. Earnings retained within co-operatives also become a source of capital (both working and equity) to support local and regional economic development and business expansion. Most co-operatives support through purchases other businesses within their community. The presence of a local co-operative along with other businesses may even mean more competitive pricing of products and services.

The seventh co-operative principle - *Concern for Community* - is expressed in a wide variety of ways. Local co-operatives often help by funding community schools, care homes, day care centres, hospitals, community parks or local community centres. It is not unusual to see a local co-operative or group of co-operatives actively supporting other service organisations, the arts, charities, sports, science initiatives, educational activities and a host of other philanthropic endeavours in their community or region. Co-operatives are well regarded by the communities in which they operate. This is in fact an understatement as many co-operatives are regularly recognized as community leaders and at the leading edge of supporting their community and its social and economic development. The presence of local directors, officers, and committee members also means hundreds and in fact thousands of individuals are receiving hands on experience in leading and governing some very complex co-operative enterprises. This contributes substantially to the pool of skills and talent available locally to undertake other business and community leadership endeavours.

In addition to illustrating the value which co-operatives create for themselves and their communities, we wish to emphasize that co-operatives around the globe are impacting the social and economic lives of women. "I am able to be self-sufficient," "I am able to feed and educate my children," and "I am able to plan for a brighter future," are common statements made by women who have learned about and benefited by joining a co-operative. The variety and diversity of women's co-operatives around the world is amazing. Women have organized themselves using the co-operative enterprise model to address issues ranging from powerlessness and HIV all the way to obtaining financing for women entrepreneurs. The outcomes are clear: greater equality and empowerment as well as financial strength for women members. Here we list just a few of the many women's co-operative that exist around the world:

- **DamDam Haiti- Women's Handicraft Cooperative in Léogâne, Haiti**
- **Womens Co-operative Bank in Larnaka, Cyprus**
- **Women's Co-operative Guild in Sheffield, England**

- Songtaab-Yalgré Association in Ouagadougou, Burkina Faso
- Women's Co-operative Bank in Goa, India
- Deir Bzei Women's Cooperative of Deir Bzei, Palestine
- Durbar Mahila Samanwaya Collective (Sex Trade Workers Co-operative) in Calcutta, India

While the above list illustrates co-operatives that have been organized and run by women, we must recognize that women also play important roles in the leadership and management of many co-operatives. It is common to see women serving as general managers and as elected directors of savings and credit co-operatives around the globe. Accepting and promoting gender diversity allows co-operatives to be more adaptable and to strengthen communities by ensuring that the needs and interests of all members are fairly represented in the organization.

Readers wishing to see the impact that women are having can see an extensive research report describing experiences in more detail from India and Nepal. It is available for download from the Canadian Co-operative Association website using this link: www. coopscanada.coop and searching for the author whose name is Smita Ramnarain.

Across society from India to Rwanda, to the Philippines, to Australia, to France, the Ukraine, Canada and Chile, and in all of the countries in between, co-operative forms of enterprise are helping to build a better world. In and through co-operative forms of enterprise, people of almost every nation on the globe are able to participate in discussions and in debates about their organizations and about policies and issues that are of concern to them. Equally important, they are able to do so peacefully.

Co-operatives and the Pursuit of Peace

In Chapter 1 we discussed how competition, conflict, and co-operation are all aspects of human behavior. We also learned earlier in this chapter that co-operative principles and values are key elements of a business model by which various interests can successfully work together to achieve common purposes.

For three days in 2006, 38 co-operative representatives from 16 different countries met in Victoria, British Columbia, Canada,[7] for the first time to review the historical record of how co-operatives have addressed conflict and to reflect on current practices of co-operatives operating in areas deeply divided by political, economic, and social tensions. The result was a growing recognition of the significant ways in which co-operative organizations can contribute in real and practical terms to the peace making process.

The possibilities which are described in the book entitled *Co-operatives and the Pursuit of Peace* include specific cases from South America as well as from Asia and Africa.[8] The cases presented describe ways in which people with different ethic, social, gender, and educational backgrounds have succeeded in achieving common goals through their co-operatives.

One of the participants at the 2006 Victoria conference, Dr. Yehudah Paz, summed it up best by stating, "Peace and social well-being are not only relevant to co-operatives, but co-operatives are relevant to the peace making process in communities and societies throughout the world."[9]

Following on the heels of the Victoria conference and further debate and discussion with co-operative leaders and officials, more than 2,000 delegates at the Annual General Assembly of the International Co-operative Alliance in November 2011, in Cancun, Mexico, approved the creation of an institute for the Promotion of Peace and Social Cohesion. This new institute will undertake further research, promote ways to educate co-operative leaders and employees around the diverse ways co-operatives contribute to creating more peaceful communities, and demonstrate the role co-operatives can play in the pursuit of peace globally. We look forward to further reports respecting outcomes of this initiative.

United Nations Declares 2012 the International Year of Co-operatives

At the global International Co-operative Alliance General Assembly held in Cancun, Mexico, in November of 2011, the United Nations Secretary General Ban Ki-Moon via video congratulated the co-operative movement for its contribution to the global common good.[10] The message came a little over two weeks after the United Nations' launched the International Year of Co-operatives in New York. The Secretary General said, "Co-operatives are a unique and invaluable presence in today's world. They help to reduce poverty and generate jobs." In his message, Moon emphasised the important role that co-operatives play in strengthening communities socially and economically. He also noted co-operatives are value-based businesses that are rooted in their communities because they are owned by their members. In closing, he called upon the audience and the worldwide co-operative movement to "create better businesses and a better world" through co-operative enterprises.

You can learn more regarding what co-operatives around the worlds have done by logging on to the United Nations website at www.un.org/en/ also on the International Co-operative Alliance special website at www.2012.coop/ , and search for the international year of co-operatives.

Not Going Away Anytime Soon

In this chapter, Co-operative Enterprise has been introduced as an alternative way of doing business. It is a business model rooted in a handful of practical principles welded together with some basic long standing human values. Co-operative enterprise is a business model proven to work within a wide variety of social and economic circumstances, and across any number of cultures. Those who have experienced it know that it can mean the difference between plenty and poverty, and the difference between fairness and inequity. Co-operative enterprise, through democratically elected officials, gives owner-members their say in the affairs of the organization and its role in the community it serves. Co-operative enterprises are gaining ground around the globe. The potential seems almost limitless. They are not expected to be going away anytime soon. You decide!

Tangible and Intangible Benefits and Contributions

The table below summarizes the various benefits referred to earlier in this chapter.

Figure 3.3

	Some Tangible Benefits	Some intangible benefits
For Members	Provides a needed service or product which may not be available, and often at a lower cost.	Leadership development of elected officials and workers.
	Provides a practical means for pooling resources and creating sustainable livelihoods.	Aids in poverty reduction and improved standard of living and independence.
	Supports individual and family savings and wealth accumulation.	Helps develop attitudes of self-help and empowerment.
	Payment of patronage dividends based on use and or contribution.	Enhances recourse and ability to address issues and or concerns.
	Policies which provide for fair and equitable treatment of all members (i.e. gender equality).	Limited liability and risk sharing across members of the co-operative.

Continued on next page

	Some Tangible Benefits	**Some Intangible Benefits**
For Society	Avenues for greater social and economic equality and empowerment of women globally.	Demonstration that co-operative efforts can lead to peaceful relations.
	Avenues allowing for broad involvement and participation of people in the discussion and debate of policies and issues of concern.	Provides a constructive mechanism for motivated individuals and groups to take action to address issues of concern.
	Tangible contribution to the overall quality of life through poverty reduction around the world.	Clear demonstration of co-operative democracy in action.

Take Aways

1. Co-operatives share some similarities with other forms of enterprise, but are quite different in their purposes, in their underlying structures, in the way they make decisions, and in the way they manage earnings. At the same time, co-operatives must be organized and managed just as carefully as any other form of business enterprise.

2. The co-operative business model is based on a set of ten values and seven principles. These values and principles serve to guide the growth and development of co-operatives around the world.

3. Co-operatives are often created to satisfy a need that no one else is willing or prepared to satisfy.

4. Co-operatives create and add value wherever they exist. Co-operative forms of enterprise continuously create a number of tangible and intangible benefits for their members, for the communities in which they operate, and for society as a whole.

5. Across the world, co-operatives are being recognized for their contributions. In 2012, the Secretary General of the United Nations Ban Ki-Moon acknowledged that co-operatives are a unique and invaluable presence in today's world. He called upon the worldwide movement to "create better businesses and a better world" through co-operative enterprise.

Chapter Four - The Public, Private, and Co-operative Sectors

An Orange is not an Apple or a Pear

In Chapter Two and Three we saw how the 'purpose' of a co-operative could be similar to, yet very different from, that of a private sector corporation. We also saw how the 'control structure' and the 'allocations of earnings' were different in a co-operative sector enterprise than in a private sector corporation. It is these differences that have made co-operatives the preferred and sometimes the only option for millions of people around the world today.

In this chapter we will begin by looking more closely at the different organizational dynamics that exist in a co-operative as compared to the private sector (privately held as well as publically traded corporations) and to organizations in the public sector (i.e. government agencies, departments, government enterprises). In particular, we will consider the various ways in which wealth is owned. We will conclude by comparing how co-operatives have performed during the most recent economic downturn.

> *Some Quick Definitions -* We ask the reader to note carefully the distinctions between the public and the private sectors. For us the "public sector", or the government sector, is that part of the state that deals with the production, ownership, sale, provision, delivery or allocation of goods and services, by and for the government or its citizens, whether national, regional, or local. On the other hand, when we talk about the "private sector" we are talking about corporations, which may be privately held or publically traded. The private sector can also include individuals or groups operating as partnerships in the conduct of businesses.

Organizational Dynamics

As we have stated, co-operative organizations come in an almost endless range of sizes, types, and colors. Every co-operative has distinctive elements and thus it is somewhat difficult to compare them precisely to other forms of enterprise. The materials following are intended to help us make such comparisons.

First, while we might on some occasion wish it to be otherwise, we must state in very practical terms what people everywhere need to understand - and that is that the "ownership and the control of assets" does indeed make the world go around. Those of you who have studied economics will know this. You may substitute the term "wealth" or "capital" or one of its many manifestations for the term "assets". Those of you who have bought and sold produce in local town markets in the Philippines, or in Mexico, or in Uganda will know that money is necessary for any enterprise anywhere to perform. In one way or another, everything in our world with some few exceptions (i.e., people, the air, the oceans and seas, the wild animals, and the heavens) is owned in some manner. As you might imagine the ownership and control of assets varies quite significantly across the globe.

Second, when we look at the "ownership and the control" of assets we learn that in a macro sense most ownership of wealth falls into one of four, and possibly five overlapping arenas. Please note we are referring to both "ownership and 'control"!

- **The first arena is the private sector, which includes assets owned by companies like WalMart, General Electric, Toyota, TelMex, Siemens, ADF, Nike, Rio Tinto, Barclays Bank PLC, Google, and AIG, as well as national and local corporations, some of which are family owned. These corporations in turn own various assets, most of which are used to produce further assets. Most of these enterprises operate on a scale and in a manner many of us find difficult to imagine. They may be described with expressions such as "a fully integrated and differentiated supply chain". Most operate and are owned in multiple regions of the world. We ask you to especially note that the private sector also includes private investment banks and pension plans, which also manage trillions of dollars invested in various enterprises spread around the globe. Most private sector ownership is in the form of shares held directly or indirectly in private corporations, and in the marketplace in forms of tradable shares.**

- **The second arena of ownership and control refers to state or what we call public ownership and control. This typically refers to properties or entities or resources either owned or controlled by government - or the state. We are sure you can think of a government marketing agency, a department of tourism and national parks, or the armed forces of a country, the national parks, the US CIA, or even the city-run local fire brigade, as examples. However, please pause for a moment and remember that the same government of each nation state also includes in its capacity the ability to "control" all manner of taxation and licensing of its citizenry, all of its corporations, and all of their various resources. Of course, this assumes a government is actually able to collect taxes so levied, which in some places of the world is not necessarily the case, since institutional jurisdictions decide whether funds are private and as such not treated as taxable in any particular manner.**

- The third arena of ownership is co-operative or collective ownership. Co-operative ownership is sometimes seen as representing a rather minute portion of global wealth. However, as we shall show later in this book, this is no longer the case. The extent of co-operative ownership is significant and continues to increase around the globe each year. A co-operative's assets initially come from local shareholders who share some common bond. They may be local farmers, employee workers, everyday consumers, business people, investors, professionals, or simply members of a local community. There are even co-operatives whose members are private sector businesses. In each case, a co-operative exists to serve a particular purpose or multiple purposes, and it does so by pooling members' funds and resources in an enterprise which members own and control. In some cases, co-operatives have grown so large that they are able to issue preferred non-voting shares or private debentures similar to government debentures as well as to borrow funds from financial institutions. Funds raised in this way are not considered speculative, and are based on underlying tangible co-operative assets. Co-operative capital may also grow (and usually does) through earning allocations of the co-operative based on its overall financial performance during a given period. Democratically elected boards of directors govern the co-operative and its assets. They are accountable for their actions and policies to the co-operative's membership.

- A fourth area of ownership is individual or personal ownership. Sometimes this may be referred to as household wealth. This type of ownership can involve personal assets (i.e., house, car, personal effects, and personal savings) as well as business assets (i.e., investments, small and medium size proprietorships, and real property). We do not intend to examine individual ownership in detail, since such ownership often exists in shares held in major private corporations. We do wish to direct interested readers to research statistics concerning global household wealth available from Credit Suisse. You may need to contact them to request a copy of the *Credit Suisse Global Wealth Report 2012,* otherwise go to: http.credit-suisse.com/ select a country and then go to Research Institute and then Publications to download a copy.[1]

- There is a fifth arena of ownership and control of assets which we will mention in passing. We will call this fifth arena "the unreported wealth" that exists around the world. Often such wealth is held outside taxable jurisdictions, or is hidden from public record. It is a matter of public knowledge that dictators and criminal elements such as drug cartels often possess billions of dollars. In many cases, both corporations and individuals move funds to legal off shore banking centres such as are established just off the coast of England on the islands of Jersey and Guernsey. Funds may also be held in countries that provide banking deposit secrecy such as Luxembourg and Andorra.[2] In other cases, as with the Vatican, institutional jurisdictions determine that funds are private and as such are not subject to be taxed or reported in any particular manner. For our purposes, this arena of wealth ownership and control is best left to others to

explore, but this break-out by ownership does serve to illustrate whose particular interests are being served depending upon where assets are held around the globe.

We have described the major arenas in which wealth is owned and controlled around the world. The way in which wealth is held and used has a significant impact upon the lives of those who helped to create the wealth in the first place.

Let's Make Money - *You may wish to watch a copy of the video documentary 'Let's Make Money' and to learn more concerning tax havens that are today sheltering trillions of dollars click on: www.topdocumentaryfilms.com/ and search for "let's make money"*

Co-operatives are Distinct - *While some authors and researchers may choose by definition to categorize non-profit forms of co-operative enterprise as social sector enterprises, it is questionable as to whether or not all co-operatives or even the majority of co-operatives around the world should be considered as part of the social sector. In our view and in the view of many, co-operatives, because of their nature and their scope and scale globally represent a distinct form of enterprise worthy of being called a sector.*

We accept that the matter may remain open for further debate for some time.

Finally, one of the factors that make comparisons between sectors challenging is that co-operative enterprises, like the private sector, can be and often are structurally complex. At times co-operatives may use private sector structures to achieve their purposes. For example, second-tier co-operatives (owned by local co-operatives) may join together to set up a private company whose sole purpose is to support some service aspect (i.e., technology for credit and debit cards). When second and third-tier co-operatives are formed, ownership and control may be based on economic investment rather than one member one vote – provided there is agreement and support from the co-operatives involved to do so!

Please see the table below (Figure 4.1) to see the important distinguishing organizational features and related dynamics in the first three arenas. In the fourth arena, that of personal ownership we expect the reader will already know the dynamics involved. In the fifth arena, that of unreported wealth, we make no comparisons since the ownership and control of such assets are typically unreported (sometimes known as 'offshore') and may be hidden so as not to attract tax, or are not disclosed for other unknown reasons. We will expand upon each of the organizational features after the table.

To illustrate, let us assume we are comparing a public health clinic, to a private health clinic, to a co-operatively operated health clinic in Canada or the US. The comparison is not perfect, but does help us to see the unique differences. We might make similar comparisons to waste management services, or perhaps educational institutions. Again, these comparison help us to see - and therefore to appreciate - the unique differences. The materials following are intended to do just that.

We also recognize particulars may vary to some extent from jurisdiction to jurisdiction, as well as internationally. We appreciate in recent years, particularly in the US, that there has been increased blurring in the lines separating what we are describing as distinct sectors. Therefore, the reader is cautioned to look to their own jurisdiction to verify the extent to which the descriptions as provided apply. Figure 4.1 which follows provides a high level comparison of the organizational dynamics involved in the private sector, the public sector, and the co-operative sector.[3]

Figure 4.1

Organizational Dynamics - Sector Comparisons

ORGANIZATIONAL FEATURES	PRIVATE SECTOR (ENTERPRISE PRIVATELY HELD & PUBLICALLY TRADED CORPORATIONS)	PUBLIC SECTOR (GOVERNMENT AGENCY / CROWN CORPORATIONS / PARASTATALS)	CO-OPERATIVE SECTOR (LOCAL AND NATIONAL CO-OPERATIVES / INTERNATIONAL & OTHERS ALLIANCES)
OWNERSHIP	Stockholders.	Government (public).	Members.
SOURCES OF FUNDS	Investors / public markets / private debt.	Taxes / public debentures / private debt.	Members / private debt / sometimes public markets.
GOVERNANCE AND CONTROL	Board appointed by shareholders (1 share - 1 vote).	Board (if any) appointed by government.	Board elected by members (1 member - 1 vote).
EMPLOYEES PROVIDE SERVICE TO	Customers.	Public (now often called clients).	Members and, as appropriate to the public.
DISTRIBUTION OF PROFITS AFTER RESERVES (SURPLUS)	To shareholders, unlimited on shares.	To treasury (if any).	To members, limited on shares, and based on patronage.
RATIONALE FOR DECISION MAKING	Profit/return on investment.	Profit/service/other.	Member service.
MANAGEMENT OF DECISION MAKING	Involve dominant shareholders. Delegate decisions to levels closest to problems. Monitor results & change quickly.	Involve politicians & government officials. Establish criteria & rules so employee decision making is closely regulated.	Involve board & as many members as possible. Delegate decisions to levels closest to problems. Monitor results and adapt to external changes.

MANAGEMENT OF INFORMATION	Limited disclosure of financial information to investors & potential investors.	Open disclosure of financial/operational information to government. Limited open disclosure to public.	Open disclosure of aggregated financial information & open disclosure of operational information to members.
MANAGEMENT OF ASSETS	To accumulate wealth for major investors.	To use wealth (and debt) for public service.	To provide quality member service.
MANAGEMENT OF ASPIRATIONS	Aspirations of dominant owners and of management are central.	Aspirations of public as represented by politicians are central.	Aspirations of active members & elected officials are central.
PLANNING & PARTICIPATION	Involves dominant owners & management.	Involves politicians, management & senior employees.	Involves active members, elected officials, management & employees.

The OWNERSHIP of a co-operative organization is in the hands of its members. All co-operative organizations require prospective members to apply for the purchase of a minimum number of membership shares in order to become members of the organization. The number of shares to be purchased may be as few as one or two and may only have a nominal value of $5.00 or less depending on the country involved. This is the most common situation. In other cases, the share purchase (number and value) may be significant depending on the co-operative's capital needs. Some worker co-operatives, for example, have a single share price of more than $50,000. The minimum and maximum number of shares that may be purchased by a member is stated in the co-operative's bylaws or in that jurisdiction's co-operative legislation or regulations. Common or voting shares in a co-operative are not traded in the open market; thus the *"one member one vote"* principle is protected, regardless of the number of shares held by individual members. Membership shares in a co-operative may increase in value based on allocation of surplus earnings to shares, or on appreciation of the co-operative's business volume and assets. Member shares are non-redeemable and are only to be paid out to the member when he or she leaves the community or quits using the co-operative, and after the required application for redemption of the share or shares and the required approvals are granted by the organization. Membership shares help to provide the equity base for the organization as well as to encourage ongoing interest in, and use of, the co-operative by its owner members.

Ownership of private sector corporations is based on the purchase of common shares, which may be held privately or traded publicly on the open market. The number of shares held determines the number of votes each shareholder is able to exercise in the major affairs of the organization. Management of private sector corporations are also typically major shareholders.

Public sector or state entities are owned collectively by the state. State entities include government agencies (at various levels from local to national) and can include parastatal enterprises, such as marketing boards, crown corporations and public service utilities. Citizenship or sometimes proof of residency is the normal requirement to be able to vote for one's choice in representative democracy elections.

The SOURCES OF FUNDS in new co-operatives initially come from member share purchases. However, co-operatives may find additional funds are required for operations and look elsewhere for some of their working capital. Shareholder loans may also be used during the start-up of the co-operative. Once established, co-operatives may seek additional financing from traditional sources of business financing, including bank loans, or may even issue preferred shares in the open market. In addition to membership share capital, a co-operative may also elect to retain a portion of its earnings as equity capital either in the form of general reserves or special allowances needed to manage growth and risk.

The private sectors will use similar forms of financing but larger corporations frequently use an IPO (or initial public share offering). Larger established private sector corporations will also use various forms of shares as well as corporate debentures and bonds.

The public sector uses its taxation powers to obtain funding but can also issue debentures and bonds. It can also participate in joint ventures or partnerships with others in initiatives it sees as being beneficial for the larger community. Nationally most countries also use a central banking facility through which they issue a national currency and thus control the money supply within their borders.

GOVERNANCE AND CONTROL in the co-operative sector is in accordance with co-operative values and principles. In a co-operative at the primary or community level, governance is based on the principle of *"one member one vote"*.

Each year, co-operatives hold their annual general membership meeting. Here members have an opportunity to discuss issues, hear reports, and vote on pressing matters. Members may also be asked to review or approve bylaws for the organization. Elections are held prior to or in conjunction with the co-operative's annual general membership meeting. The general membership democratically elects board members from their ranks to represent their interests in the operation of the co-operative. More and more co-operatives are now using Internet or other electronic voting systems in advance of the co-operative's annual meeting. Co-operative members may, depending on the bylaws approved by the membership, also elect a supervisory and governance committee to oversee selected aspects of the board. Each co-operative must ensure that it is operating within the legislation and regulations in its jurisdiction, and typically must file annual and statistical reports with the designated government department responsible for monitoring it.

Multi-Stakeholder Co-operatives - *Multi-stakeholder co-operatives (MSCs) are co-operatives that allow for governance by representatives of two or more "stakeholder" groups. They can include consumers, producers, workers, volunteers or general community supporters. Multi-stakeholder co-ops are typically formed to pursue social objectives and are particularly strong in the area of healthcare*

The board of a co-operative organizes itself and elects the various members of the executive, including the president, vice president, and so on. The board also hires a general manager who in turn hires the other employees of the organization. The size of the co-operative and the nature of its activities dictate the degree of complexity and sophistication that will be required. Boards may meet monthly, bi-monthly or quarterly. Co-operative boards are required to establish clear roles and responsibilities for themselves and for their management. They also establish policies and practices needed to guide and direct management.

Governance and member control structures vary considerably, depending on the type of co-operative and its scale of operations. It is not uncommon for larger co-operatives to establish delegate structures and processes as a way of engaging members in the affairs of the organization. The election processes for delegates are designed in such a way as to ensure fair and equitable representation of all members. Such processes must typically be dealt with in the bylaw of the co-operative. It is from the elected delegate body that the board of directors are in turn elected. Delegates and directors will have fixed terms of office. Most boards of directors and elected delegates are active throughout the year, discussing issues and sharing information as well as establishing longer term direction and policies needed by the co-operative. In all cases, the board of directors and delegates are accountable to the general membership during the year and at annual or special general membership meetings. In other cases the co-operative may be organized as a multi-stakeholder co-operative (MSC) and include members representing community groups and organizations, civic bodies or agencies, as well as private corporations.[4]

In some countries such as the Philippines, it is not uncommon for a co-operative's annual meeting to last for two, even three, full days. In many instances, some three or four thousand or more members attend. The reason co-operatives are sometimes criticised for taking longer than others to make major decisions is because they often choose to dialogue with a broad cross section of members before taking action.

The EMPLOYEES PROVIDE SERVICE TO owner-members of the co-operative. Employees include management and staff. They should be aware that the organization is owned by its members and one of the primary reasons it exists is to provide services to its members; "membership" is a vitally important concept, the benefits and duties pertaining to it are significant in demonstrating the co-operative difference and in providing future possibilities. In the case of private sector organizations, employees provide services to customers. In the public sector, employees provide services to the general public.

The DISTRIBUTION OF PROFITS AFTER RESERVES (SURPLUS) is dictated by four factors (not in any order of priority) in the co-operative sector:

First - the size of surplus funds (earnings after required taxes and statutory reserves have been provided for), which is generally based on how well the co-operative has performed during the period.

Second - how much of the services of the co-operative each member actually used, or contributed. In some cases, the payout may be entirely in cash and in other cases may be cash in part directly to the member and a portion as an allocation to the member's share holdings.

Third – the amount considered fair and equitable, as may be spelt out in the co-operative's operating policy, to reward employees for their contribution to the success of that period.

Fourth - the amount the co-operative needs to set aside for future development and risk.

The above allocations are typically planned and budgeted for annually. Where unforeseen circumstances impact the co-operative's performance, and it is unable to achieve the performance as planned, then it is the duty of the board and management to carefully weigh how they wish to allocate remaining earnings after meeting statutory obligations. Ultimately, it falls to the board of directors to make the decision on allocations after due consideration and consultation with its executive management.

In the private sector, the distribution of profits after taxes and reserves is intended to maximize the net wealth of shareholders and is typically paid out as a declared cash dividend on shares, or is used to buy back existing shares, thus increasing the value of existing issued and outstanding shares. In some instances, private sector corporations are rewarding customers with reward points based on their total purchases. Most airlines and some credit card companies follow these practices as a way of encouraging customer loyalty. Public sector entities typically do not distribute profits or surplus funds although in some instances they may selectively reduce tax rates or reduce fees for fee based services such as licenses.

The RATIONALE FOR DECISION MAKING is always based on delivering, improving, and in some cases sustaining member services in the co-operative sector, usually over a specific planning period such as one year, three years, or five years. In the private sector, the primary basis for making decisions is usually the impact they will have on the price of the corporation's shares in the upcoming quarter end. Return on assets or return on equity figures may also be used as a rationale for some decision-making in co-operatives --but the quality, value, and reliability of service to members over the longer term will be the primary rationale for more day-to-day decisions within the co-operative. A public sector entity may use a variety of rationales for its decision-making. Public acceptance or pushback, shifts in policy frameworks, trends in political polls, creation of jobs or conversely unemployment rates, inflation and public indebtedness, environmental implications, media reporting, business endorsement, and lobbying efforts may all play into public sector decision-making.

The MANAGEMENT OF DECISION MAKING is all about how decisions are made within an organization. In the private sector, the decisions of the dominant shareholders can play a major role. Often senior management are the major shareholders. In private sector corporations it is usually prudent to delegate decisions to those most knowledgeable and to those who are closest to problems. When decisions are being made in the public sector, it is essential that elected politicians and senior government officials are involved as needed or required by law. In the public sector, criteria and rules are often created so employee decision making can be closely regulated. In the co-operative sector, decisions are taken within a broader planning framework which involves both board and management in the creation of high level vision strategies, policies, and tactics. Board members, managers, and as many employees as possible are involved in decision-making. Decisions are delegated to those most knowledgeable and closest to the situation. However major decisions typically require approval by the membership before then may be implemented. In co-operative, as in the other organisations, it is important to monitor results and adapt to external changes.

The MANAGEMENT OF INFORMATION is handled quite differently in the co-operative sector than elsewhere. In the private sector, information is power. In privately-held, private sector corporations, there will be only limited disclosure of financial information to existing investors and potential investors. In many publicly traded companies, depending upon their jurisdiction, high level plans and targets as well as high level operating results will be disclosed. Where subordinated debt is involved, more detailed quarterly reporting may be provided. Inside the public sector there will be disclosure of financial and operational information to top bureaucrats and senior elected officials, although there may be limited disclosure of particulars to the general public. In the co-operative sector, there tends to be open disclosure of aggregated financial information and of longer term business plans and goals as well as open disclosure of operational information to members. At the same time, though, the confidentiality of individual member information is always a top priority of co-operative employees and officials.

The MANAGEMENT OF ASSETS varies widely and is one of the biggest differences amongst the three sectors. The private sector manages its wealth in order to create wealth for its major investors. The public sector uses whatever assets and wealth (including public debt) that are at its disposal to provide public services. Public services can include spending on defense and military, education and health care, public infrastructure, internal security, the justice system, and social security spending. In the co-operative sector, assets are used to provide quality member service and to mobilize for future development.

The MANAGEMENT OF ASPIRATIONS has a lot to do with whose interests are being represented and whose time frame is being considered. Here again, while there are similarities there are also some stark differences. In the private sector (both closely held corporations as well as publicly traded ones) the aspirations of the principal shareholder or shareholder group and of the executive and senior management group will be most evident in the plans that are set, and in the results expected. In the public sector, the aspirations and desires of the senior politicians and the senior bureaucrats tend to be central concerns. In the co-operative sector, the aspirations of active members and the elected officials tend to be central, followed in turn by those of management and other employees. Active members serve on the board of directors and committees, as well as special task forces and other development work of the co-operative. In keeping with the seventh co-operative principle, these same active members and elected officials will reflect the needs and interests of the community to which the co-operative might respond.

PLANNING & PARTICIPATION activities are more extensive in the co-operative sector than in the other sectors. Co-operatives often use interest study groups, focus groups, study circles, member surveys, special task forces, member committees, suggestion boxes, employee discussion groups and feedback, and other member service satisfaction research tools to learn what members think and to plan for the future. Planning sessions involve active members, elected officials, management and employees as well as community leaders and organizations. In the private sector, the senior management prepares the plans and goals for the organization; they, in turn, are approved by board members. Traditional market research methods (such as customer satisfaction surveys and focus groups) together with confidential, externally conducted, employee feedback surveys may also be used. The extent of other participation in the private sector is the result of the particular management style that is used. In many countries, planning and participation in the public sector involves selected politicians, senior party members, senior bureaucrats and senior employees. In western countries, media research, market polls and other forms of research may be used by senior civil servants to assess citizen sentiment prior to decisions being taken by governments. As well, public sector entities may entertain private dialogue and lobbying efforts prior to finalizing future plans.

A noteworthy point is that in today's world, co-operatives everywhere have started to use technology to communicate with each other and to engage members. More and more people are connecting electronically via the internet. Facebook and LinkedIn have numerous discussion groups discussing co-operative issues and opportunities. More and more people are sharing papers, reports and proposals through whatever means are available. The real story about what co-operatives are doing and what they can do is being shared much more widely today. This trend was substantially expanded as a result of the activities of the United Nations' International Year of Co-operatives in 2012. Today many co-operatives are communicating and working collectively with each other via online surveys, emails, SMS, Skype, Twitter, via Google Blogger and other social media sites. The positive influence that co-operatives are having is more widely publicized than it has ever been in the past.

Nevertheless, there is still a large portion of the world's population from the United States to China to India that are not aware of the sometimes subtle but important differences between private sector, public sector and co-operative sector entities. While the differences as described are many and are important for the reasons described, they are not always readily visible to or understood by those outside of the co-operative movement or system. This is something which co-operatives around the world and the Global Co-operative Development Group Inc. through this publication are attempting to remedy.

Some Early Illustrations and Comparisons

Although there are relatively few research reports that illustrate the scale and scope of the co-operative sector in comparison to the private sector, there are selective studies pointing out what co-operatives have achieved in recent times. As well, work has now begun across the globe to access a wider range of sources. We shall draw upon some of these sources to help illustrate what has been, and is being, achieved.

One of most interesting studies, entitled *Resilience of the Co-operative Business Model in Times of Crisis* by Johnston Birchall and Lou Hammond Ketilson, was published by the International Labour Organization in 2009.[5] In referring to the actions taken by many governments around the world to the acute economic challenges that emerged amid the financial crisis of 2008, the report states:

> **The recent massive public bail-out of private, investor-owned banks has underlined the virtues of a customer-owned co-operative banking system that is more risk-averse and less driven by the need to make profits for investors and bonuses for managers. Savings and credit cooperatives also known as credit unions or SACCOs, building societies and co-operative banks all over the world are reporting that they are still financially sound, and that customers are flocking to bank with them because they are highly trusted.**

While the study reports on all forms of co-operative enterprise, much of its focus is on financial co-operatives. While a small number of co-operatives have experienced losses because of significant down turns in regional economies, the report explains that "not a single credit union, anywhere in the world, has received government recapitalization as a result of the financial crisis and they remain well capitalized".[6]

The report goes on to explain that in Canada and the United States some of the national and regional financial co-operative organizations have sustained losses and "in other parts of the world, co-operative banks have also posted losses, but again only at the highest level of their structures and their subsidiaries, not at the level of the local banks. The write-offs have so far been bearable in relative terms."[7] On the whole, co-operative forms of enterprise do better than others during periods of crisis because they are locally owned and controlled and because they tend to be more risk averse. The report, in referring to the economic downturn over the past five years states that "... co-operatives have to compete with bankrupt investor-owned banks that have been recapitalised by governments which are offering very high deposit rates and forcing others to follow; this is unfair competition."[8]

Let us turn to co-operative banks in Europe. A research paper entitled *European Co-operative Banks in the Financial and Economic Turmoil – First Assessments* by the European Association of Co-operative Banks, 2010, summarized their situation as follows:[9]

> **In their long tradition, they have served more than 160 million customers, mainly consumers, SMEs and communities. Europe's co-operative banks represent 50 million members and 750,000 employees and have an average market share of about 20%. In some countries, such as Austria, Germany, Finland, France, Italy and the Netherlands, the market share is well above this figure, ranging from 30% to 50%. Their resilience during the crisis makes co-operative banks a key driving force in the economic recovery.**[10]

It remains to be seen to what extent co-operative banks will be able to contribute to recovery within the Eurozone and elsewhere, but the early indications are positive. In a 2012 International Labor Office Research Report, entitled *Resilience in a Downturn: The Power of Financial Co-operatives,* the author found that financial co-operatives had survived the downturn as well and in many instances better than their private sector competitors. The report's author, Johnston Birchall, states: "Before the crisis, financial cooperatives were competing successfully against investor-owned banks. During the crisis, in general they were not badly affected, though losses were made by central banks in several countries".[11] Birchall goes on to conclude "Now, after the crisis nearly all the indicators show that they have bounced back and are growing again, though not at the same pace as before the crisis; the worldwide economic slowdown and the Euro crisis are to blame for that. There must be something about the customer-owned business model that makes it so resilient in a downturn".[12]

While it is true that in many countries following the events which began in 2008, the private sector and the public sector where contracting, in most instances the co-operative sector was either holding its own or expanding is size. To add flavour to these comparisons, we will note the following statistics reported by the International Co-operative Alliance in 2012:[13]

Co-operative Stories - *To get a further sense of what co-operatives have done and are successfully doing you can use the internet and the following link to get up close and personal: Co-operative Stories: www.stories.coop/*

- Co-operatives provide over 100 million jobs around the world, 20% more than multinational enterprises.
- 30,000 co-operatives in the United States that operate 73,000 places of business throughout the country own more than United States Dollars (USD) 3 trillion in assets, and generate over USD 500 billion in revenue and USD 25 billion in wages.
- In Switzerland, the two largest consumer co-operatives - Migros and Coop - are responsible for 8% of the Gross Domestic Product (GDP) of Switzerland.
- Co-operatives and mutuals in Scotland account for 4.25% of the Scottish Gross Domestic Product having an annual turnover of British Pound Sterling (GBP) 4 billion and assets of GBP 25 billion.
- In Kuwait, the Kuwaiti Union of Consumer Co-operative Societies, whose members are 6.5% of the Kuwaiti population, handled nearly 70% of the national retail trade in 2007.
- In Kenya, co-operatives are responsible for 45% of the GDP and 31% of national savings and deposits.
- In Iran, co-operatives contribute 6% of the Gross Domestic Product.
- In France, Co-operatives handle 60% of retail banking, 40% of food and agricultural production, and 25% of retail sales.

- In Colombia, the 8,124 co-operatives are responsible for 4.96% of the GDP in 2009.
- In Brazil, co-operatives were responsible for 5.39% of GDP in 2009.
- In Spain, co-operatives provided jobs to 21.6% of the labour market in 2007.
- In New Zealand, 22% of the Gross Domestic Product is generated by co-operative enterprise. Co-operatives are responsible for 95% of the dairy market and 95% of the export dairy market.
- In Vietnam, co-operatives contribute 8.6% of the Gross Domestic Product.
- In Japan, the agricultural co-operatives report outputs of USD 90 billion with 91% of all Japanese farmers in membership.
- In Singapore, 50% of the population (1.6 million people) are members of a co-operative.
- In Canada and the USA, 4 in 10 individuals are members of a co-operative.
- In Germany, 1 out of 4 people are members of a co-operative.

Another research report compares the control of private sector enterprises to co-operative enterprises. The report, entitled *Global Business Ownership 2012: Members and Shareholders Across the world; Co-operative Insight 9*, is published by Co-operatives UK.[14] Here are some of the reporting highlights:

- There are three times as many member owners of co-operatives as individual shareholders worldwide. There are 328 million people who own shares, compared to 1 billion who are member owners of co-operative enterprises.
- There are three countries where over half the population have co-operative memberships and they are all in Europe. These are Ireland (70%), Finland (60%), and Austria (59%).
- The countries with the most significant numbers of people in co-operative membership, however, are predominantly in Asia and the Americas. These are India (with 242 million members), China (with 160 million members) and the USA (with 120 million members).
- One in five people across the Americas (North and South) is a member of a co-operative.
- One in thirteen people in Africa is a member of a co-operative and there are six times as many co-operative owners as there are shareholders of investor-led firms.
- In the fast-growing BRIC countries (Brazil, Russia, India and China), there are four times as many co-operative members as direct shareholders. 15% of their population are co-operative members, compared to only 3.8% who are shareholders.

In this section we have sought to illustrate how well co-operatives have survived globally during the recent economic downturn. We have also included in an abbreviated form some of available statistics to illustrate the scope and scale of co-operatives globally. We intend to expand upon these statistics later in this publication.

Take Aways

1. The ownership and control of wealth has a significant impact on people's lives. There are four and perhaps five ways in which wealth is owned globally. Co-operative ownership and control of wealth is one such way.

2. Organizationally the private sector, the public sector, and the co-operative sector each have similar but different organizational dynamics. Understanding each of the differences helps one to appreciate the distinctive nature of co-operatives.

3. In comparative terms co-operative forms of enterprise have performed very well during the recent economic downturn, in part because of their conservative nature. Losses have been minimal and governments globally have not been called upon to inject funds into ailing co-operative or credit unions.

4. Co-operative forms of enterprise are flourishing as an alternative form of ownership and control across the globe. For example:
   - Globally there are now over one billion member-owner shareholders.
   - Co-operatives provide over 100 million jobs around the world, 20% more than multinational enterprises.

Chapter Five - Leadership and Management Effectiveness in Co-operatives

Managing the Co-operative Difference

In this section we introduce you to the core elements (but certainly not everything!) that make up one model of co-operative management. Our model is based in large measure upon research which was first conducted in the early 1980s and published in *A Contingency Theory of Management Effectiveness in Co-operatives*.[1] Our model is intended to aid the reader in understanding what it means to be an effective leader or senior manager in a co-operative enterprise. The content is applicable not only to those interested in co-operative management, but also to any elected director or official, any committee member, appointed manager or executive officer, as well as all employees of a co-operative. In some instances we use (elected) leader and manager interchangeably. In other cases we clarify to whom we are referring.

Co-operative leadership, whether it is at the elected official level or at the executive management level, and whether it is in very large national co-operatives or at the grass roots level, is as complex as it is challenging. Part of the reason that the job is so difficult is that there are few road maps, models or guidelines to follow. A great many successful officials and managers have acquired their know-how from mentors and personal experience. Another reason is that many of the guidelines and text books are based on business school logic and (sadly) business schools generally only instruct on how to lead or manage within private sector corporate enterprises. This is not to suggest business school content is irrelevant. Instead, we suggest business school content should be used as a supplemental to a more primary set of educational materials based on the co-operative values, principles and practices that are in place in successful co-operatives today.

We shall propose one basic framework for leadership and management effectiveness based on primary research previously conducted across a large co-operative system. The model of leadership and management effectiveness is also based upon your authors' collective years of experience in and across a variety of co-operative enterprise settings.

First, to begin, it is helpful (if you haven't already done so) to appreciate that, while co-operative organizations are very much like other forms of enterprise, they are also fundamentally different. In some respects, it is like comparing a helicopter to an ultra-light, or ice cream to apple pie. In the first case, both are aircraft and both involve flight – but at the same time "some of the fundamentals involved are quite different". In the case of ice cream and apple pie... they are both food, and they may even complement each other, but they taste different and they are prepared from different ingredients. If you have not yet grasped some of the major differences, please review the first four chapters of this publication, with particular attention to the statement on the co-operative identity as provided in chapter three.

Second, if you aspire to become an elected official or a management employee of a co-operative (that also includes becoming its president or its CEO), then you are encouraged to take a careful look into who you are and what you stand for as a person. What are your values? Is there or might there be a good fit? Successful co-operatives are always looking for good people! If you have a basic level of maturity, if you have either significant life experience or business training or experience, if you have a credible background, if you have an interest in the welfare of others and in your community, and if you are not satisfied with the status quo, then you will probably find co-operative leadership to be both interesting and rewarding for you. If you believe that there must be a better way and if you are willing to put the time and effort into learning, then co-operative leadership is probably right for you. If on the other hand, you prefer owning your own business, taking your own risks, making your own decisions, and running your own show, then you might find working with others in a co-operative setting to be a little frustrating.

As you may have learned, co-operative leadership is multi-faceted and may at times appear a bit confusing for newcomers to co-operatives - and especially to newcomers fresh out of most business schools. Also, one should not assume that an extensive background or experience in public administration or in the private sector will automatically equip you for a role in co-operative leadership. In today's world, public administration dogma has in great measure swung towards private sector teaching as espoused by Davos consultants and gurus. And as we have already seen in the previous chapter, private sector leaders and management will want to serve different purposes and to focus on different priorities.

Third, and finally, we wish to state that co-operative leadership is a shared responsibility. It is a co-operative responsibility. For example, as a credit union president you share responsibility for the success or failure of the enterprise with the other board members and with general manager or CEO. If you are a board member or you are on a board level committee, you share your responsibility for success with other board members or other committee members and management, regardless of your position. That does not mean everyone is responsible and therefore no one is accountable. Successful co-operatives make it a point to clearly establish in their governance practices what roles the board of directors are accountable for and what roles management is accountable for. Understanding each other's roles is an important aspect of being able to work together effectively. First time co-operative CEO's who feel they can succeed by themselves are - as you might guess - typically are not around for the long a term.

First Things First

We will begin by asking you to set aside, just for the moment, any stereotypical notions or assumptions you might have respecting leadership and management effectiveness.[2] We ask you to do so because a great deal of what people have learned about leadership and management has been developed for those operating in the private sector, and involves "how to" formulas and methods, a number of which are not appropriate in co-operative organizations. You will see in this section that leadership and management in a co-operative enterprise is in many ways more challenging because of the organizational dynamics that are involved.

Our framework is made up of a few basic elements which we hope, when combined, will provide a useful illustration of management and leadership effectiveness in a co-operative form of enterprise.

Mind the Gap

We will begin with the broader social, economic, political, natural and technical environments. It is within these environments that conditions of needs and wants arise. Needs and wants may be stated or unstated. In all instances needs and wants will exist as gaps between what is and what might be. A gap between "what is" and "what might be" often becomes the future vision for the enterprise. In turn, when well-conceived and thought out, the vision becomes the basis for purposeful action. We shall return to matters of purpose and actions later in this chapter.

Here are some examples.

- There appeared to be a gap between what cell phones did and what cell phone users wished they could do. A smart cell phone provider (Apple under Steve Jobs) found the way to satisfy the want and earned a significant return for doing so.

- Thinking more generally, there may be a gap between living in poverty and earning a living income. An individual or group of persons with a good idea, the needed resources, and a willingness to work might be able to start a successful business and thus generate a living income.

- There may also be gaps in terms of what some leaders feel should be done and what others think needs to be done when it comes to addressing environmental degradation. Environmental activist organizations such as "Greenpeace" and "Earthwatch" are established to demonstrate and advocate in hopes of narrowing the gap.[3]

- In 1985 Rotarians around the world saw the need to eradicate polio, and since then, have led the charge to do so. Rotary International has contributed over US $850 million and hundreds of thousands of volunteer hours, leading to the inoculation of more than two billion of the world's children. Rotary and its partners such as the World Health Organization, UNICEF and the Bill and Melinda Gates Foundation, succeeded in reducing polio-endemic countries from 93 countries in 1988 to three countries (Nigeria, Afghanistan, and Pakistan) in 2012. Plans are being developed to address the challenges in those three countries so that polio, once a horrible scourge for many people, especially the young, can be entirely eliminated around the globe.[4] It is a remarkable example of how people working together can close what once seemed like an impossible gap.

- Most governments around the world see the need for things such as copyright protection, uniform building codes for construction, and occupational health and safety regulations, and so act to ensure those needs and wants are satisfied.

So our starting point or gap is something that at least initially exists outside of any organization and may be expressed in terms of a need or a want. Most who have taken Marketing 101 might point out that on the surface, there seems to be little new in what has been stated. They would be correct. However, readers must realize that where and how a co-operative works to identify and close a gap makes all the difference in the world!

Where and How Co-operatives Come In

Many of today's successful co-operative organizations were created to close a gap between "what was" the case and what some people perceived "should be" the case. Co-operative movements first flourished when needs and wants were well articulated (by co-operative leaders), and ordinary people were convinced to work together to achieve common goals. Those who decided to support the initiative agreed to contribute financially by purchasing a share or the minimum number of shares required to start the enterprise. Getting organized also involved establishing a minimum basis for decision-making and participation. Often the basis for decision-making was spelt out a little more formally in the bylaws of the co-operative.

So what was or is different? The difference is that co-operative enterprises are almost always formed where a sufficient number of people in a community consciously decide that they need to work together co-operatively to achieve their goals. In the beginning, everyone invests a little in terms of time and money to become a member and each member has one vote in important enterprise decisions. Over time, those same members through their co-operative manage to change their lives from something they were dissatisfied with into something that they know is better. Members sometimes humbly, and sometimes proudly, call what they do "self-help"!

Here are some examples:

- In the early twentieth century orange growers in California were facing difficult hurdles in getting their crops to market, at the same time many people wanted to have easy access to oranges at fair prices. Under the leadership of Aarin Sapiro, a Chicago lawyer, they organized a marketing co-operative with several features for assuring good supply at fair prices and supported by an increasingly innovative way to reach out to markets across the United States and, ultimately Canada. They called their co-operative – and the fruit they sold – "*Sunkist*".[5] They filled a gap.

- Savings and credit co-operatives (credit unions) were formed in the prairie regions of Canada in the late 1930s when banks were willing to accept deposits from people but were unwilling to lend money to many of those who needed and deserved it. In addition, the banks made their services less accessible by closing branch offices. Local community members agreed to pool their savings and created their very own people's bank. They closed a gap! You are encouraged to see the 1962 black and white video on this story here: Click on www.youtube.com/ and search for "LaFleche Anniversary".[6] The credit unions from this part of Canada have gone on to serve as inspiring examples to other credit unions around the world.

- In China in the township of Bihu, which is only a few hundred kilometers from Shanghai, farmers had long struggled to find a market for their produce. Bad roads and the small scale of individual production made trade impossible. The Bihu Co-operative, created in 1999, is among the first agricultural co-operatives established in recent times and it is a classic example of a shareholding co-operative in China.[7] Thanks to a huge market place (the biggest one in the area) supported by the co-operative, more than 150 jobs in rural areas are provided, half of which are part-time employment for local women. As well, through training, new types of seeds and consolidation of products, co-operative members have seen a massive increase in annual income. Most Bihu members are making twice as much as the best urban salary provides. See: www.ica.coop/en/ , then Co-op Stories, and select China for more details.

- A recent co-operative example involves idle factories and idle workers in Argentina.[8] Abandoned factories needed workers, and workers needed jobs. The gap between idle factories and productive factories was closed when worker co-operative were organized to bring the factories alive again. As a result jobs were created and sustainable incomes were created, and factories became productive once again. See: www.ica.coop/en/ , then Co-op Stories, select Argentina, and then see "Argentinean workers take destiny in the own hands".

We provide these examples, which are typical of co-operatives around the globe, to illustrate that because of the reasons co-operatives are formed, the way in which co-operatives are owned and controlled, and the three results areas (for the member, the co-operative, and the community) that the enterprise must strive to achieve, *means that how they must be managed to be sustainable is considerably different and more involved than in either the public sector or in the private sector.*

What Co-operative Leaders Must Do

We will touch briefly on the four domains on which co-operative leaders must focus to ensure future success.

1. **Satisfy Member Needs**

Satisfying member needs successfully usually requires a great deal of knowledge and experience on the part of co-operative leaders or management. That is why most co-operatives prefer to engage experienced and proven functional professionals when they are recruiting.

How one goes about satisfying members will be as different in a credit union in Saskatchewan as it will be in electricity co-operative in Wisconsin or in a Women's Handicraft Co-operative in Mexico. Different types of skills and knowledge are required in each instance. In most cases co-operatives are operating in highly competitive or regulated environments. If for example you are involved at the leadership level in a credit union and you are competing with banks, then you and your management need to understand the business and the business environment just as well as your business competitors. If, on the other hand, you are involved with a woman's handicraft co-operative in Mexico, you will probably also need some other specialized kinds of knowledge and skill.

In simple terms, the leadership in the co-operative needs to know as much as possible about what it is doing if it intends to satisfy member needs. If your co-operative has been operating for some time, you also need to know how well you are succeeding in satisfying members' needs. It is always important to know where you are doing well as well as where you need to do better. It is also important to know how you are doing in relationship to existing and possibly new competitors. Leaders within the co-operative must actively understand and appreciate what member needs and wants are, and then acquire and organize the human, financial, and technical resources required to effectively satisfy those needs and wants.

In co-operative enterprises, functions are always centred either directly or indirectly around satisfying member needs. Functions may be theories, models and concepts which relate to processes. Functions are typically a conceptualization of a particular set of activities. They can illustrate what is, what has been, and what will be performed. Think of any aspect of management for a moment. Traditional management theory as taught in the business schools included the management functions of planning, organizing, directing, and controlling.[9] During the 1960s, they were the theories that were taught at universities about how one should think and act to succeed as a manager or corporate leader. Those theories have since been replaced by more advanced theories, all of which describe how to lead or manage in the public sector or more commonly in the private sector. In most instances, it had been assumed that such theories could be applied universally to any form of enterprise. The use of private sector assumptions, including "maximization of shareholder returns", and "growth is a primary avenue to profit," are generally not applicable within well managed co-operatives. We wish only to point out that such assumptions can at times be dangerous to those leading or managing a co-operative enterprise.

However, interspersed with some of private sector management teachings are numerous theories of management which are of great importance to co-operatives. To explain... if one wishes to succeed in marketing produce, then one should attempt to know everything there is to know about the marketing function as it has evolved and developed, and of course to know generally what works and what doesn't. One needs to know everything there is to know about banking functions, such as credit granting and collections, and asset and liability matching, and margin management if one wishes to successfully manage a credit union. Basically, the knowledge required depends upon the specific business functions performed by the co-operative. In a competitive and usually regulated environment, that means thoroughly understanding the regulatory structure as well as knowing everything that your competitors know about how to run their organization. It is through the ongoing management of various business functions that most co-operatives succeed financially by satisfying member needs.

Some examples of business functions include human resource function, business planning functions, credit and collections functions, marketing and communications functions, information and technology functions, transportation and logistics functions, and of course the accounting function. Given that functions are often complex and require special training and knowledge, they often fall to management and employees to either perform or to support. In large multi-unit or diversified co-operatives there may be a large number of functions (i.e., research and development functions, government relations functions, procurement assembly and distribution functions), all of which need to be well organized and carefully managed.

There are three additional functions within co-operatives which are not typically covered in business schools or in management texts. These are the *member participation functions*, the *co-operative education functions* and the *democratic control and governance functions*. These functions, while important to all co-operatives, may on occasion not be well developed or well understood. Failure to give adequate attention to these functions can, over time, lead to a loss of "the co-operative identity" by the enterprise.

In almost all co-operatives, satisfying member needs and wants is a top priority If it is not, you may wish to ask why it is not and then weigh the answer you receive carefully.

2. Generate Co-operative Effort

Leaders cannot be expected to know everything, or to do and to see all of the things that need doing. At the same time boards engage management, management engages employees, boards work with and appoint committees and task forces, members want to be heard, other co-operatives ask you to work together, community leaders expect you to contribute, and staff wish to be respected and treated fairly. Furthermore, different interest groups sometime see things from different – and even develop opposing - points of view. As a leader or leaders, it isn't always easy finding common ground - on the other hand, taking sides may be detrimental to the various interests reaching agreement and ideally reaching consensus. It is important for the leadership of a co-operative to help foster and encourage co-operative effort. This means getting things done through groups, finding areas of agreement to build upon when differences occur, ensuring work is organized and rewarded fairly, seeing roles and responsibilities across the organization are clearly defined and are understood, and of course seeing that counterproductive behavior is addressed. However, it means much more, it also means ensuring various interests both inside (especially including members) and outside the organization know and understand what the co-operative is doing and why it is doing it. It means group efforts are valued and focused on solving problems and moving forward. It means communicating and it means sharing. It means give and take and at times compromise. Generating co-operative effort involves managing relationships in a collaborative and mutually supportive manner. It also involves knowing and engaging in a clear and positive manner with all stakeholders who have an interest in your co-operative.

In a broad sense, 'interest' implies an attraction to or a stake in something or somebody. Interest may be used to describe who is involved in various activities, as well as why. A concern for people will often involve relationships between and among different interests. In a co-operative, internal and external interest groups include members, employees (management and staff if so designated), elected officials, committee members, local or other community leaders, political actors, unions, competitors, suppliers, researchers, regulators, other special interest groups, other co-operatives, the various forms of media, and so on. Co-operative leaders are encouraged to think of all these individuals, groups and organizations as having their own specific interests. In a co-operative, how interests are managed and involved, or sometimes deliberately not involved, will be of critical importance to the short as well as the long term success of the enterprise.

The leadership and management of the co-operative must strive to generate co-operative effort amongst the various, and at times, competing interests in the co-operative. For example, employees might like higher salaries, savers might like higher savings rates, borrowers lower interest rates, and financial regulators might wish to see earnings being allocated to increase financial reserves. There is no single technique to use or course to follow regarding the generation of co-operative effort amongst various interests at various times. Sometimes it involves carefully bringing together those people or groups who share some similar concerns yet may have competing interests and helping them to find common ground, define joint objectives, and determine actions or a course of actions that can work best for all concerned. Co-operative effort amongst interests involves teamwork and co-ordination, but it requires more; it requires due consideration of each person's or each group's interest in the matter to be addressed. Successful leaders and mangers in co-operatives must become skillful in areas such as group facilitation, group planning, communicating (presenting and listening), empathy, and when required being aware of what at times may involve "small p politics" amongst various interests that are in or around the co-operative.

If you are involved in a co-operative, and your co-operative is a part of a larger co-operative group, you may well come to appreciate the principle of "co-operation amongst co-operatives". Often there really is too much for one organization's leadership group to try to know and to do by itself. Having a second-tier co-operative organization owned and controlled by like co-operatives is one way to support the management functions at the local co-operative level. In this case, it is important to ensure that your co-operative's interests are properly and well represented. Other avenues such as alliances with third parties can, at times when there are shared interests, also be beneficial. It is essential for co-operative leaders and managers to be conscious of the interests that others have - particularly in working arrangements or partnership relationships which the co-operative does not own or control.

It is helpful to remember that your competitors or others may also be actively seeking to influence those who already have an interest in the co-operative. How your co-operative chooses to build relationships locally and otherwise can influence both your short term and your longer term success. It is important that co-operatives avoid becoming aligned with any political interest or other non-co-operative interest group, regardless of how appealing such possibilities might first appear.

3. Ensure Operational Efficiency

Creating a culture of efficiency across an organization is always important and is particularly important in situations where the co-operative is facing strong competition. As a co-operative leader, it is your responsibility to see that all resources of the organization are used in the very best way possible. This need not mean cutting corners or trimming expenses, but it does mean ensuring that work is well organized, that productivity is measured and compared to benchmarks, and that appropriate technology is employed. Activities that do not have a productive purpose or that can be done elsewhere need to be scrutinized. Operational efficiency can mean working with other similar co-operatives in order to reduce costs and to gain efficiencies. It may mean becoming creative. It may mean making numerous small changes instead of one or two major ones. Ensuring operational efficiency is essential for the survival of any co-operative. The world continues to change. It is important for all co-operative leaders to periodically consider how their organization may need to adapt itself to do a better job.

Any set of organized activities may be equated to a task. When one describes how an observable task is being performed, he or she is describing an activity. One can observe or monitor the performance of activities. Activity represents particular actions which together make up courses of action and which in turn constitute a function or functions. "Balancing the books" is a task, actually a series of activities, which together with other accounting tasks make up the accounting function.

So why are activities of particular importance to co-operative leaders? If activities are not well organized from a workflow perspective, or if they do not employ appropriate technology, or if they are simply not monitored or controlled, they may well result in poorly performed functions (i.e. , credit granting, inventory management, human resource management) and lead to a drain on the co-operative's overall performance. Over time, when functions are not well performed, the organization loses its ability to serve its purpose successfully. Typically, in larger co-operatives the board of directors will see their general manager or CEO employs a team of experienced professionals to manage the core function or functions of their business.

In a co-operative, leaders and managers must manage activities so as to ensure operational efficiency. This focus area is in almost all respects similar to what any private sector or public sector enterprise must do. It can be more complex within co-operative organizations because it requires co-operative leaders and managers to think competitively, to think long term, and to act in keeping with co-operative principles. Introducing a new technology can sometimes eliminate positions, or it can facilitate new growth and new positions. Failing to introduce a new technology when others are can quickly put the co-operative in an uncompetitive position. These are the kinds of decisions that managers must carefully work through while bearing in mind the impact any decision is likely to have on co-operative functions and on the overall level of member service.

4. Pursue Collective Ideals

This may sounds easy to do but it is not. It is both a handful and a mouthful. Not everyone is able to do it. It involves individual sentiments as well as group sentiments. For a leader it may simply mean being able to tell others why your co-operative is important. Sometimes it may involve lengthy debates. Sometimes it involves really listening and really trying to understand what it is that members are saying about their needs and wants. Sometime it involves examining what members might need today - while imagining what they might want tomorrow. For larger co-operatives, the idea of pursuing collective ideals as an organization can involve a considerable amount of research and enterprise planning, competitive and external analysis, members' needs analysis, board and committee meetings and discussions, feasibility analysis, business cases, etc. Sometimes it may involve an extensive period of soul searching before a co-operative or even a group of co-operatives in the same market are finally able to agree on what is needed. One large co-operative in the Netherlands described its ideal seeking process as "re-inventing itself."[10] Regardless, the leaders within the co-operative must be able to articulate to the membership at large what it is that the organization is reaching out to achieve and why what it is doing is important to the membership and perhaps to the surrounding community. Leaders must also be able to articulate, in their own words and in their own way, why having a successful co-operative really matters both to its members and to their communities.

There are also many ways and means through which co-operative leaders can emphasize or renew their sense of purpose. For example, defining a co-operative's purpose may be done as a part of their longer term enterprise planning process, or as something the co-operative formally decides to communicate to the world in its websites or annual reports, or it may be something that is so self-evident it only requires revisiting and re-consideration on occasion. Nevertheless, given the purposeful nature of co-operatives, it is important for co-operative leaders and managers to give thoughtful oversight to this domain to ensure that the collective ideals for which the enterprise was created will continue to exist and remain relevant.

Michelle Chevalier was an early proponent of co-operative management.[11] He, like others, including Peter Davis,[12] and Jack Craig,[13] felt the management of purpose was an essential element in the management of any co-operative. Chevalier elaborated his views on co-operative management in the early 1980s as part of a master's level program on Co-operative Management at York University. Collective ideals are always an expression of purpose. Purpose in this case represents particular desired achievements that together meet the demands of an interest or interests. Purpose can exist at the highest level of abstraction, or can be profoundly simple. Purpose relates reason to direction. Purpose answers the question "why?", thus satisfying particular (and/or various) interests.

Often, the purpose or purposes of a co-operative are described in a purpose statement which may be in the form of a vision and or mission statement, and sometimes includes more specific statements of aims or high level objectives.

We will include some examples to illustrate some of the distinct statements of purposes of various types of co-operatives. For example, the Co-operative Group in the UK states their purpose this way: "To serve our members by carrying on business as a co-operative in accordance with co-operative values and principles. Our vision --- To build a better society by excelling in everything we do."[14]

A second example is also from the UK and is from the Co-operative Women's Guild: The Purpose of the Guild Aims and Objectives:[15] 1. To promote through the expansion of Co-operation such conditions of life as will ensure for all people equal opportunities for full and free development. 2. To educate women in the principles and practice of Co-operation in order that they shall be loyal members of their Societies and play a full part in the control of the Co-operative Movement. 3. To encourage and prepare women to take part in local, national and international affairs. 4. To work for the establishment of world peace. 5. To provide social, cultural, and recreational activities through which members may live a full and interesting life.

Our third example is from the SEMO Electric Co-operative in Bloomfield, Missouri, USA, whose purpose is contained in their mission statement:[16] "Through a partnership with our members, we will provide the safest and most reliable service, for the lowest possible price."

As Yair Levi and Peter Davis have emphasized, co-operative elected leaders and management must recognize that it is the distinctive purposes (socio-economic) of co-operative organizations that separates them from other forms of enterprise.[17] As the environment changes, successful co-operatives must adapt themselves and often their purposes to remain relevant to their membership. Davis further explains that co-operative leaders must successfully manage purpose otherwise the democratic aspects of their organization will be undermined and its strategic focus will become problematic.[18]

Perhaps you've heard statements such as the following: "The local co-operative store is the same as Tesco or – it is a part of it ... isn't it?" or "The credit union is just like a bank... isn't it?" There may be many reasons why a person might ask such questions, but often it is because of the way he or she was treated when dealing at a co-operative or a credit union. In either instance it involves an opportunity for the leadership and the management to clearly distinguish themselves as something quite different from private sector corporate entities. Even more important, it offers the leadership an opportunity to examine to what extent their co-operative's purpose is relevant to the membership and to the community.

Co-operative Enterprise Sustainability

We will turn to sustainability, since any organization's ability to sustain itself and thus survive over the longer term is a reasonable indicator of its ability to achieve its purpose on an ongoing basis. One of the greatest responsibilities of the board of directors have is to ensure the short and long term sustainability of their co-operative.

A co-operative leader or manager must learn that a co-operative's survival depends on two inter-related but sometimes opposing outcomes. As an economic enterprise, every co-operative must perform well financially to ensure its survival. A sudden drop in cash flow from sales, a series of unprofitable financial periods, or a major default in payments can wipe out member equity and retained earnings held by the co-operative, and therefore can put the organization's survival in question. At the same time, if the members stop using or supporting their co-operative, and board members and employees stop caring for how the organization is doing, failure will soon result. In the long term, a successful co-operative requires two outcomes in order to survive, and indeed to succeed.

The two longer term outcomes that every co-operative enterprise needs to be sustainable are 'Financial Strength,' and 'Communities of Support'. Successfully achieving these two outcomes occurs as a consequence of the four leadership behaviors described below and on the host of decisions and actions by the co-operative's leadership.

Financial Strength occurs over time when all of those factors (e.g., profitability, liquidity, equity, and growth) that any business enterprise must tend to are being well managed. How well the co-operative and its core functions are managed determines the performance in each of these inter-related factors.

Communities of Support occur when those persons and groups who have an interest or a stake in the co-operative [e.g., members (individually, as groups, and as a collectivity), board members individually and as a group, employees individually and as a group, community leaders, special community or interest groups, elected officials and law makers, government regulators and even other co-operatives] feel positive towards the enterprise. The extent to which sometimes small and specific communities within a co-operative's larger community actively like and support the enterprise can influence an organization's sustainability over time. This factor was identified in research into co-operative leadership and management effectiveness in credit unions more than 30 years ago. It has also been identified in 2012 by author Dave Kerpen in one of his latest books, *"Likeable Business: Why Today's Consumers Demand More and How Leaders Can Deliver"*.[19]

In a co-operative, it is not enough to do well financially as an enterprise; the organization must also garner the support (active and passive) of those who have an interest in what you are doing. For co-operative leaders and managers, this can create a natural tension between ensuring that the enterprise performs well financially while ensuring continuing communities of support.

To explain why these two outcomes can at times be in opposition to one another, consider this hypothetical case:

A financial co-operative (credit union) declares a year-end staff bonus for work well done, and announces:

1. a reduction in already competitive interest rates to be charged on loans,
2. a higher than planned dividend on shares plus better than market rates of interest on savings, and mentions this in its annual report to members,
3. that it has made a sizeable donation to the community hospital to purchase new imaging equipment, and
4. that the co-operative's overall equity has reduced 10% because of tighter margins and recent growth.

In this case, the positives (bonus for staff, low interest rate loans, a very favourable share dividend and savings rates, and support for the community hospital) would in most cases find favour with the various communities involved, at least in the short term. Levels of member and community support could be expected to rise over time as these actions are taken. However, at the same time, doing all of these various things will tend to weaken the co-operative's overall equity position and thus its financial strength. What might be seen as positive in many eyes would at the same time weaken the organization financially. Result: An increase in support for the co-operative by its various communities coupled with a weaker financial position.

The flip side can also occur. In this second hypothetical case a financial co-operative's leaders decide to:

1. set aside large reserves out of earnings for potentially bad loans,
2. increase its lending rates to widen margins,
3. not provide staff salary adjustments or performance pay at year end in order to set aside a reserve fund for future automation,
4. pay a small share dividend or no dividend at all on member shares savings, and, finally
5. offer slightly below market interest rates on regular savings accounts.

In the short term, all of these actions will tend to slow growth while increasing profitability and perhaps help to improve equity when expressed as a percentage of assets. Future automation should help improve profitability. With better profitability and improved reserves, one could expect the co-operative will be able to increase its financial strength. Result: An increase in financial strength coupled with weaker support for the co-operative by a number of its various communities.

Sometime such action, or at least some of them, may be necessary. Often the outcomes depend in large measure on how such decisions are taken, and how they are communicated. When people know that measures are being taken to strengthen their co-operative, they may continue their support and loyalty to the enterprise. Otherwise, it is highly likely that the level of support from the various communities (i.e., employees; savings clients) who have an interest in the co-operative can naturally be expected to decline over time.

In any co-operative it is in situations such as this that the collective good thinking of the board and management must come into play. It is up to decision-makers to do what is best for the members and for the co-operative, in the short term and in the longer term as well, depending on circumstances both within the co-operative and in its environment. In our experience, the leadership group of successful co-operative organizations tend to be extremely skilled at dealing with tough trade-offs.

When both financial strength and community support are trending positively in the long term, almost everyone will attest to the fact that the co-operative is sustainable and is doing well. However, when either or both outcomes continue to trend negatively for some time, it is likely that the co-operative's days are numbered unless corrective actions are taken.

Putting the Pieces Together

By pursuing collective ideals and by working to generate co-operative effort amongst various interest groups in the co-operative, the leadership and management of the co-operative can expect to gain support from its various communities. By satisfying member needs and ensuring operational efficiency the co-operative can expect to gain financial strength from its operations. Both outcomes help the co-operative to be able to contribute to its larger community, and to be sustainable.

How best to succeed in the four domains or fields described earlier depends to a considerable degree on the nature, type, and size of a co-operative, and as well on its broader environment. There are many avenues, approaches, methodologies, strategies, tactics, etc., that the leadership of co-operative can use. The key in tending to these four domains is ensuring that the approaches employed towards the first and third domains (member needs and operational efficiency) complement the co-operative principles and values which come into play in the second and fourth domain (co-operative effort and collective ideals)! You may wish to jump from here to Chapter 9 to see thoughts on best practices intended to help co-operative enterprises succeed across all four domains.

Management cannot be a passive passenger on the co-operative vessel. Management has a responsibility and an obligation to participate in leadership. A strong board or chairperson should not be making its strategic decisions independent of management. This requires sound communication and collaboration skills on the part of management. If you as elected leaders have, as part of your leadership team, a passive manager who sees himself or herself merely as a duly paid administrator, then you may best spend time considering his or her future. The exception of course may be the inexperienced but potentially strong new manager or the voluntary incumbent who is filling the role temporarily. As elected leaders you should look to building a collaborative relationship with mutually agreed but clearly defined performance expectations.

Time and circumstances always change. Chevalier states that effectiveness depends upon a leader's ability to successfully cycle through periods of continuity (times when performance and results are trending positively) and discontinuity (times when conditions have deteriorated or external challenges arise), while managing all the relevant activities, functions, purposes, and interests accordingly.[20] This is one of the main reasons most successful co-operative boards of directors today seek to involve professional, experienced managers in their leadership group.

We hope this basic framework may assist in your understanding of some of the unique aspects of co-operative leadership and management, and has added to your understanding of co-operative forms of enterprise.

The various pieces, when put together, appear as shown in Figure 5.1. As you may recognize, most co-operatives began as movements and attend more to items one and four. As co-operatives grow and mature, their functions and activities become more important and so focus often has shifted to items one and three. Co-operatives are encouraged to consciously allocate their time and energy across all areas, depending on circumstances within their co-operative and the environment within which it exists.

Further illustrations and examples of leadership and management effectiveness will be available for discussion on the Co-operative Enterprise website at www.co-operativeenteprise.coop. Chapter Nine will provide some strategies and tactics for co-operative enterprise success.

Figure 5.1

Co-operative Leadership and Management Effectiveness Framework

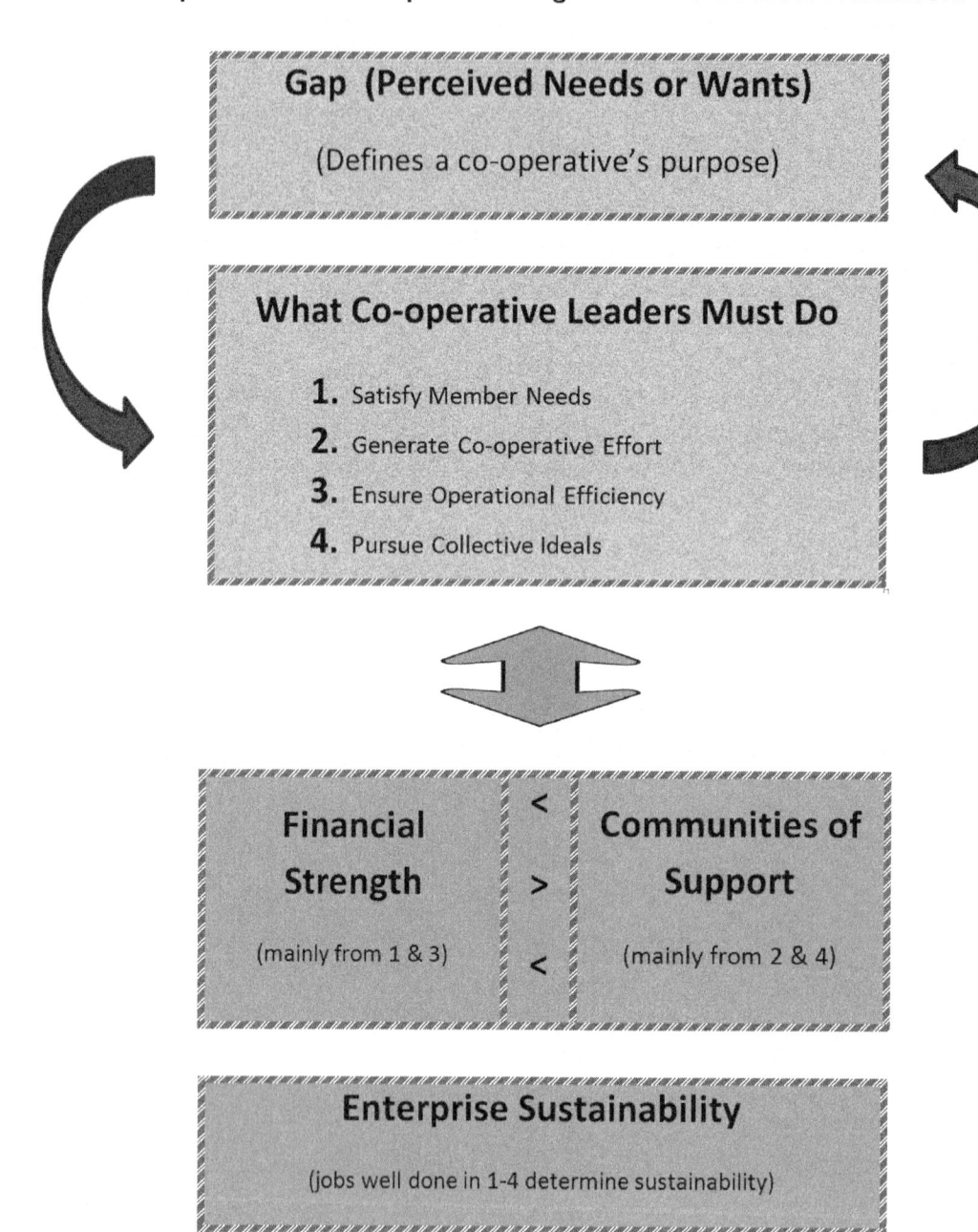

Gap (Perceived Needs or Wants)

(Defines a co-operative's purpose)

What Co-operative Leaders Must Do

1. Satisfy Member Needs
2. Generate Co-operative Effort
3. Ensure Operational Efficiency
4. Pursue Collective Ideals

Financial Strength	Communities of Support
(mainly from 1 & 3)	(mainly from 2 & 4)

Enterprise Sustainability

(jobs well done in 1-4 determine sustainability)

Take Aways

1. Leading and managing a co-operative is different because co-operatives are different. Care needs to be taken by leaders and managers when using best practices normally prescribed for private sector enterprises or public sector bodies.

2. There are four key domains which leaders and managers must attend to in a co-operative. How managers balance these four domains is contingent upon the circumstances within and around the co-operative.

3. The effectiveness with which leaders and managers carry out their roles will determine how sustainable their co-operative will become over time. Two success factors will vary over time (frequently inversely) depending upon the decisions and actions of leaders and managers - financial strength and community support. Taken together these two factors determine the long term sustainability of any co-operative.

4. It is the responsibility of elected leaders and employed managers to do what is best for the members and for the co-operative, in the short term and in the longer term as well, depending on circumstances in the co-operative and in its environment.

PART THREE - CO-OPERATIVES TODAY

One Billion Strong

Chapter Six - National and International Co-operative Development

Overview

When we started this book, we thought writing this chapter would be relatively straight forward. All that would be required was to describe a handful of international organizations, provide some brief statistical highlights, and discuss some examples of international co-operative development. It certainly seemed as if it could be completed quickly. Surprisingly, that has not proven to be the case! First, over the past year (2012) there has been a relative explosion of information concerning co-operative development around the world, in part because of the International Year of Co-operatives.[1] Second, co-operative development is in reality a wide and a deep subject, one that is difficult to touch upon lightly without missing important factors or details. Third, when one takes a global perspective on co-operative development, it soon becomes clear that because of historical and cultural differences, lumping such developments into a single or even a few sections becomes virtually impossible. Fourth and finally, it appears very difficult to describe co-operative development without looking to the future and in particular to opportunities and to challenges. Very quickly, we faced the questions of where and how to begin, and where to end.

As a result, this chapter in particular should best be seen as a work in progress.

All we will attempt to do is to provide the reader with an understanding of the different types of co-operatives that exist, the various organizational structures and arrangements that are in use, the scope and scale of co-operatives globally, a description of some of the co-operative support organizations that exist, and take a brief look at some of the trends we see in terms of co-operative development in various places around the world today. Our thoughts on co-operative development in the future are included in later chapters.

We intend to supplement this content with additional supporting details in our website located at: www.co-operativeenteprise.coop.[2]

Types of Co-operatives

Co-operatives can be formed by individuals, businesses, or communities. The different ownership models of co-operative enterprise are described in some detail below.

Consumer-Owned Co-operatives

Consumer co-operatives are owned by the people who buy the goods or use the services of the cooperative. Consumer co-operatives include credit unions and some co-operative banks (the others are owned by co-operatives), child care co-operatives, electric and telecommunications co-operatives, food co-operatives, health care co-operatives, housing co-operatives, and many more.

This is the most common form of co-operative and it is organized by individuals who seek to purchase goods and services. By organizing a co-operative, consumers are either able to access products or services not otherwise available to them, or access the products or services at prices and/or quality that are not available from for-profit businesses.

Producer-Owned Co-operatives

Producer co-operatives are typically owned by producers of farm commodities or various crafts (e.g., handicrafts, jewellery, and textiles) who band together to process and/or market their products. Producer-owned co-operatives are most common in agricultural regions, where farmers often must band together to survive in an industry that is increasingly industrial and centralized. Before co-operatives were organized, farmers were often trapped in a situation in which processors could dictate the prices paid for crops. Today, as fewer and fewer for-profit businesses assume increasingly significant control over the production, processing, and marketing of farm commodities, one could argue the need for existing agricultural co-operatives and the value of creating new ones is once again abundantly obvious and necessary.

Worker-Owned Co-operatives

Worker co-operatives are owned and democratically governed by their employees. They operate in numerous industries, including childcare, commercial and residential cleaning, food service, health care, technology, consumer retail and services, manufacturing, wholesaling, and many others.

Purchasing/Shared Services Co-operatives

Purchasing or shared services co-operatives are owned by individuals, small independent businesses, and municipalities, or other like organizations that band together to enhance their purchasing power or to improve their performance and competitiveness. Members of these co-operatives have found that they can adapt quickly to changing economic conditions rather than become victims of them. They can lower their operating costs by pooling their purchasing power to obtain goods and services.

Some examples include Best Western, which is the world's largest hotel chain, owned by the independent operators of more than 4,000 hotels in 80 countries. ACE Hardware and True Value are both purchasing co-operatives, which collectively are owned by more than 13,000 independent hardware stores.

Hybrid Cooperatives and Multi-stakeholder Co-operatives

Co-operatives are generally made up of people with a common interest, but that hasn't stopped some innovators from developing multi-stakeholder hybrids which seek to balance their members' sometimes conflicting needs—for example, between consumers' desire for affordable products and producers' desire for higher prices for their goods. In many cases, these co-operatives are tied to their members' dual roles as producers and consumers, most often in agricultural co-operatives, but not always. In other cases, stakeholder co-operatives formally expand their governance systems to include employees, representatives of communities, and government officials.

Mutuals and Co-operatives

Mutuals primarily exist in the insurance sector, and are governed by different legislation than co-operatives. They operate under a slightly different business model depending upon their ownership.[3] Both mutuals and co-operatives are independent associations of individuals who have voluntarily come together to fulfill their economic or social needs through co-ownership in a democratically-run organizations. Mutual insurance companies may be owned by their policy-holders, just as co-operatives are owned by their members, or they may be owned by second or third-tier co-operatives.

Co-operatives for Everyone!

There are car share and transportation co-operatives (buses and taxis), school co-operatives, restaurant co-operatives, pub co-operatives, cable and internet services co-operatives, business support services co-operatives, credit and payment card processing and settlement services co-operatives, funeral co-operatives, and sex trade workers co-operatives. The scope of co-operative enterprise is almost endless. Sometimes, the same kind of co-operative may be owned and controlled differently as is the case with health care co-operatives, which may be consumer-owned, worker-owned, producer-owned, or even multi-stakeholder owned.

The above detail describing different types of co-operatives has been adapted from the USA 2012 IYC website.[4] For further details please see: www.ncba.coop/ and click on "About Co-ops".

Co-operative Structures

Just as co-operatives operate in and sometimes across different ownership models, they also operate in different levels of co-operative structures.

Local Co-operatives

The local co-operative is what many think of when they think of co-operative organizations. It is the kind of co-operative we have generally referred to throughout this book. People think of many individual members working together to satisfy their needs. Structurally, the ownership begins with one member owning at least one share and each member having one vote in electing a board of directors and in passing bylaws and special resolutions to govern the affairs of the enterprise. Local co-operatives may on some occasions be referred to as societies or as collectives.

Second-Tier Co-operatives

It is common in many countries for local co-operatives to work together to achieve objectives that they cannot achieve alone, often through second-tier co-operatives. Such co-operative organisations can undertake a wide range of functions, including the provision of technical services, advocacy, training and capacity building, production and marketing, risk management, and finance. In some cases second-tier co-operatives also help support individual and group governance through peer group performance monitoring and reporting.

Second-tier co-operatives may be formed at the district, provincial, state, or regional levels, and may be referred to as unions, federations, or centrals. Second-tier co-operatives may also be referred to as societies. Second-tier co-operatives typically will have more complex democratic ownership and control structures. Member co-operatives who own and control second-tier co-operatives must act to ensure they are structured and operate in a manner that is as fair and equitable as possible given the variations in the membership numbers and in the asset size of the various local co-operatives.

Third-Tier Co-operatives

In many countries, there are also third-tier co-operatives which may be referred to as federations or centrals, and in some instances as alliances. When they operate on a national level, they may also be referred to as confederations, alliances, associations or apex organizations, depending upon the legislation under which they are governed. Third-tier co-operatives are often owned and controlled by second-tier co-operatives.

International Co-operatives

At a global level there are two distinct co-operative flavours. First, there are national co-operatives which have expanded their operations internationally. As well, there are hybrids. For a description of some of the larger co-operative organizations we suggest you refer to the section of this publication entitled "Co-operative Movements and Systems around the World." Again please appreciate there are now a great many international co-operatives, and more being created each year. Second, there are the developmental organizations that help promote and advocate for the broader co-operative brand and that support co-operative development. We shall give examples of some of the more well-known developmental organizations with which we are familiar. Typically, such developmental organizations are owned and controlled by co-operative organizations from numerous countries.

The **International Co-operative Alliance** (ICA) (www.ica.coop/) is the best known and most widely recognized such organization.[5]

The ICA is an independent, non-governmental organisation established in 1895 to unite, represent, and serve co-operatives worldwide. It provides a global voice and forum for knowledge, expertise, and co-ordinated action for, and about, co-operatives. ICA's members are international and national co-operative organisations from all sectors of the economy, including agriculture, banking, consumer, fisheries, health, housing, insurance, and workers. ICA has members from one hundred countries, representing one billion individuals worldwide. The ICA is the guardian of the co-operative identity, values, and principles.

The ICA has numerous sectoral organizations. This allows those co-operatives that are members of the ICA and have similar business functions to work together and to bring forward their particular concerns and interests.

The International Cooperative and Mutual Insurance Federation (ICMIF) (www.icmif.org) is a specialized promotion, advocacy, and development organization of the ICA. Its focus is on co-operative insurance, and it serves to represent the interests of co-operative and mutual insurance providers to the ICA.

The International Co-operative Banking Association (ICBA) (www.icba.coop) is made up of co-operative banks from around the world. It deals with matters in the banking industry, and serves to represent the interests of co-operative banks to the ICA.

International Co-operative Agricultural Organisation (ICAO) (www.agricoop.org) . The International Co-operative Agricultural Organisation (ICAO) is the democratic organisation representing agricultural co-operatives and farmers world-wide. Founded in 1951, it is a sectoral organisation of the ICA. This organisation represents 27 agricultural co-operative organisations from over 24 countries. ICAO works closely with the Food and Agriculture Organisation of the United Nations (FAO), World Trade Organization of the United Nations (WTO), the General Committee for Agricultural Co-operation in the EU (COGECA), the International Federation of Agricultural Producers (IFAP), European Confederation and other professional groups in the agricultural sector.

CCW

Consumer Co-operatives Worldwide (CCW) (www.ccw.coop). Consumer Co-operatives Worldwide (CCW) is the sectoral organisation of the International Co-operative Alliance (ICA) which brings together consumer co-operatives within the ICA membership. CCW has the basic philosophy that the consumer has a right to a reasonable standard of nutrition, clothing, and housing; adequate standards of safety and a healthy environment; unadulterated merchandise at fair prices with reasonable variety and choice; access to information on goods and to education on consumer topics; and that s/he should have an influence on the economy through democratic participation. In accordance with its philosophy, CCW strives to disseminate information among its members and provide a forum for the discussion and exchange of valuable experiences. It also promotes business between its members.

IHCO

International Health Co-operative Organisation. The IHCO (IHCO) (www.ica.coop/en/ihco) is a voluntary association of consumer (user), producer (provider), and multi-stakeholders health co-operatives. Its objectives, as a sectoral organisation of the ICA, are to provide a forum for the discussion and exchange on issues of relevance to its member organizations; to provide information about the nature and role of health co-operatives to international agencies and bodies, specifically United Nations bodies, to national governments, to the media and to public opinion; to promote the development of health co-operatives and collaborate with ICA Regional Organisations, ICA Thematic Committees, and other ICA sectoral organisations.

CICOPA

International Organisation of Industrial, Artisanal, and Service Producers' Cooperatives (CICOPA) (www.cicopa.coop), or CICOPA, has been a sectoral organisation of the International Cooperative Alliance (ICA) since 1947. Its full members are representative organisations of producers' cooperatives from different sectors: construction, industrial production, services of general interest, transport, intellectual services, artisanal activities, health, social care, etc. Its associated members are support organisations promoting cooperatives in those sectors. Many of those cooperatives are worker cooperatives, namely cooperatives where the members are the staff of the enterprise, i.e., worker-members. Because of this, those enterprises are characterized by a distinctive type of labour relations, called "worker ownership", different from the one experienced by conventional employees or by being self-employed.

IFCO

International Co-operative Fisheries Organisation (IFCO) (website not available). The IFCO is a specialized organisation of the International Co-operative Alliance. This committee was originally founded in 1966, as a sub-committee of the ICA's Agricultural Committee, but it became an independent body in 1976. The Fisheries Committee has 23 member organisations from 21 countries. It considers its main goals to be the following:
- creation of new co-operative fisheries organisations,
- co-operative training and education by the co-operative movements of advanced countries, including the production of educational materials,
- the exchange of "fisheries technical information movements" on a global basis, and
- the promotion of trade.

ICA Housing

ICA Housing (ICAH) (www.icahousing.coop). ICA Housing is a sectoral organisation of the International Co-operative Alliance. It was established to promote the development of co-operative housing in all countries, and in particular developing countries, as an economic and social contribution to the problem of providing shelter. Their mission is to unite, represent, and serve the international movement for co-operative and mutual self-help housing.

The ICA also has a number of thematic committees which carry out work in a variety of fields. They include: Gender Equality, Human Resource Development, Research, Communications and Youth. To learn more about ICA's thematic committees see: www.ica.coop/en/ and under About Us click on "Thematic Committees".

The European Research Institute on Co-operative and Social Enterprises (Euricse) is a research centre designed to promote knowledge development and innovation for the field of cooperatives, social enterprises, commons, and non-profit organizations.[6] Although _not_ a co-operative, it has worked closely with the ICA in the past and particularly during the 2012 International Year of Co-operatives. It has taken on the role of gathering co-operative statistics (the World Monitor) for the ICA. It also publishes many of its research reports which may be accessed from this link: www.euricse.eu/en/. Euricse is located in Trent, Italy.

The World Council of Credit Unions (WOCCU) is a world-wide co-operative development organization.[7] See: www.woccu.org/. WOCCU specializes in promoting, advocating, and developing savings and credit co-operatives and credit unions around the world. WOCCU's members represent some 51,000 credit unions in 100 countries.

The International Association of Co-operative Banks (CIBP) (www.cibp.eu) has member institutions from around the world.[8] It has held annual co-operative banking conferences and meetings of co-operative banking institutions since 1949. It has a number of specialized working groups and much of its focus is on small and medium sized enterprises (SMEs).

The European Association of Co-operative Banks (EACB) (www.eacb.eu) focuses on the interests of European Co-operative Banks.[9] It has a number of working groups which deal with matters such as: banking regulation, supervision, payments systems, consumer policy, social affairs, financial markets, accounting and audit, corporate social responsibility, and co-operative affairs on behalf of its members.

The International Raiffeisen Union (IRU), established in 1968, links banks and financial institutions and promotes agricultural and savings co-operatives.[10] It has 61 affiliates in 36 countries and an estimated total of 190 million local members. See: www.iru.de/

Co-operative News is a specialized second-tier information co-operative. See: www.thenews.coop.[11] The Co-operative Press Limited publishes the printed Co-operative News, which is distributed in Britain. The Press manages the on-line co-operative news media, The Global News Hub for Co-operatives. The Global News Hub is a collection of articles, features, and opinion pieces submitted by co-operatives and co-operators from around the world. As well as text, the website hosts picture, audio and video content. The site includes a wide range of resources such as presentations, annual reports, and academic papers.

The Global Co-operative Development Group Inc.[12] is incorporated as a non-profit co-operative whose purpose includes research and development and co-operative enterprise awareness building. It is the co-operative's purpose to put forward ideas and criticism which might not normally be voiced from within any one co-operative entity, such as the notion that there may be "more competition amongst co-operatives than co-operation when it comes to international co-operative development." This book is the Group's first publication. See: www.co-operativeneterprise.coop .

Some Co-operative Statistical Highlights

In 2010 the International Co-operative Alliance partnered with the European Research Institute on Cooperative and Social Enterprises (EURICSE) and collected survey data from 2,190 co-operatives from 61 countries. The details and figures which follow have been taken from the 2012 World Co-operative Monitor,[13] which was published following the analysis of the data.

Analysis of data collected indicated:[14]

- **Total net banking income = $185.3 billion USD**
- **Turnover (sales) in 2010 excluding banking and insurance sector = $1,155.1 billion USD**
- **Total insurance co-operatives and mutuals premium income = $1,101.8 billion USD**

The data collected was from countries around the world.[15]

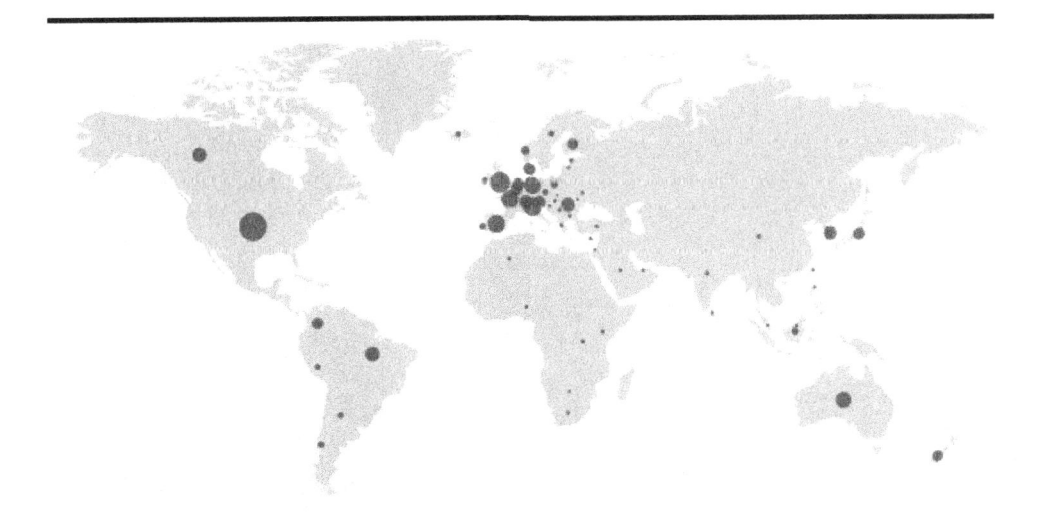

Figure 6.1 Co-operatives by Country

The co-operatives who particpated in the survey are active in nine sectors.[16]

Other International Co-operative Alliance statistics indicate the extent of co-operative membership.[17]

Figure 6.2

Co-operatives by Sector of Activity

28% Insurance co-operatives and mutuals

26% Agriculture and food industries

21% Consumer and retail

7% Banking and financial services

7% Industry and utilities

4% Other services

3% Other

3% Health and social care

1% Housing

Figure 6.3

Some Countries with Co-operative Membership Globally

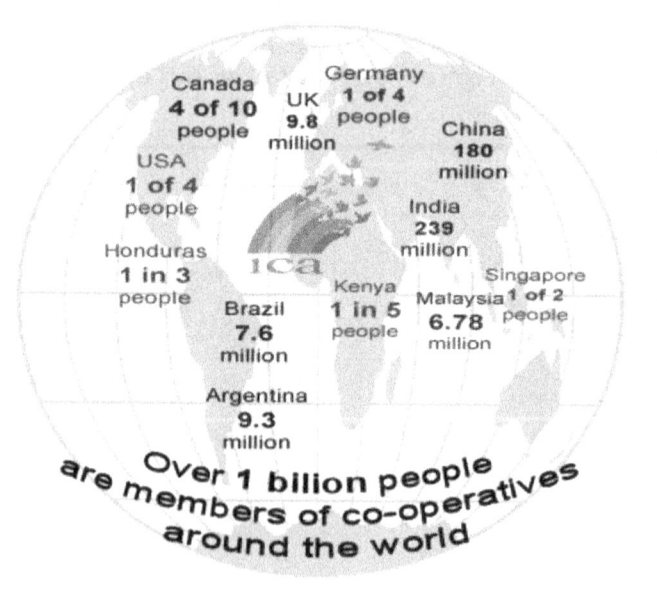

Canada 4 of 10 people
Germany 1 of 4 people
UK 9.8 million
China 180 million
USA 1 of 4 people
India 239 million
Honduras 1 in 3 people
Brazil 7.6 million
Kenya 1 in 5 people
Singapore Malaysia 1 of 2 people
6.78 million
Argentina 9.3 million

Over 1 bilion people are members of co-operatives around the world

Major countries with co-operative memberships in the International Co-operative Alliance are shown in the two graphics in Figure 6.4 following.[18] Please note, as we have stated elsewhere, one member may have more than one co-operative membership! Also note that one membership may also be for a family, this is common with consumer co-operatives! For further details see: www.ica.coop/en/ and click on "What's a co-op", then on Facts and Figures.

Figure 6.4

Countries With Largest Co-operative Memberships

	Millions
United States	305.6
China	160.8
India	97.6
Japan	75.8
Indonesia	40.6
France	32.4
Iran	25.5
Canada	18.1
United Kingdom	11.5
Bangladesh	11

Looking at co-operatives and the mutual, member-owned, insurance market share we see significant global penetration in Figure 6.5 below.[19]

Figure 6.5:

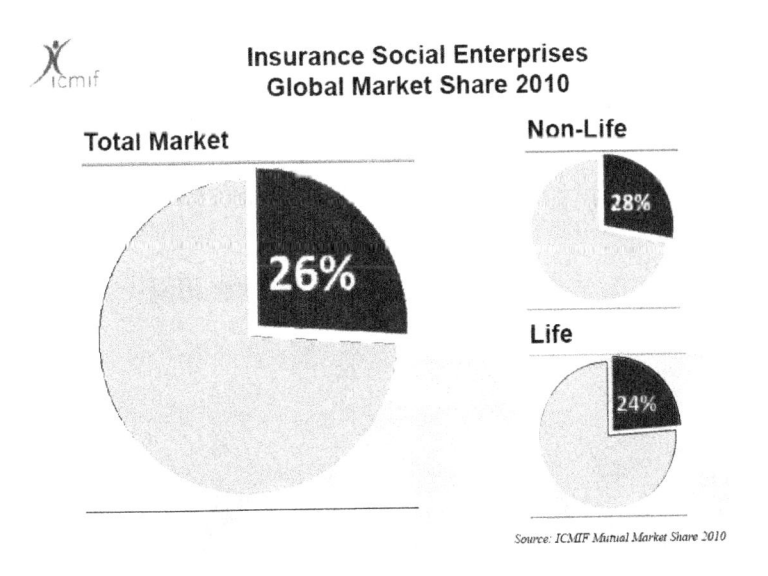

Insurance Social Enterprises Global Market Share 2010

- Total Market: 26%
- Non-Life: 28%
- Life: 24%

Source: ICMIF Mutual Market Share 2010

Credit Unions and Savings and Credit Co-operatives Statistics are shown in Figure 6.6 below.[20]

Figure 6.6

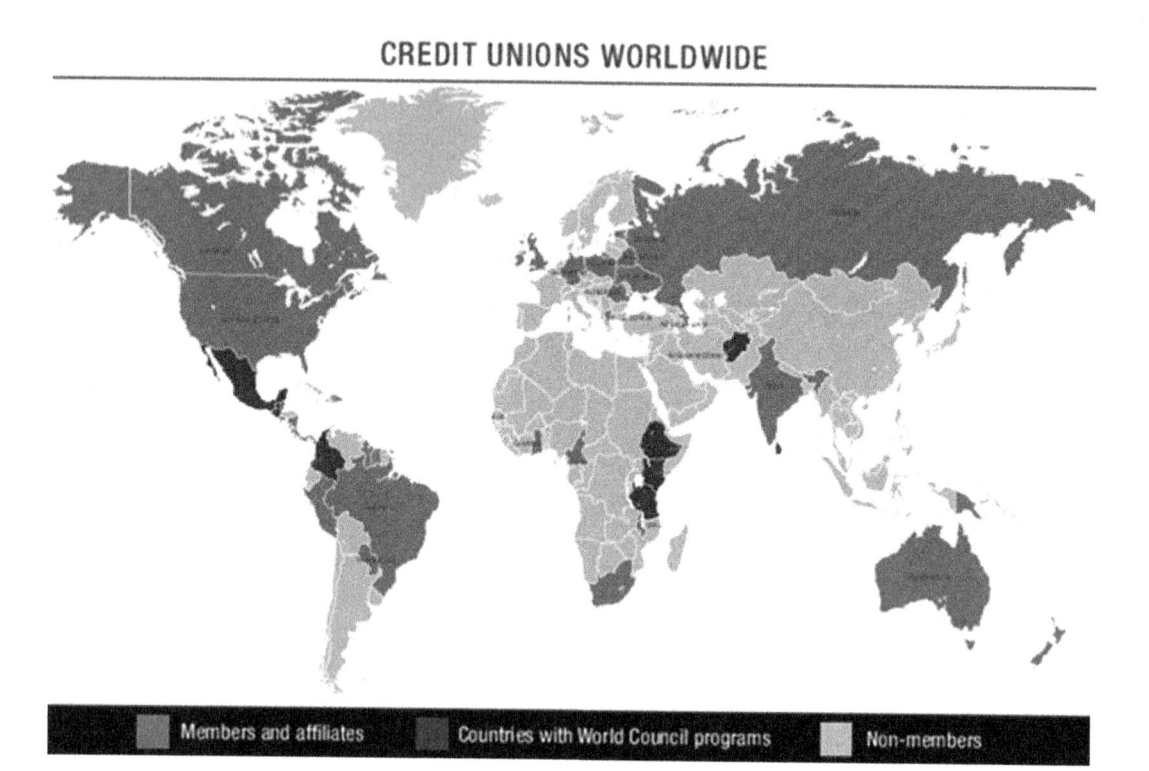

CREDIT UNIONS WORLDWIDE

Members and affiliates | Countries with World Council programs | Non-members

Source: www.woccu.org/

Figure 6.7

Credit Unions at a Glance[21]

Credit Union Countries*	100	Savings & Shares (USD)	1,221,635,067,922
Credit Unions	51,013	Loans (USD)	1,016,243,687,594
Members	196,498,738	Reserves (USD)	141,314,921,924
Penetration**	7.8%	Assets (USD)	1,563,529,230,920

Source: www.woccu.org/

So that you may see credit union growth trends over the past decade, we have included both membership and financial statistics from around the world.

Figure 6.8

Member Statistics

Year	Countries	Credit Unions	Members
2010	100	52,945	187,986,967
2009	97	49,330	183,916,050
2008	97	53,689	185,800,237
2007	96	49,134	177,383,728
2006	96	46,367	172,007,510
2005	92	42,705	157,103,072
2004	82	41,042	128,338,297
2003	84	40,457	123,497,445
2002	78	40,258	118,268,624

Source: www.woccu.org/

Shown below in Figure6.9 are the financial statistics for the same countries over the same 9 year period.[22]

Figure 6.9

Financial Statistics

Year	Savings (USD)	Loans (USD)	Reserves (USD)	Assets (USD)
2010	1,229	960	132	1,460
2009	1,146	912	120	1,353
2008	996	847	115	1,194
2007	988	848	115	1,181
2006	904	758	107	1,092
2005	764	612	92	894
2004	707	531	83	825
2003	656	483	75	758
2002	589	425	67	676

Source: www.woccu.org/

For many people, when they hear the word "share price," they think of stock exchanges, such as the New York Stock Exchange or the Hang Sheng Stock Exchange. Surprisingly, the actual number of human beings who own a share or shares in a co-operative is actually greater than the number of people who own shares that are traded on world stock exchanges. A study by Co-operatives UK and prepared by Ed Mayo in 2012 entitled *Business Ownership Worldwide* concludes that: "There are two tribes of business ownership. Indeed, there are perhaps many more if you consider informal ownership, family firms and micro-scale enterprises. Despite the focus of attention being on stock markets, however, it is co-operative enterprise that touches the lives of more people as owners worldwide." The report analyses and compares the number of people who have an ownership stake in a co-operative enterprise (tribe one) with those who have an ownership stake through company shares (tribe two).

Highlights from the research report on Global Business Ownership are shown below in Figure6.10.[23]

Figure 6.10

Business ownership worldwide – share companies and co-operative enterprise

Form of ownership	Numbers of people
Share owners – direct ownership	328m
Share owners – indirect ownership	565m
Member owners – direct ownership	1,000m

Co-operative member ownership and share ownership as a percentage of population – by region

Region	Co-operative members	Indirect shareholders	Direct shareholders
Africa	7.4%	4.1%	1.3%
Americas	19.4%	16.7%	9.2%
Asia Pacific	13.8%	6.9%	4.4%
Europe	16%	12.9%	7.5%
Worldwide	13.8%	8.7%	5%

Share ownership and co-operative member ownership for a selection of countries

Country	Direct share ownership	Percentage of the population	Co-operative member ownership	Percentage of the population
Brazil	3,123,425	1.7%	8,252,410	4.4%
Canada	12,396,020	38%	11,000,000	33.7%
China	78,318,000	6%	160,000,000	12.2%
Finland	761,674	14.5%	3,164,226	60.1%
Germany	10,317,000	12.5%	20,509,973	24.9%
Ghana	345,000	1.5%	2,400,000	10.7%
India	21,794,832	2%	242,000,000	21.8%
Japan	39,284,500	30.7%	17,000,000	13.3%
Kenya	110,000	0.3%	8,507,000	23.1%
South Korea	4,441,000	9.2%	7,600,000	15.7%
Portugal	323,237	3.1%	2,000,000	18.9%
Spain	2,152,969	4.9%	6,960,870	15.8%
United Kingdom	9,060,260	14.9%	12,800,00	21.1%
United States of America	62,880,000	21.1%	120,000,000	40.2%

Source: Global Business Ownership 2012: Members and Shareholders Across the World, Ed Mayo, by Co-operatives UK, 2012.

Please note: the figures shown refer to the number of co-operative memberships that exist in a country. Co-operative members may have memberships in more than one co-operative. For example, in the USA every 1 out of 4 persons is a co-operative member (120,000,000 persons). Those same co-operative members, on average, belong to 1.5 co-operatives. It is important to distinguish between the number of persons who are members of a co-operative, and the number of co-operative memberships that exist.

Co-operatives and the Global Economy

According to the International Co-operative Alliance and the National Co-operative Business Association:[24]

- **Worldwide, more than 1 billion people are members of co-operatives.**
- **Co-operatives provide 100 million jobs worldwide, 20% more than multinational enterprises.**
- **The economic activity of the largest 300 co-operatives in the world equals the 10th largest national economy.**

- In India and China combined, more than 400 million people are members of co-operatives.

- In Germany and the United States, one in four people are co-operative members while in Canada that number is four in 10!

- In Japan, 1 out of every 3 families is a member of a co-operative.

- In Indonesia, co-operatives provide jobs to 288,589 individuals.

- In Kenya, 250,000 people are employed by co-operatives.

- Canadian maple sugar co-operatives produce 35% of the world's maple sugar production.

- In Colombia, 8,124 co-operatives were responsible for 4.96% of the GDP in 2009. They employ over 137,888 people - 46% of which are men and 54% women.

- In Kenya, co-operatives are responsible for 45% of the GDP and 31% of national savings and deposits. They have 70% of the coffee market, 76% dairy, 90% pyrethrum, and 95% of cotton.

- In Poland, dairy co-operatives are responsible for 75% of dairy production.

- In the UK, the largest independent travel agency is a co-operative.

- In Vietnam, co-operatives contribute 8.6% of the Gross Domestic Product (GDP).

- Costa Rica counts over 10% of its population as members of co-operatives.

- In Germany, 20 million people are members of co-operatives, 1 out of 4 people.

- In Singapore, 50% of the population (1.6 million people) are members of a co-operative.

Co-operatives Celebrate Financial Success

- In Manchester, United Kingdom on 31 October 2012 the world's largest ever co-operative exhibition was held.[25] More than 10,000 visitors from 36 countries attended
- Essential Trading is a Bristol-based whole food producer and wholesaler and is one of the largest successful worker co-operatives in the UK.[26] The company has a turnover of approximately £12 million and employs 85 people. 2012 saw Essential Trading celebrating its 40th anniversary year. Essential Trading's vision is to be a sustainable, scalable business, providing secure employment and satisfactory remuneration to its members whilst benefiting the global community.
- One of this year's Financial Times prestigious awards for *"Boldness in Business"* goes to Mondragon Co-operative Group, in Spain, which has shown the world that co-operative enterprises can do as well - and in many respects better - than the slumping private sector.[27] Like other companies, Mondragon suffered during the downturn. Revenues rose modestly by 0.5 per cent year on year to 14.83 billion Euros for 2011. Its most recent published annual results showed consolidated profits falling from 178 million to 125 million Euros as the recession in Europe weighed on the company. However, even in this period it still managed to keep its headcount steady and increased its presence abroad, with international sales rising from 4.1 billion Euros to 4.5 billion. At its 2011 year-end, Mondragon co-operative had 94 overseas plants, including 13 in China. We expect the award will have many in the private sector questioning how a co-operative could actually pull something like this off. Amazing!
- IFFCO is the world's largest fertiliser co-operative federation based in India.[28] It was ranked as the 37th largest company in India in 2011 by Fortune India 500. IFFCO has made strategic investments in several joint ventures. The number of co-operative societies associated with IFFCO has risen from 57 in 1967 to more than 39,800 at present. Indian Farmers Fertiliser Cooperative Limited (IFFCO) was registered on November 3, 1967 as a Multi-unit Co-operative Society. The Society is primarily engaged in the production and distribution of fertilisers. The bylaws of the Society provide a broad framework for the activities of IFFCO as a co-operative society. Revenue and net income for the 2010-11 year is shown below:

    Revenue 211.9 billion INR (US$ 3.86 billion) (2010-11)

    Net income 7.914 billion INR (US$ 144.03 million) (2010-11)

- The US National Co-operative Bank produced its own country specific statistical report in 2012. It is entitled: *The NCB Co-op 100 -The secret is out on the impact of co-operatives*. It lists the top 100 co-operatives in the USA including total revenues, total assets, industry sector, website addresses, and names of President /CEO. What is amazing is that the top 100 co-operatives had total revenues of more than $216 billion US in 2011, which was an increase of 11% over 2010. You can down load the full report as well as instructions on how to download a free co-operative app for your mobile from: www.ncb.coop/ [29]

Take Aways

1. In the past two years, there has been an explosion of information about co-operatives. This is in large measure because the United Nations declared 2012 as the International Year of Co-operatives.

2. There are many different types of co-operatives. Types include: producer-owned, consumer-owned, worker, purchasing and shared services, hybrid and multi-stakeholder, and mutual co-operatives. There are so many different forms of co-operatives, that grouping them is difficult.

3. There are a number of widely different co-operative structures in use. People are often familiar with their local co-operative but are not aware that there are other co-operative structures. Some structures include: local, second-tier, third-tier and international co-operatives. Many of tiered co-operatives have large and complex ownership and management structures.

4. There are a number of widely different co-operative structures in use. People are often familiar with their local co-operative but are not aware that there are other co-operative structures. Some structures include: local, second-tier, third-tier and international co-operatives. Many tiered co-operatives have large and complex ownership and management structure.

5. Co-operatives take seriously their commitment to international co-operative development. A significant number of co-operative organizations from Europe and North America are involved in supporting co-operative development internationally.

6. Co-operative enterprises are a significant factor around the globe in terms of co-operative membership, individual income and employment, share ownership, savings and loans, income generation, and economic contribution.

- More than 1 billion people are members of co-operatives around the world.

- Co-operative enterprises employ more than 100 million people world-wide; this is 20% more than multi-national corporations.

- Co-operatives are growing and succeeding across the entire globe from India and China to the USA and Canada, from Germany and France and the UK to Columbia and Kenya and Vietnam, and to many countries in between!

Chapter Seven - Wealth Creation, Community Development, and Poverty Reduction

Connecting the Dots

A word of warning to readers! This chapter covers a lot of ground, in that each of the major subsections could be a book by itself. Further, while we are attempting in this publication to provide a global perspective, in most cases, and especially in this chapter, we are, of necessity, only able to give selected individual, local, regional, or national details. This means a great amount of detail recognizing particular co-operative cases and entities has sadly not been included, although such detail is ripe for sharing.

In this chapter we have deliberately chosen to touch on three topics (wealth creation, community development, and poverty reduction) which may seem disparate, but which from a co-operative perspective all involve use of the co-operative enterprise business model.

Incidentally, for those of you who may be economists, students of economics, or those who may look to economists for enlightenment, please forgive our perhaps too rudimentary perspectives regarding how wealth is created and distributed, locally and globally. This chapter is only intended to look at and to describe matters as we see them from a co-operative enterprise perspective. The fact that others may choose to see matters from a different perspective is quite acceptable and is even anticipated.

We all know and accept that wealth has to do with value. However one's definition and understanding of value is determined by one's place of birth, or at least one's place of residence. At a fairly broad level of definition, wealth can be in evidence by observing the extent to which processes, enterprise, people, or commodities contribute to such benefits as eliminating pain and suffering, enhancing self-sufficiency, improving the quality of life, and providing needed basics such as food, water, and shelter. Especially in this context, consideration of wealth must extend to individuals, families, and communities who experience a higher standard as a result of the "wealth" created by a wide range of processes, enterprises, people, and commodities. Examples of this include having choices in housing, purchasing, work, entertainment, health care, and education.

What has all this has to do with co-operatives? Simply stated it is through co-operatives that a great many people are able to provide needed goods and services for themselves. Through and because of co-operatives, they are able to generate wealth (and value) for themselves and their families.

Just how do co-operatives create wealth in the first place? How much co-operative wealth are we talking about? What roles do financial co-operatives play globally? These are questions we shall answer in the first part of this chapter, supported by a variety of examples.

Co-operatives and Wealth Creation

When members join a co-operative and purchase shares in the co-operative, they are able to obtain something of value in return, directly or indirectly. In most cases, members are able to receive something of value by joining together with other members and thus adding to the pool of funds available to help support and strengthen the enterprise. Initially, a certain number of members must agree to work together in the belief that the enterprise can succeed in helping them to achieve their goals. The "joining together" typically involves becoming an equal owner of the enterprise through the purchase of whatever minimum number of shares the co-operative requires. In addition the "joining together" may involve utilizing the co-operative for most ongoing purchases, or most marketing of produce. When many members act in this way, they are able to achieve the advantages that come with scale, including pricing and methods of access that are generally not available to individuals. At some point, when the co-operative has achieved sufficient scale, its functions and activities can become self-sustaining. When this occurs, the co-operative is in a position to not only provide valuable products and services to its members at competitive rates, but also to begin retaining some of its surplus earnings to offset normal business risks and to help fund future growth.

We know of thousands of cases around the world where co-operatives provide individuals and households the option to pool often meagre resources, thereby allowing them to do things and overcome barriers to entry that otherwise would prohibit them from undertaking successful endeavours. To learn more, click on www.ica.coop and use the search term "examples"; for more personal and often more detailed illustrations, click on www.stories.coop. Many of these cases illustrate what can happen when individual members of co-operatives are able to work together.

The creation of wealth can become substantially leveraged when co-operatives themselves begin working together for purposes of creating endeavours that ultimately add value and therefore generate wealth. This line of thought should include the investments made internally by co-operatives as part of their brand, as well as pure capital type investments in support of community/regional/provincial/national economic development. These range from making equity investments in start-ups or growing enterprises, to financial co-operative lending philosophies that tolerate an additional element of risk "because it is good for the community". The measurement of this type of activity has rarely been undertaken at a national or international level as far as we know, but we do know that co-operative endeavours range from small community projects (fresh water wells) to mega-sized undertakings (from Federated Co-operatives' $2.6 billion dollar expansion to their oil refinery in Canada,[1] to the purchase of private banking operations in the US by Rabobank of the Netherlands).[2]

Given limitations in statistical gathering regimes around the globe, we are only able to capture glimpses of the extent to which co-operative forms of enterprise are contributing to wealth internationally. The statistics which follow have been gathered by the ICA, which in turn has gathered them from a host of other sources, including in many cases from co-operative organizations themselves. They are intended to give you a sense of the actual extent of co-operative wealth creation activities.

CO-OPERATIVES TODAY

Co-operatives are significant economic actors in national economies:

- In Belgium, co-operative pharmacies have a market share of 19.5%.

- In Benin, the savings and credit co-operative federation FECECAM provided USD 16 million in rural loans in 2002.

- In Brazil, co-operatives are responsible for 40% of the agricultural GDP and for 6% of total agribusiness exports. In 2006, Brazilian co-operatives exported 7.5 million tons of agricultural products to 137 countries for a value of USD 2.83 billion.

- Co-operativa de Ahorro y Crédito "Jesús Nazareno" Ltda. (CJN) handled 25% of the savings in Bolivia in 2002.

- In Côte d'Ivoire co-operatives invested USD 26 million for setting up schools, building rural roads, and establishing maternal clinics.

- In Colombia, over 7,300 co-operatives were responsible for 5.61% of the GDP in 2007 - up from 5.37% in 2006 and 5.25% in 2005. They employ over 110,000 people and some sectors are providing a significant proportion of the jobs - 24.4% of all health sector jobs are provided by co-operatives, 18.3% of the jobs in the transport sector, 8.3% in agriculture, and 7.21% of the jobs in the financial sector. Co-operatives provide 87.5% of all microcredit in the country; they provide health insurance to 30% of all Colombians, and they are responsible for 35.29% of Colombian coffee production.

- In Cyprus, the co-operative movement held 30% of the market in banking services, and handled 35% of all marketing of agricultural produce.

- In Denmark, consumer co-operatives in 2007 held 36.4% of consumer retail market.

- Finnish co-operative groups within Pellervo were responsible for 74% of meat products, 96% of dairy products; 50% of the egg production, 34% of forestry products, and handled 34.2% of the total deposits in Finnish banks.

- In France, 9 out of 10 farmers are members of agricultural co-operatives, co-operative banks handle 60% of the total deposits, and 25% of all retailers in France are co-operatives.

- In Hungary, the members of the consumer co-operative Co-op Hungary are responsible for 14.4% of the national food and general retail sales in 2004.
- In Iran, co-operatives contribute 6% of the Gross Domestic Product (GDP).

- In Japan, the agricultural co-operatives report outputs of USD 90 billion with 91% of all Japanese farmers in membership. In 2007, consumer co-operatives reported a total turnover of USD 34,048 billion with 5.9% of the food market share.

- In Kenya, co-operatives are responsible for 45% of the GDP and 31% of national savings and deposits. They have 70% of the coffee market, 76% dairy, 90% pyrethrum, and 95% of cotton.

- In Korea, agricultural co-operatives have a membership of over 2 million farmers (90% of all farmers), and an output of USD 11 billion. The Korean fishery co-operatives report a market share of 71%.

- In Kuwait, the Kuwaiti Union of Consumer Co-operative Societies, whose members are 6.5% of the Kuwaiti population, handled nearly 70% of the national retail trade in 2007.

- In Latvia, the Latvian Central Co-operative Union is responsible for 12.3% of the market in the food industry sector.

- In Mauritius, in the agricultural sector, co-operators play an important role in the production of sugar, vegetable, fruit and flowers, milk, meat, and fish. Nearly 50% of sugar-cane planters are grouped in co-operatives and the share of co-operatives in national sugar production is 10%. Co-operative Societies account for more than 60% of national production in the food crop sector – 75% of onions, 40% of potatoes, and about 70% of fresh green vegetables are produced by co-operatives. In addition, the co-operative bus sector (or "bus co-operatives") represents some 30% of the national bus transport.

- In Moldova, the Central Union of Consumer Co-operatives is responsible for 6.8% of the consumer market.

- In New Zealand, 22% of the gross domestic product (GDP) is generated by co-operative enterprise. Co-operatives are responsible for 95% of the dairy market and 95% of the export dairy market. They hold 70% of the meat market, 50% of the farm supply market, 70% of the fertiliser market, 75% of the wholesale pharmaceuticals, and 62% of the grocery market.

- In Norway, dairy co-operatives are responsible for 99% of the milk production; consumer co-operatives hold 24.1% of the market; fisheries co-operatives are responsible for 8.7% of total Norwegian exports; forestry co-operatives were responsible for 76% of timber, and 1.5 million people of the 4.5 million Norwegians are members of co-operatives.

-
- In Poland, dairy co-operatives are responsible for 75% of dairy production.

- In Portugal, approximately 3000 co-operatives are responsible for 5% of the Gross National Product of the country.

- Co-operatives and mutuals in Scotland account for 4.25% of the Scottish Gross Domestic Product, having an annual turnover of British Pounds Sterling (GBP) 4 billion and assets of GBP 25 billion.

- In Singapore, consumer co-operatives hold 55% of the market in supermarket purchases and have a turnover of USD 700 million.

- In Slovenia, agricultural co-operatives are responsible for 72% of the milk, 79% of cattle, 45% of wheat and 77% of potato production.

- In Sweden, consumer co-operatives held 17.5% of the market in 2004.

- In the UK, the largest independent travel agency is a co-operative.

- In Uruguay, co-operatives produce 90% of the total milk production, 34% of the honey, and 30% of the wheat; 60% of co-operative production is exported to over 40 countries around the world.

- In Vietnam, co-operatives contribute 8.6% of the GDP.

- In the United States more than 30 co-operatives have annual revenue in excess of USD 1 billion. In 2003 the top 100 US co-operatives had combined revenues of USD 117 billion. In addition, approximately 30% of farmers' products in the US are marketed through 3,400 farmer-owned co-operatives.

The information provided above has been collected from a variety of sources including ICA's statistical questionnaire, information published by co-operative organisations, presentations made by co-operatives, and government statistical offices.[3]

To this partial list we add the following additional examples:

- In India the Indian Farmers' Fertilizer Co-operative (IFFCO) is a massive co-operative enterprise operating across India and elsewhere around the world.[4] It is owned by 39,862 member shareholders. Member shareholders are local agricultural co-operative societies. IFFCO's total sales and other income for the 2011-2012 year were 4.7 billion USD. Retained earnings after taxes, dividends, educational funds, and donations were approximately $123,700,325 US.

- In India, dairy co-operatives generate employment for 13.4 million rural households. AMUL is the apex organisation of the Dairy Co-operatives of Gujarat.[5] AMULis India's largest food product marketing organisation with annual turnover (2011-12) of US $ 2.5 billion. Its daily milk procurement is approximately 13 million litres from 16,117 village milk co-operative societies, 17 member unions covering 24 districts, and 3.18 million milk producer members. Despite the global recession, AMUL had a turnover of £750 million in 2008-9 and sales growth of 27%. (You can learn more about AMUL by clicking www.amul.com/m/about-us . From there, you can even link to their TV podcasts located under menu Fun@AMUL.)

- In Argentina, "Co-operativa Obrera Ltda. de Consumo y Vivienda" was created in 1920 by a group of 173 train workers of the city of Bahia Blanca (a city in the Province of Buenos Aires) in order to lower the price of bread.[6] They successfully built a bakery, and after ninety years it has become the most important consumer co-operative in Argentina, and the second largest in Latin America. At present, it has 90 supermarkets, 26 in Bahia Blanca; the others are located in different cities in the Province of Buenos Aires and three other provinces (La Pampa, Río Negro, and Neuquén).

- In Argentina, La Riojana Co-operative is a wine producer co-operative located in the Province of La Rioja.[7] Founded in 1940, it includes more than 450 wine producers and it has evolved based on the idea of sustainable development and values such as solidarity and the equal distribution of benefits. Also in Argentina, the Asociación de Co-operativas Argentinas (ACA) was established 90 years ago and it comprises about 150 co-operatives which sell and export their products through ACA.[8] ACA handles around 15 per cent of the total grain production of the country.

- In the USA in 2009,[9] more than 29,000 co-operatives helped create $652 billion in revenues resulting in jobs and wages affecting more than 2.1 million employees. The majority of the country's 2 million farmers are members of the nearly 3,000 farmer-owned co-operatives. They provide over 250 thousand jobs and annual wages of over $8 billion. More than 7,500 credit unions provide financial services to 91 million US consumers. In the US more than 900 rural electric co-ops deliver electricity to more than 42 million people in 47 states.
- Electric co-operatives are important providers in rural areas. In Bangladesh, rural electric co-operatives provide service for 45 million people.[10] In the United States, 900 rural electric co-operatives serve 42 million people in 47 states.[11] This makes up 42 percent of the nation's electric distribution lines and covers 75 percent of the country's land mass. In Argentina, co-operatives provide 58% of rural electricity.

- In Colombia, the health co-operative Saludcoop provides healthcare services for 20% of the population.[12]

- In Japan, 9 million family farmers are members of co-operatives.[13]

- In India, the needs of 67% of rural households are covered by co-operatives.[14]

- In Germany, Greenpeace Energy is the largest national energy co-operative.[15] Founded in 2000, it has 21,000 members and supplies over 110,000 clients with clean energy.

- **In Switzerland, the largest retailer employer is a co-operative.**[16]

Today, more than 50% of global agricultural produce is marketed via co-operatives.[17] It must be obvious that agricultural co-operatives are by no means small potatoes!

The examples above illustrate the significant economic contribution co-operative forms of enterprise are making around the world.

In all cases we are illustrating the significant contribution to wealth creation that co-operatives are making. While we are sure you are beginning to see the picture, we are not yet finished!

Co-operative Ownership and Control of Financial Resources

While co-operatives may compete within a global marketplace, members continue to retain local ownership and control of their assets and their various resources. This is particularly the case when it comes to using resources and distributing earnings locally. In financial co-operatives, the ownership and control of wealth rests with local members. Policies, and thus decision-making processes, are typically created to maximize service quality (including financial returns) to all members rather than maximizing financial returns for a small number of often distant shareholders. Earnings in financial co-operatives typically remain in the region or location in which they were generated. Surplus earnings in co-operatives are usually returned in part to members based on patronage and use of the co-operative, while a portion is retained by the co-operative to help offset future growth and business risk. In either case, profits are retained within the community, area, or region in which they were generated. Over time, the re-investment and retention of earnings by co-operatives means the enterprise can in turn positively support economic growth and development within the areas they serve.

We include the following statistics (Figure 7.1) to illustrate the extent to which financial co-operatives are able to gather savings and, in turn, fund loans for their members. We have included the three largest groups for which statistics are generally available. These figures from 2011 are incomplete in that they do not include various other forms of co-operative financial aggregation or figures for co-operative insurers.

Figure 7.1

Selected Co-operative Bank and Credit Union Statistics

European Association of Co-operative Banks

Total Members	Total Assets (Trillion USD)	Total Deposits (Trillion USD)	Total Loans (Trillion USD)
55,734,193	$9.0	$5.1	$5.2

World Council of Credit Unions

Total Members	Total Assets (Trillion USD)	Total Deposits (Trillion USD)	Total Loans (Trillion USD)
196,498,738	$1.6	$1.2	$1.0

Japanese Co-operative Banks (Shinkin Banks)

Total Members	Total Assets (Trillion USD)	Total Deposits (Trillion USD)	Total Loans (Trillion USD)
9,316,044	$3.0	$1.5	$0.8

Combined Totals

Total Members	Total Assets (Trillion USD)	Total Deposits (Trillion USD)	Total Loans (Trillion USD)
261,548,975	13.5	7.8	7.0

Note: These figures have been derived from a variety of sources and are intended to serve as indicators of scale only. The figures are understated as details of operations and statistics are not available for some countries.

Source: Global Co-operative Development Group Inc. based on the year ending 2011.

In the majority of cases the loans made by financial co-operatives are in support of some form of small or medium sized income generating enterprises owned by members. The greatest use of co-operative finance around the world is in support of agricultural production.

Globally, "financial co-operatives" of all types serve an estimated 857 million people, or 13 per cent of the world population.[18]

Co-operatives and Community Development

Community development - loosely defined here - refers to various processes and activities by which interested parties within the community can successfully pursue common social, economic, and even cultural objectives. To be successful, co-operatives must focus on sustainability while continuing to adapt their organizations to changing circumstances. Implicit in our definition is the narrower definition of community *economic* development – which focuses more particularly on matters such as job creation, wealth creation, and value-added activities. We include this definition to illustrate the connections that can develop between a co-operative and its community.

Many years ago, it was with some surprise that a credit union leader in Saskatchewan, Canada,[19] explained that she had suddenly realized that her organization succeeded when the community in which it was located succeeded - and vice versa. She said it was as if a light had somehow suddenly come on in her mind. At that time, she was managing a medium-sized credit union. Prior to that insight, she had always perceived that what was important involved delivering top quality financial products and services to satisfy member needs while ensuring the financial strength and well-being of the organization. Her new insight revealed the synergy that can exist between a co-operative and its community, if and when the co-operative is being well managed. It is interesting that the definition of "community development" can still hold true when one substitutes the word "co-operative" for the word "community" and various interests within the definition, thusly:

"Co-operative development - loosely defined here - is that group of process and activities by which various interests within the co-operative can successfully pursue common social, economic, and even cultural objectives." It is not surprising then to find that the processes and activities, interests, and objectives often overlap between a community and its co-operatives".

It is from this general definition that one comes to fully appreciate the importance of the seventh principle in the Statement on the Co-operative Identity referred to earlier in Figure 3.2, which is "Concern for Community".

The following is our short list of avenues through which a co-operative can care for its community:

- **Help develop leaders and community members – opportunities for leadership experience.**

- **Acts to inform the community – openness and transparency as well as member education.**

- **Cares for the environment and its sustainability – environmentally sound practices.**

- **Pays to the community its fair share of any taxes due – enterprise responsibility.**

- Helps finance the community – through loans, purchase of community bonds, debentures, etc.

- Serves to fill gaps not satisfied by public or private sector bodies – I.e. worker co-operatives.

- Invests in communities – helps fund community facilities such as community centres.

- Provides meaningful work/liveable wages – required to carry out enterprise functions.

- Creates tax accruing activities – be they corporate, employment or services based.

- Educates and trains – members', and employees' knowledge and skill development.

- Allows members to experience democratic decision-making - e.g. *one member one vote*

- Builds social capital - empowering, team-work, networking, empathy, equity, civic participation.

- Leverages wealth – financial co-operatives can increase community money supply up to 18 times!
- Advocates on behalf of members and the community – in policy and legislative matters, such as in the cost of credit disclosure, and environmental protection.

We quote Jessica Gordon Nembhard, who in turn is quoting from a paper prepared by Gordon Nembhard 2004a; Fairbairn, Bold, Fulton, Hammond Ketilson, and Ish in 1991, when she states:[20]

> **Co-operative economic development solves many problems created by market failure, economic discrimination, and under development. Co-operative businesses are group-*centered, needs-based, and asset building local development models based on pooling of* resources, democratic economic participation, and profit sharing. They are locally controlled, internally driven democratic institutions that promote group learning, economic interdependence, and consolidation of resources, development of assets, and protection of people and the environment. Co-operatives stabilize their communities - increasing economic activity, creating good jobs, increasing benefits and wages, and encouraging civic participation. Community-based, co-operatively-**

owned enterprises are characterized by greater community input and participation in the planning, development, and governance of commercially viable socially-responsible businesses. Co-operatives provide a mechanism for low-resourced people with few traditional opportunities, to create new economic opportunities for themselves and their co-workers and/or neighbors.

The following are just a few particular illustrations of co-operatives that are actively involved as an integral part of their communities.

- In the US, Evergreen Co-operatives of Cleveland, Ohio are pioneering innovative models of job creation, wealth building, and sustainability.[21] Evergreen's employee-owned, for-profit companies are based locally and hire locally. Evergreen Co-operatives is an innovative partnership between public and private stakeholders intended to support the creation of worker co-operatives as a means for creating living wage employment in low income neighbourhoods. Started in 2008, the Evergreen Co-operatives Initiative is based on a vision of "community wealth building."

- In Spain, Mondragon Corporation is a complex worker-owned, co-operative system that has over 100 global businesses, more than 80,000 employees, and annual sales of over $25 billion USD.[22] It is very much a part of its social, economic, and cultural community. It takes its contributions seriously and invests 10 percent of its profits annually into socially oriented activities. In 2008, Mondragon contributed 35.3 million euros - earmarked for backing socially-oriented activities - as follows:

  -

  • Projects in training and education: 10.4 million euros, channelled into higher education, professional training, and general education.

  • Promoting cultural activities: 2.2 million euros.

  • Research and development projects: 7.8 million euros.

  • Promoting the use of the Basque language and other minority languages: 1.7 million euros.

  • Care schemes (programmes in support of the disabled, caring for the elderly, reinsertion of substance abusers, etc.) and backing for the activities of NGOs and development projects in emerging economies: 6.3 million euros.

  • Other activities: 6.9 million euros.

You can learn more about Mondragon and about Evergreen Co-operatives by using www.youtube.com and searching for "shift change - putting democracy to work".[23]

- **In Bolivia, the Co-operativa de Servicios Publicos Santa Cruz Limitada provides water and sewage services in the city of Santa Cruz, Bolivia.[24] It has been in business for over 30 years and serves 750,000 people. Over the years performance has been very good by international standards, with water available 99% of the time. Membership is open to all its customers and its co-operative structure has helped the utility stay focused on consumers' needs.**

- **In Canada, in the province of Saskatchewan, credit unions use their resources to help make dreams real for individuals and for communities.[25] Every year, credit unions support a broad range of local and provincial initiatives that contribute to growing Saskatchewan communities. In all corners of the province, credit unions sponsor educational initiatives, arts and culture programs, sports teams, health care, economic development projects, and many other causes. Credit unions provide gifts or inkind services for special events and reduce, or waive, service fees for thousands of community groups. Over the past four years (thru to the end of 2011) Saskatchewan credit unions contributed $26.6 million to growing communities; fundraising efforts brought in nearly $2 million for causes like the Children's Hospital Foundation of Saskatchewan, Red Cross Disaster Relief, Terry Fox Run, and Telemiracle; and credit union employees logged more than 285,000 hours of volunteer time for community organizations.**

The seventh co-operative principle requires that co-operatives not only serve their members, they must also contribute to the growth and development of the communities of which they are a part. In addition to purchasing locally, providing gainful employment, and paying various taxes, co-operatives serve to improve their communities by contributing to local facilities such as schools, hospitals, public parks, local charities, sporting events, and at times, even infrastructure such as sidewalks and roads. Co-operatives can also choose to spark local economic development through offering assistance to other groups and providing some funds for the development of local community-based enterprises.

- **An innovative approach supported by the UK's Co-operative College involves establishing Co-operative Trust Schools and a companion co-operative schools network across England.[26] You can learn more using this link from the national association: www.co-operativeschools.coop/**

Co-operatives Create and Maintain Employment

One of the most important things co-operatives do in communities is create employment.[27] Here are some eye opening numbers to consider.

- Co-operatives provide over 100 million jobs around the world, 20% more than multinational enterprises.

- In Argentina, co-operatives are responsible for providing direct employment to over 233,000 individuals.

- In Bolivia, 1590 co-operatives provide 32,323 direct jobs and 128,180 indirect jobs.

- In Canada, co-operatives and credit unions employ over 155,000 people. The Desjardins movement (savings and credit co-operatives) is the largest non-governmental employer in the province of Québec.

- In Colombia, the co-operative movement provides 123,643 jobs through direct employment and an additional 537,859 jobs as worker-owners in worker co-operatives - providing 3.74% of all jobs in the country.

- In France, 21,000 co-operatives provide over 4 million jobs.

- In Germany, 8,106 co-operatives provide jobs for 440,000 people.

- In Indonesia, co-operatives provide jobs to 288,589 individuals.

- In Iran, co-operatives have created and maintain 1.5 million jobs.

- In Italy, 70,400 co-operative societies employed nearly 1 million people in 2005.

- In Japan, a consumer co-operative, the Seikatsu Club, has fostered the development of over 600 worker collectives (essentially co-operatives) in recent years.

- In Kenya, 250,000 people are employed by co-operatives.

- In Slovakia, the Co-operative Union represents more than 700 co-operatives which employ nearly 75,000 individuals.

Were there space and time available, many more examples could be provided.

Co-operatives and Poverty Reduction

Fighting poverty and creating wealth are in many ways the opposite side of the same coin. It is well known that "economic activity" and in particular "economic growth" are the major ingredients in wealth creation. These are the same ingredients necessary in fighting poverty. A well regarded African co-operative leader and author once stated (and we paraphrase here), that *if the aim is to help fight poverty, then one should make sure one is not poor.* Emmauel Darko's wisdom has proven sound.[28] In strictly non-economic jargon - money is at the heart of the matter. How value is created, and who gets paid for what part of the value chain generally determines where wealth lies. Darko goes further in asserting that fighting poverty should not be an exercise focused on finding and acquiring someone else's money, but rather should be focused on using and creating your own wealth. Such a simple yet fundamental truth is worthy of explanation, so in this section we will revisit the matter of co-operatives and fighting poverty. The numerous examples we have provided previously in this chapter show beyond question that co-operatives can, and are, successfully fighting poverty around the globe.

For more than 50 years, co-operatives have been strengthened in less developed countries through accessing foreign aid budgets from developed countries. This was particularly true of developed countries with a strong co-operative sector, such as Canada, US, UK, Sweden, and Germany. Many strong partnerships have developed between co-operatives in more developed and less developed countries to strengthen co-operatives and communities through the application of best practices and efforts to increase community solidarity. Communities were strengthened as a result, and members and their families reaped lasting economic and social improvements. There are examples where co-operatives have provided leadership and served as change agents locally and nationally in such important areas as gender equality. It has not been surprising to find co-operative leaders adopting principles of gender equity far ahead of national awareness or of public policy.

To learn first-hand how the Co-operative Group in the UK is helping to tackle poverty by pioneering avenues such as Fairtrade, you can use www.youtube.com and search for "Tackling Global Poverty - The Co-operative".[29]

Globally, financial co-operatives are the largest providers of microfinance services to the poor.[30] It is estimated that financial co-operatives reach 78 million clients living below a poverty line of $2 per day. In South Asia, for example, 54.5 per cent of borrowers living below $2 per day are served by co-operatives, compared to 19 per cent served by other microfinance providers. Clearly, financial co-operatives play a central role in the achievement of an inclusive financial sector that encompasses the poor.

At the same time, we know of well-meaning but ill-informed NGOs who have sought to introduce co-operative enterprise into their projects as a method of fighting poverty. Sadly, some have failed because there was insufficient understanding of the nature of co-operatives and of their requirements. Successful co-operatives need:

- an appropriate legislative framework which permits formal registration of co-operatives;

- a macroeconomic climate and a marketplace that are conducive to the viability of the enterprise;

- strong elements of member education, ownership, and control; and

- time to develop and grow.

There are cases where co-operatives have been started by international development groups or agencies as philanthropic projects. Although well intended, in the absence of co-operative technical expertise and external co-operative system linkages, such initiatives have in many cases proved to be unsustainable. Unfortunately, their failures tend to create mistrust, confusion, and misunderstanding in the minds of governments and in the eyes of the general public.

In many ways, the keys to co-operative success are the same in less developed settings as they are in developed settings. The key involves instilling the notion of local ownership (and thus control) coupled with the notion of self-help. Any local co-operative start-up or support initiative in any setting which does not at a minimum instill these two elements initially, and continue to emphasize them over the longer term, we believe, is prone to fail.

While there is considerable good case by case evidence, we regret that there is not at this time any definitive research illustrating more precisely the impact (positive and otherwise) that co-operative enterprises are having in reducing poverty levels globally. We are hopeful that research work will begin appearing and supporting our contentions within the not too distant future.

It may be helpful to look briefly at some of the longer-term players that have been active in the co-operative development arena. Many of them are the same players described in chapter six who have achieved their own success and are willing to support the development of co-operative enterprises in less developed settings.

There are two major groupings: those from within the co-operative sector, and others from groups or agencies who are significant supporters of co-operative development as an avenue for reducing poverty globally. We will describe each grouping in general terms and then consider briefly some of the major or key players involved in each grouping.

Co-operative Agents Support International Co-operative Development

Regardless of their democratic structure, the following organizations are structured within or as a part of the co-operative system. These organizations or entities were created by and are answerable to local, regional, national, or international co-operatives. While these organizations do share a common culture and a common set of values, each one is different from the others in the ways they operate and make decisions. We know that there are numerous co-operative groups supporting in-country co-operative development. The list that follows includes those agents who we see are supporting co-operative development internationally as a means for reducing poverty. We expect there are other co-operative groups supporting international co-operative development, and we will be pleased to include them in any future publications if so requested.

While various non-co-operative organizations, institutions and agencies are active throughout the world supporting co-operative development, we will make note of various co-operatives with which we are familiar and which are actively engaged in co-operative enterprise development internationally.

The National Co-operative Business Association (NCBA) (www.ncba.coop/) is the primary co-operative organization promoting, advocating, and developing co-operatives across the United States of America. The Cooperative League of the USA (CLUSA) is an international arm of the National Cooperative Business Association, and it provides significant technical assistance to develop cooperatives internationally.

The US Overseas Cooperative Development Council (OCDC) (www.ocdc.coop) helps to promote co-operatives internationally through various initiatives as a practical means for income development, food security, and democracy building. The OCDC receives direction and support from nine other major co-operative development organizations. Its two main initiatives at this time are: the Cooperative Law and Regulation Initiative (CLARITY) which assists developing countries to create a legal and regulatory environment that enables cooperative businesses to flourish, and the Measurements for Tracking Indicators of Cooperative Success (METRICS).

In Canada, the Canadian Co-operative Association (CCA) (www.coopscanada.coop/), and the Desjardins Group's international arm, Développement international Desjardins (DID) (www.did.qc.ca/) carry out significant co-operative development work in Africa, the Americas, and Asia. Both organizations deliver a wide selection of programs and projects ranging from co-operative partner education and capacity building and technical support for livelihood income generation, through to local co-operative growth and development, to women's co-operative credit union coaching programs, to food security, to support for legislative and regulatory frameworks for financial co-operatives.

The Co-operative College (www.co-op.ac.uk/) In the United Kingdom, Co-operatives UK is the central membership organization for co-operative enterprise in the United Kingdom. Under Co-operative UK's trusteeship, the Co-operative College supports co-operative development work locally and internationally. The College is the UK's leading knowledge centre on co-operation, drawn from nearly 100 years' experience of working with co-operatives throughout the world. The College is a unique educational institution focused on providing world class learning programmes and research to support the development of a successful and diverse co-operative sector. The Co-operative College works in countries in Africa and the Asia/Pacific region.

In Ireland, the Irish Credit Union League Foundation (ICUL Foundation) (www.ilcufoundation.ie/) supports various credit union and co-operative projects internationally. Through support for the development of credit unions in low-income countries, the Foundation is helping people to help themselves through the credit union model. This support is made possible through the generous support of Irish credit unions and their members, whose annual contributions enable the Foundation to share the success of the Irish credit union movement with credit unions, and similar type movements, in countries in Africa and Eastern Europe.

Please appreciate that the list of organizations described is incomplete and does not include numerous national and regional co-operative development organizations. It does not include a number of co-operative and non-co-operative organizations that support development in Asia and in Central and South America. If there is sufficient interest we will be pleased to expand this listing in future.

Other Groups or Agencies Supporting Co-operative Development

Following are some, certainly not all, agencies and partner agents, who are not themselves co-operative entities, but which, as part of their mandate, are actively supporting international co-operative development.

ILO - The International Labour Organization (ILO) is a United Nations Agency. It was founded in 1919, in the wake of a destructive war, to pursue a vision based on the premise that universal, lasting peace can be established only if it is based on social justice. The ILO became the first specialized agency of the UN in 1946. The ILO is actively engaged in both research and advocacy in support of the co-operative development model internationally. The ILO has played a very significant role in co-operative enterprise awareness building and in supporting the development of co-operative legislation in many countries around the world.

USAID - The United States Agency for International Development (USAID) supports the development of co-operative organizations because co-operatives embody aspects of the principles of voluntarism, democratic choice, and the economic effectiveness of private enterprise that historically have shaped the United States national development.

DFID - The Department for International Development (DFID) leads the UK government's fight against world poverty and works with specific co-operatives, providing financial aid and technical assistance, and with governments and regulatory bodies to facilitate the setting up of co-operatives.

CIDA - The Canadian International Development Agency (CIDA), has, since 1968, supported co-operatives in their efforts to reduce poverty around the world. This relationship is considered by many to be one of Canada's greatest achievements in terms of international aid. As of mid-2013 efforts are underway to merge CIDA with Canada's Department of Foreign Affairs and International Trade in a new department to be called Foreign Affairs, International Trade and Development. It is perhaps too early to assess the full implications that this restructuring may have upon Canada's support for international co-operative development.

Norges Vel - The Royal Norwegian Society for Development (Norges Vel) is an independent, non-governmental and non-profit organisation, presently consisting of 33 member organizations and 1,100 individual members. Norges Vel works to strengthen sustainable business development, including co-operative development, nationally and internationally.

GTZ - The Deutsche Gesellschaft für Technische Zusammenarbeit (GTZ) is an international arm of the German government. GTZ offers customised solutions to complex challenges. GTZ is an experienced service provider and assists the German Government in achieving its objectives in the field of international co-operation. GTZ projects and programs often include support for co-operative forms of enterprise.

SCC - The Swedish Cooperative Centre (SCC) is a development organisation that works on the principle of: *help to self-help*. They work to achieve a world that is free from poverty and injustice. They support study circles, microfinance projects, and co-operative partnerships in 25 countries across the world. Activities are financed via corporate and individual fundraising, as well as grants, mainly from the Swedish International Development Cooperation Agency (SIDA).

The list of organizations and agencies working in support of co-operative enterprise development is, we know, much longer. However, these are some of the major entities of which we have knowledge.

We will endeavor to add additional entities on our website at: www.co-operativeenterprise.coop.

Co-operatives are Not a Quick Fix

In this chapter we have given you a glimpse into co-operative wealth creation, co-operative development, and the use of co-operative enterprise in poverty reduction from a global perspective. We hope you have found the information and the links provided to be both interesting and useful.

Finally, while we might wish it to be otherwise, we know that co-operatives are not a quick fix to poverty. Co-operatives often take longer to start and typically take an even longer period of time to become viable than other forms of enterprise. On the other hand, though, they do have longer term success and greater resilience in periods of economic crisis.[31]

Take Aways

1. Co-operative enterprises are significant wealth creating engines operating across the globe.

2. Co-operatives create wealth, in their own ways, by:
    a. Aggregating member capital and contributing volume,
    b. Retaining local ownership and control of capital,
    c. Investing in communities, and by
    d. Fighting poverty.

3. Co-operatives can serve as active community development actors.

4. Co-operatives are active in supporting international co-operative growth and development.

5. Co-operatives through their local and national organizations are major players in fighting poverty globally.

Chapter Eight - The Pivotal Role of Government in Enabling Co-operative Development

Creating Legislation

In most democratic countries, it is a given that one of the roles of government (government here meaning elected or other legislators and their administrative agencies and ministries) is to enact and enable laws, policies, and practices which served to protect citizens and to promote various forms of development which government feel will be in the best interests of its citizens. Typically, such laws, policies, and practices are cast as being, if not for the benefit of all citizens, at least for the benefit of the nation as a whole.

Various pieces of business corporation legislation and related regulations, as well as banking legislation and capital markets and securities legislation, trust service and insurance legislation, labour standards legislation, and of course, tax legislation and regulation all have a significant influence over how a society develops. Of course there are also the civil and criminal codes, human rights and freedoms legislation, health and safety legislation, and so on, which serve to govern human affairs and behavior and to protect individuals and groups within society.

In many western countries, it has become common for legislators to enact statutes which favour the actions and activities of corporate and public sector bodies over the interests of the average citizen. By far the most complex and extensive bodies of legislation to be developed over the past 150 years around the world concern trade, market behavior (competition), and the corporation (principally the private corporation). While it has morphed slightly in various forms, the corporation (including those traded in the marketplace) still has as its stated primary purpose the maximization of returns on capital to shareholders, while at the same time limiting liability for its actions to the value of shares held. In most cases, such laws and regulations were seen as being for the common good and in the interests of a country as a whole. In this way, governments in a general sense, regardless of their political stripe, have acted to legitimize certain behaviors and beliefs and to delegitimize other behaviors and beliefs. They have put in place policies, formal legislation, and regulations which have shaped educational institutions, intelligence and military communities, policing and security agencies, private and public corporate bodies, national and international institutions, national banking systems, justice systems, and have, of course, spelt out who will be taxed, and how they will be taxed through various tax regimes.

Recognizing the increasingly interlinked and interdependent nature of nations, major government institutions and major multi-national corporations, particularly in the West, have succeeded in great measure in marketing their cultural value systems globally. This in turn supported the exporting of related economic goods and services as well as desired political beliefs. The marketing and corresponding export of economic systems and associated beliefs is what many people think of today when they talk about the negative effects of globalization. As John Raulston Saul explains in *The Collapse of Globalism and the Reinvention of the World*, major western governments and government civil servants have without question begun to ascribe private sector thinking and private sector values to public sector policy decisions and direction.[1] The World Bank, the International Monetary Fund (IMF), and the Organization for Economic Co-operation and Development (OECD) have all been created to help governments tackle the economic, social, and governance challenges of a globalised economy. This, in and of itself, is not something which is undesirable, except we feel that there needs to be more to humanity than private sector values and private sector thinking.

What does any of this have to do with the role of governments and the development of co-operatives? The answer in social, economic, and even cultural terms is that it has a great deal to do with co-operatives, because it helps to explain why governments, from time to time, either support co-operatives or they do not. It further introduces a tendency which Hagen Henry, a specialist in international co-operative law, describes as the "stock companisation" of co-operatives.[2] By this Henry means there is a generalised perception that stock companies can be, and are being used as, yardsticks by which to measure and evaluate the performance and efficiency of all types of enterprise.

This chapter will use the above backdrop as a way of explaining why some governments and legislators may think and act as they do and why some governments may from time to time either choose to ignore co-operatives, or may seek to label them, or wish to categorize them as being something that they in fact are not. It is therefore essential that co-operative leaders themselves fully appreciate the personal and political dynamics involved when engaging in discussions with government leaders. We trust that the content of this chapter will be of interest to both co-operative leaders as well as political and government officials currently concerned with government/co-operative relations. This chapter concludes by proposing ways in which co-operatives and governments might seek to dialogue with each other and to think about how they can work together most effectively over the longer term.

Co-operative Law - The World Over

While historically there are different instances where countries have established co-operative legislative frameworks, there are, as Hagan Henry states, three more recent and widely recognized instances (or instruments as he describes them) that have a direct bearing on the subject of co-operative law.[3] They are:

- **the 1995 International Co-operative Alliance (ICA) Statement on the Co-operative Identity,**
- **the 2001 United Nations Guidelines aimed at creating a supportive environment for the development of co-operatives, and**
- **the 2002 International Labor Organization (ILO) Recommendation No. 193 concerning the promotion of co-operatives.**

Henry goes on to explain:[4]

> "These instruments emphasise the need for adequate legislation as a necessary, albeit not sufficient, element of co-operative development. This emphasis is taken up by the UN declaration of the IYC and by the subsequent draft International Plan of Action for the IYC [International Year of Co-operatives]. The UN Guidelines and the ILO R. 193 re-affirm what the ICA Statement reformulated, namely that which most co-operatives have always been and should (in law) continue to be: associations of persons serving their members through the activities of their own enterprise. This (re-)affirmation can only be understood against the background of a long history in which co-operatives have been instrumentalised for (party) political and/or developmentalist purposes, whereas, co-operatives should be formed at the initiative of their members and their operations should be determined by these same members".

> "The shift in how co-operatives are perceived goes beyond this reaffirmation. It also recognises that, more and more, co-operatives are chosen by (potential) members for being a specific, distinctive type of enterprise and that this choice needs attending to by policy and law-makers. The argument does not overlook the fact that the formation of co-operatives often remains the only "choice" that disadvantaged people have."

While Henry makes compelling arguments why co-operative law should not be "stock companionized", he warns co-operative leaders that the current evolution of co-operative law is diluting the difference between co-operatives and stock companies. We propose that one of the underlying reasons co-operative legislation has been, and is, being diluted in various parts of the world is that in strictly economic terms, many political leaders do not appear to be able to see much to be gained from devoting time and attention to co-operatives. In fact, some of them seem to believe that there may be ground to be lost if governments give too much attention to co-operatives – especially when major private corporations begin to see co-operatives as competitors instead of as small local players within the larger marketplace.

At the same time, it may seem reasonable for governments and legislators, especially those who know little about co-operative forms of enterprise, to prefer, for economic and practical reasons, to slot co-operatives into existing legislative frameworks used to govern private sector entities (i.e. "stock companies"), rather than to create new and sometimes more complex laws and regulations through which such organisations can be regulated.

Although it may not be an accurate assessment, some governments tend to view traditional local co-operatives as generating little or no tax revenues. Co-operatives are thought of as small and local; thus they are dismissed as more expensive and more difficult to regulate than larger, more integrated entities. Interestingly, co-operatives, because of their nature, tend to be less likely to spend money on lobbyists or on political patronage than larger, less transparent corporate entities. While all of the above circumstances may at times may valid, none of them are legitimate reasons from a members' perspective for legislatively treating co-operatives as private sector entities. Even in authoritarian settings, (e.g., Afghanistan, Cuba, Iran, and Zimbabwe) successful co-operatives exist as visible examples of how people can and do work together democratically to help themselves.

The reality in the past has been that governments in some countries around the world either tolerated co-operatives by adopting basic "one time, then forget it," cookie cutter legislative frameworks and regulations for governing them, or they sought to "mobilize co-operatives" through legislation and regulations that moulded co-operatives into political agencies under their control. Admittedly, this is not the case everywhere, and in recent years many governments have been focusing more on co-operatives than in the past.

It is for these reasons that co-operatives and co-operative legislative frameworks sometimes fall below the radar for those charged with setting political and government agendas. It is for these same reasons that co-operatives and co-operative leaders must understand what is happening, and where possible must press forward to ensure sound legislative footing.

Co-operative Law in Development Settings

In many development settings, governments are not aware, or do not appreciate, the extent to which co-operatives can and do provide an avenue for poverty alleviation and wealth creation. Government officials and leaders may see publically supporting co-operatives as a popular way in which to garner political points and constituent votes at minimal costs. Those readers who are familiar with co-operatives, however, will appreciate that a top down, short-term approach is unlikely to be sustainable once government development funding ceases to be available. It is true that as long as resources or subsidies are being provided, co-operative groups may be gathered, co-operative training may be provided, and co-operative organizations may be established and registered. However, once development funding and/or party support is no longer provided, it is common to see the number of co-operatives that had been created decline or die. This occurred in Uganda in the earlier 1980s, and in Vietnam in 1990s through to 2010, when co-operatives which had been broadly supported by governments (more so than by member owners), lost favour and then gradually fell into decline. In cases such as this, co-operatives may continue to exist in name only as statistics in the government's registration system.

Short-term, donor funded and donor supported development projects that are not carefully aligned with and linked to new or existing co-operative movements may do more harm than good. In some development settings, it is not uncommon to see more energy and effort put into creating projects and finding external donors than into supporting local co-operative growth and development. Successful development of co-operative movements and system depends upon many factors. Even when circumstances and environments are favourable, the time required for a co-operative movement to become self-sustaining as a system may easily extend from a dozen to two dozen years. A fledgling co-operative movement may require a similar number of years to mature into an efficient and organized co-operative system of enterprise. There are no guarantees that just because an organization is established as a co-operative that it will succeed. Externally funded short-term projects as well as government initiated projects often do not extend past five years. As a result, it is not surprising for governments to find co-operative organizations collapsing one or two years after their support has been discontinued. With proper due diligence by governments and development agencies, such failures can and should be avoided.

In the first decade of the new millennium, governments in development settings were excited about what they were being told concerning micro-finance. Accordingly, legislation was drafted with advice from micro-finance experts, many of whom were unfamiliar with co-operatives. Typically, such legislation sought to regulate financial co-operatives as if they were the same as private sector, privately funded, micro finance institutions. This was the case in a number of African countries. Since this type of draft legislation typically did little to aid in the growth and development of savings and credit co-operatives, co-operative leaders openly rejected it in favour of legislation specific to co-operative financial institutions. In June of 2012 leaders from African Saving and Credit Co-operatives (SACCOs) from 12 countries met in Kenya with government counterparts to discuss legislation and the unique aspects involved in regulating financial co-operatives. The meeting was convened by the African Confederation of Co-operatives Savings and Credit Associations (ACCOSCA). The leaders met to share experiences regarding best practices that had worked and what frameworks were needed in future. Although work has been underway for some years, both Kenya and Malawi have now put in place legislative and regulatory frameworks to guide their financial co-operatives, and Ghana expects legislation for their financial co-operatives to be enacted during 2013. The African experience over the past decade, while somewhat unique, can be of good value to financial co-operatives and governments in other regions. A link to the full report of this gathering can be found at: www.accosca.org/ under the Downloads as the Regulatory Framework Workshop 2012.[5]

Thankfully, because of the efforts of organizations like the ICA, ILO, WOCCU, the OCDC, CCA, ACCOSCA, and many others, (including the International Credit Union Regulators Network – please see the sidebar for further details) co-operative leaders and governments alike in many regions of the world have today come to appreciate that it is not always practical or desirable to simply legislate all types of co-operatives within the same framework as other forms of enterprise. In our experience different legislative frameworks are appropriate for different types of co-operatives, including savings and credit co-operatives and credit unions.

> *The **INTERNATIONAL CREDIT UNION REGULATORS' NETWORK (ICURN)** - is an independent international network of credit union regulators that was formed in 2007 and currently has members in 30 countries and jurisdictions. ICURN's mission is to promote greater international coordination among regulators of financial cooperatives through the sharing of information and positions of common interest, initiating research on financial cooperatives and their oversight, identifying best practices and providing direct access to an exclusive forum for thought leaders worldwide on issues critical to sound credit union regulation. The ICURN steering committee consists of senior representatives of the supervisory authorities for cooperative financial institutions in Australia, Brazil, Canada, India, Kenya, Poland, and the United States.*
>
> *Visit: www.curegulators.org to learn more.*

While initially it is not always practical or possible for co-operatives to obtain the most appropriate or desired legislative framework, it is essential that any legislation recognize the co-operative identity and the co-operative form of enterprise as distinct from other forms of enterprise.

At the same time, there have been occasions where government's well intentioned support for co-operatives may not actually have translated into aiding development at all. Any of the following specific circumstances or approaches can invite failure:

- **Rushing the creation of a legislative framework and/or the creation of a government agency or department charged with overseeing and supporting co-operative development.**

- **Moving forward in acquiring facilities and appointing administrative personnel without a detailed well thought out plan based on longer term staged development project goals.**
- **Electing to place a co-operative department or agency within another government agency or bureau for convenience or economy's sake.**

- **Adopting the creation of a large number of new co-operatives as a primary goal. Creating a large numbers of co-operatives in a short period of time can soon exceed a government's capacity to keep track of them or to provide basic regulation for them – or the capacity of co-operative enthusiasts to develop them.**

- Failing to oversee and hold a new government co-operative department or agency accountable for the achievement of established goals and planned outcomes, and failing to attract and educate co-operatively minded personnel to oversee the agency or department.

- Supplementing or staffing a co-operative department with external business advisors who lack sufficient co-operative management experience in development, or who too easily assume that whatever seems to work in for-profit enterprises can be applied to co-operatives.

- Allowing staff within government agencies to see themselves as "administering co-operative development" rather than supporting it.

- Drafting and passing legislation without adequately educating and informing a solid cross section of elected officials and other government agencies and departments about the reasons behind, and the basis for, long term non-partisan co-operative development.

- Failing to plan for and ensure the commitment of the financial and other resources for ongoing regulation and supervision of newly formed co-operatives.

- Failing to ensure the embodiment of co-operative principles and practices within each of the new co-operatives, leading to the creation of pseudo co-operatives (i.e., co-operatives in which membership is not linked to ownership and in which self-help is replaced with external donor or other forms of financing).

Co-operatives in Western Settings

In some instances, co-operatives in the West have successfully existed and have served their members and communities alike for more than 100 years. In the West, the co-operative legislative regimes tend to be much more complex, as there are numerous other pieces of legislation that have been developed in the same time frame. For example, consumer protection legislation, privacy of information legislation, money laundering legislation, human rights legislation, environmental protection legislation, and of course, personal and corporate taxation legislation, all have the potential to affect co-operatives. Depending upon the history of the co-operatives, their position within the state or country, and their size, co-operatives may have their own specific co-operative legislation. For example, there may be different legislation for producer co-operatives, consumer co-operatives, financial co-operatives, insurance co-operatives, health care co-operatives; and they may be regulated at the local, provincial or state and national levels, or even a combination of levels.

In the West, too, there very often is legislation governing the functions and operations of second or third-tier co-operatives. These are co-operatives that have been created to serve the needs of individual local co-operatives. They are usually owned and controlled by local co-operatives. In Europe, most co-operatives will either have their own legislation or, because of their size, fall under private sector legislation. In the latter case, as in Denmark, they may adopt co-operative principles and values within the by-laws that govern how they will operate.

During the past twenty or so years, when not pre-occupied with other matters, governments and co-operative movements have been expanding and harmonizing their co-operative legal frameworks. This is always a significant and important undertaking. This has been particularly true in parts of Europe. As well, further pertinent research is underway by Hagen Henry and others looking at what has been done and on to what might be done to secure satisfactory co-operative legislation. Interested readers will find further details concerning a New Study Group on European Co-operative Law at: www.papers.ssrn.com/ and do a search for ID=2005019.[6]

Even in cases where co-operative legislative frameworks exist, of the need for specific and useful legislation for co-operative development may also exist. In the UK for example, Prime Minister David Cameron has announced plans for a Co-operatives Bill.[7] The new bill will provide a foundation for co-operative growth and development. It is expected to be brought forward in 2015.

Alignment, Non-alignment, or Other

Co-operative movements and co-operative systems must remain wary of being co-opted by political parties. New or loosely organized co-operative movements may, in some instances, find their leaders in agreement with or being supported by one or more political parties. Once established however, all co-operatives are by principle autonomous and independent entities. It therefore follows that co-operative leaders must tread carefully when invited by the state agencies or political leaders to adopt what may be perceived as pro-party practices or positions; they can easily be perceived as advocates for a particular party or as agencies of the state.

We are aware that in some countries there have been and still are political parties based upon notions of co-operative principles, values, and practices (e.g., Canada – the Co-operative Commonwealth Federation or CCF party 1944-1964;[8] United Kingdom – The Co-operative Party[9]). Any form of alignment leading up to, or at, election time creates the risk of a sudden non-alignment of the entire co-operative sector following an election, should an alternative party form the government.

> **The Co-operative Party UK – Politics for the People** - The Co-operative Party in the UK is unique in that it is a properly constituted political party and states that it is the political arm of the co-operative movement. The party was established in 1917 and has been a sister party of the Labour Party since 1927. It has some 9,000 members. The party believes people achieve more by working together than they can by working alone, and they work to promote co-operatives and all forms of mutual organisation.
>
> The risks of aligning with a political party (in this case the Labour Party) are expressed by the Chair of the Co-operative Party, Gareth Thomas MP, when he states...
>
> "After thirteen years of Labour Government which saw unprecedented change for the mutual and co-operative sector, we now face the challenge of opposition and of a coalition Conservative-led government. The Conservative Party pretends to be a friend of co-operation but would betray it as easily and as readily as it has on every single occasion it has seized power. We cannot let that happen."
>
> Learn more at: www.party.coop.

At the same time, co-operative systems should not ignore their government's efforts to develop and strengthen their region or their country economically or culturally. To avoid gaining the reputation that "if you are not with us, you are against us", co-operatives must of necessity aim to be non-aligned politically, yet be willing partners when there clearly are mutual benefits to be created or derived.

What seems to work best is to ensure that co-operatives welcome persons of all political views as members, while emphasizing politically that they are autonomous and independent entities, and that they are accountable and responsible to their owner members for their actions. It is on this type of foundation that co-operatives are often able to work successfully with government for the benefit of their members and their communities, without being seen as either aligned or non-aligned.

Co-operative leaders should recognize the importance of being politically aware and maintain ongoing contact and some means of information sharing with their elected political representatives. This may be accomplished informally or even formally. In some cases second or third-tier co-operatives can facilitate gatherings (sometimes short informal receptions) in which there are occasions for face-to-face meetings, as well as mutual sharing of day-to-day challenges and opportunities. It is important that similar meetings be held with representatives of all major parties. In that way co-operative are able to remain non-partisan. As is sometimes the case, co-operatives via their second or third-tier co-operatives, and through their democratic structures, may wish to develop or bring forward their view of a particular issue concerning a government policy or a particular piece of legislation they wish to see enacted or changed. In such cases, it is important for co-operatives to dedicate resources to researching the policy or legislation and to develop a co-operative position on the issue to be dealt with rather than focusing on any of the political parties involved. Any co-operative positions being pressed forward should first be discussed and vetted before key co-operative players at the local level. In that way, co-operative positions, on issues can be well thought out, well understood, and widely supported before being presented. Having a formal full time staff complement available (i.e., Government Affairs Office) provides a useful administrative point of contact for government officials to use as required.

To Tax or Not to Tax - That is the Question!

Modernizing and harmonizing co-operative legislation is perhaps one of the longest-standing and most difficult issues governments and co-operatives have faced. It is a thorny issue because there are no simple answers to the many questions as to whether or how to tax co-operatives. That is partly because there are now so many different types of co-operative structures and arrangements, but also because there are so many tax regimes at play in most situations.

At the danger of generalizing too much, we offer the following views for future consideration and discussion...

1. **Where and when a co-operative enterprise is creating a social or an economic benefit for its members, more so than for the community at large, and where such benefits accrue measurable value within the co-operative, and where the co-operative is openly and obviously competing with other forms of enterprise, notwithstanding that other factors may need to be considered, then the co-operative's capital and the co-operative's activities should be taxed at rates that are deemed fair in comparison with what other entities are being taxed.**

2. **Where and when a co-operative enterprise is creating a social or an economic benefit for its members, and also for the community at large, and where such benefits accrue measurable value within the co-operative, and where the co-operative is not openly and obviously competing with other forms of enterprise, notwithstanding that other factors may need to be considered, then the co-operative's activities (i.e. sales) should be taxed at rates that are deemed fair in comparisons to what other entities are being taxed.**

3. **Where and when a co-operative enterprise is creating a social or an economic benefit for its members, and also the same benefit for the community at large, and where such benefits do not accrue measurable value within the co-operative, excepting perhaps good will, and where the co-operative is not openly or obviously competing with other forms of enterprise, then notwithstanding that other factors may need to be considered, neither the co-operative's capital nor the co-operative's activities should be taxed.**

The above is depicted in table format in Figure 8.1 below.

Figure 8.1

Co-operative Taxation Considerations

Co-operative Activities and Environment	Taxable Position of the Co-operative	
Some Value Passes to Members	Co-operative's Capital and Activities Should Attract Fair Tax	We appreciate each governmental jurisdiction must decide for itself based on its policies for development (including co-operative development) what is the appropriate basis for taxation of co-operative types of enterprise. We have found the "level playing field" to be the best basis upon which to tax any type of co-operative. The table beside is intended to illustrate what might be a "level playing field" for all concerned.
Some Value Retained by Co-operative		
Other Competitor(s) Paying Tax		
Values Passes to Members & Community	Co-operative's Activities Should Attract Same Tax as Others	
Some Value Retained by Co-operative		
Few or No competitor(s) in Market Area		
Value Pass to Members and Community	Co-operative Should Not Attract Tax	
No Value Retained by Co-operative		
No competitor(s) in Market Area		

How Governments Can Enable Co-operative Development

In addition to better understanding the unique and distinct aspects of the co-operative identify, there are a number of important measures governments (co-operative legislators, administrators, or regulators) everywhere can take in support of longer-term sustainable co-operative development. They include:

1. **Following and understanding the state of co-operative development, and co-operative law locally, as well as internationally, and in particular the guidance provided in ILO Recommendation 193.**

2. **Ensuring governments respect co-operative enterprises as "autonomous self-help" entities.**

3. Time-limiting any government start-up support programs or benefits that lead towards, not away from, a level playing field for co-operatives; this avoids creating co-operative dependence.

4. Establishing periodic, preferably informal, two-way dialogue sessions with co-operative leaders regarding areas of mutual interest or concern.

5. Providing public education concerning co-operative development (history, principles, and democratic control curriculum), and recognition of co-operatives through dedicated ministries and or departments.

6. Ensuring adequate and accurate statistical tracking and reporting of co-operative activities and results, including data and research gathering by government agencies.

7. Enshrining in legislation the provision for a periodic (i.e. every 5 or 10 years) co-operative legislative review to be conducted jointly with representatives of the co-operative sector and government.

Enshrining Co-operatives Rights in India's Constitution - *In 2009, the Indian government amended its constitution through its Constitution (111th) Bill, which made the right to form co-operative societies a fundamental right. The House also accorded the right to set up a specialised agency on the lines of the Election Commission which would outline standard procedures and guidelines for elections in the co-operative societies.*

See: www.indiancooperative.com, and search for "Constitutional amendment bill 2009".

What Co-operatives Can and Should Do

In practical terms, good legislation is important to co-operatives for at least five reasons: 1) it defines the powers and authorities granted to co-operatives; 2) it stipulates the governance structure of co-operatives; 3) it stipulates many of the relationships between a co-operative enterprise and government officials; 4) it normally establishes the governance mechanisms and responsibilities of directors; and 5) it often affects the taxation position that co-operatives must face. For these reasons, it is always in the interest of all co-operatives to take seriously their overall relationship with government, as well as the legislative and regulatory frameworks within which they must work.

Locally and nationally, there are at least seven things that co-operatives can and should do:

1. **Co-operative leaders and managers should become familiar with all major aspects of the legislation regulations, bylaws, and other policies under which they must act.**

2. **Co-operative leaders should, on an informal but organized basis and through their state or national bodies, demonstrate their willingness to dialogue in useful two-way communications concerning the goals and the effectiveness of the current legislation and regulations with government elected officials and with the heads of bodies charged with co-operative oversight and regulation or development.**

3. **Co-operative organizations should, to whatever degree might be possible within their respective co-operative systems, develop the capacity to self-regulate so governments do not need to deal with insider issues, corruption, co-operative bankruptcy, legal compliance, and so on. Co-operatives have an opportunity to lead by example especially when it comes to self-dealing, insider information considerations, and patronage. The nature of co-operative ownership and governance makes it very difficult to confer inappropriate rewards on any individual or group.**

4. **Co-operative leaders and managers must actively and regularly listen to their members, as well as inform them, concerning their communications and positions with government on any issues.**

5. **Co-operatives, again through their regional or national bodies, should put time and money into policy research and data gathering to advance their interests as a system. It is also wise for co-operatives to put forward their views and their members' views concerning what they feel might or should be done by government in terms of policy or budgetary matters.**

6. **Co-operatives should do their homework in identifying and illustrating how for-profit private sector enterprises receive significant assistance and accommodations in the forms of tax holidays and incentives, start-up grants or subsidies, advisory and information services, and departmental supports that are typically not available to co-operative forms of enterprise. At the same time, co-operatives should invest time and money into researching the value which they create, the contribution which they make to the community, and the tax payments which they generate as an enterprise over the long term; and should inform government leaders and officials about these contributions.**

7. At the same time, co-operatives should look for positive, creative, and non-controversial ways through which to present their views and positions to government.

The ICA's *Blueprint for a Co-operative Decade* suggests ways in which legislative developments might be guided by the ICA and others across the co-operative system.[10] While more detailed recommendations were included, the two core recommendations were as follows:

1. Assistance can be provided to registrars and regulators through:
   a. The creation of an international network for registrars and regulators, and
   b. The development of guidance on how to apply the co-operative principles.

2. Assistance can be provided to national parliamentarians, legislators, and policy-makers through the comparative study of the way laws apply to co-operatives in different jurisdictions.

The Next Decade

It is perhaps best to sum up by simply restating words from the ICA *Blueprint For A Co-operative Decade*.[11]

> One of the great successes of the 2012 International Year is that policy-makers and regulators are finally waking up to the difference that co-operatives make and the benefits they deliver. There is much already to celebrate here. However, assistance must be provided to law-makers and regulators, if the growing enthusiasm for the co-operative form of enterprise is to be translated into the types of supportive legal frameworks that will unleash the co-operative growth from which everyone will benefit.

> We must stress at the outset that pursuing this agenda does not mean pleading for special treatment, subsidies, or favours. Co-operatives are no more dependent on government assistance than any other business form. But no business exists in a regulatory vacuum, and business growth always depends on an infrastructure of rules and policies. For much of their history, co-operatives have succeeded in spite of legal frameworks that tend to be designed with limited companies in mind. The co-operative sector does not now expect, or ask, to tip the balance in its favour. It seeks a proper understanding by governments and law-makers of the economic and social benefits which the co-operative form can bring, and an appropriate legal framework which takes account of these benefits and speaks to a broader diversity of ownership forms than is currently the case.

Take Aways

1. In today's world many of the things that governments do will likely have an impact on co-operatives (whether via incentives including subsidies or even via penalties, including fines, or any other any initiatives or legislation). Co-operatives deserved to be consulted. Co-operatives must be prepared to constructively consult with government as needed.

2. Historically co-operative law has seldom been a high priority for government or legislators.

3. Co-operative growth in development settings may be vastly different than in other settings. Governments may unintentionally actually delay co-operative development by trying to drive it by without ensuring real progress by trying to do too much too quickly.

4. Co-operative law regimes in Western countries are often complex and so require considerable effort and resources in their development, application, and over time their refinement.

5. As far as being politically aligned, what works best is recognizing and emphasizing that co-operatives are autonomous and independent entities, and that they are accountable and responsible to their owner members for their actions. Co-operatives tend to do best when they remain non-partisan and put forward positions which deal with issues rather than party politics.

6. The tax treatment of co-operatives can be a difficult and complex issue; no single treatment can be applied in all instances. It can be helpful to look at the value chain being created by co-operatives, as well as their competitive environments.

7. Governments and co-operatives can both benefit by working together to support and enable co-operative development efforts.

PART FOUR - BUILDING A BETTER WORLD

The Technology of Co-operation

Chapter Nine - Some Strategies and Tactics for Success

Starting Co-operatives for the Right Reasons

Elsewhere we said "YES" co-operatives are succeeding in serving their purposes, but we must qualify that statement by affirming that co-operatives can and do fail. In this section, we will look at some of the factors involved. We will begin by looking briefly at factors that can contribute to the failure of a co-operative, and follow by identifying factors that can contribute to a successful co-operative.

Occasionally co-operatives can fail. Sometimes a large number of failures have happened across entire countries. After all, co-operatives are economic entities and as such their revenues must meet their operating costs. Sometimes, people make mistakes; sometimes economic crises make success impossible. Co-operatives have failed in the past in some African countries and in Eastern Europe in the former Soviet Union states. Many of those that failed were "pseudo co-operatives" formed by government bureaucrats with a top-down vision of what a co-operative should be. When co-operatives fail, it is sometimes because they were established without a broader longer term purpose, or because they were created for purposes which are not in the interest of the member-owners and their broader communities. For example, co-operatives have failed over time in a number of African countries because they were conceived and implemented by colonial officials as a means of organizing commodities, like coffee or tea, for production and sale, rather than for enhancing the livelihood of owner members. While they were organized legally as co-operatives, often they were not managed or operated as such.

A second common instance where co-operatives tend to start and then wind up failing is in response to a "We will help you to get out of poverty" government policy which is "politically motivated" and which has little to do with members getting out of poverty at all, and more to do with politicians getting re-elected. For example, Uganda's 2007 "Prosperity for All" program was intended to require Saving and Credit Co-operatives in that country to serve as government's mechanism for "on-lending" of government supplied funds to members.[1] A related instance where co-operatives have failed is where an external development agency or a government decides to introduce a co-operative enterprise approach without first ensuring that there is the managerial, technical, and financial capacity available to properly do so. This also appears when externally motivated agents get involved without ensuring there is a sincere and significant interest in moving forward on the part of potential members. In many of the incidents mentioned above, new co-operatives failed, either directly or indirectly, because there was an insufficient level of member ownership and understanding, coupled with top-down approaches used by government or others external to the co-operatives or their members.

As we explained earlier in Chapter 4, **communities of support** are essential for the longer-term success of any co-operative enterprise, system, or movement.

Creating Communities of Support

There are a great many strategies and tactics for creating strong communities of support for a co-operative. The following list is not exhaustive, but will provide examples of approaches that have proven successful in various settings.

Learning from other co-operatives

There is an old pilot's saying, "Learn from the mistakes of others; you will not survive long enough to make them all yourself!" In today's information-rich world, it is relatively easy (and in most cases essential) for a co-operative to reach out and learn about the failures and success of other co-operatives. In many cases, sharing "lessons learned" is a valuable exercise that costs little and sometimes nothing.

Board, management, employee and member education

Perhaps the greatest resource a co-operative can have is an educated and informed community. Education, especially a sound understanding of co-operatives, must begin with the Board of Directors and extend throughout the organization. Those who are in positions of leadership should be an example to others.

Working together within defined communities towards a shared vision

Successful co-operatives identify themselves within communities of interest, be they local farming communities, factory workers, artisan communities, and so on. The people who become involved succeed by working co-operatively together and also with others within their larger community, which can include civic and political leaders. They often share a vision of a more ideal future state.

Branding and brand promise

Co-operatives must not only say what they do, they must do what they say, and they must do so consistently. To do so, they must adhere to established co-operative principles and values. A failure of one co-operative can have a negative impact on the co-operative brand and thus on all co-operatives.

Personal commitment and leadership by elected officials and management

Those in positions of influence, whether elected board or appointed committee members or employees, should see their work and their performance as a sacred trust given to them by the membership which they are there to serve.

Managed community, government, and political relationships

Co-operative leaders must take good care to foster and maintain good will relationships within their communities, including relationships with others who are not members of their organization. However, good will relations are more than public relations, since care must be taken not to become aligned or co-opted into serving any interest not committed to the long-term, best interest of the co-operative.

Support across the system for ongoing co-operative development
Co-operatives seldom enjoy "once and done" development. Product and service research and development, technical development, new market development, and of course human development are all aspects of organizational activities that require ongoing attention and resources. Often such development is expensive and requires working closely with other co-operatives and co-operative support organizations in order to be done efficiently.

Member ownership, involvement, and education-/-use of social media
Ensuring a sense of member ownership and involvement may sometimes be seen as an unnecessary expense, especially in larger narrow margin co-operative organizations. It may even be seen as opening a can of worms, creating more problems than the effort is worth. Finding avenues for engaging members as members, and not merely as consumers, can be done successfully, including by using interest study groups, study circles, and focus groups – although focus groups can easily become a very one-sided way to elicit responses from people. Today, too, more than ever before, co-operatives are in a position to utilize social media to engage specific member groups or broad cross sections of the membership – doing so can be undertaken quickly and efficiently.

Taking an "interest" in "member interests" to better understand unsatisfied needs
While a co-operative can use a member survey to understand how well its products and services are being received, face to face meetings can often help the co-operative gain a greater appreciation of members' unsatisfied needs, while at the same time reinforcing the "member owner" concept. Interest study groups, for example, can often help to identify new unmet service needs or new market opportunities for co-operatives.

Democratic governance-/-transparency
A good co-operative can become and remain a great co-operative by ensuring that its governance is both democratic and transparent. Important decisions must be made in an informed manner. When they have a significant impact on the co-operative, they must be taken to the larger membership for direction. While for competitive and confidentiality reasons, not everything can be shared publically, the co-operative must continue to honestly inform its members and employees of important internal matters as well as news of external matters affecting the organization or its members. Boards have an obligation to keep the members informed about the ways in which their co-operative is developing and the kinds of issues it is facing.

Patronage rewards and community support projects when practical

Many co-operatives have discovered how positively members respond to patronage rewards, and to support provided for local community groups and projects. It is important to anticipate and plan in advance for such rewards and community support undertakings. Equally, co-operatives must ensure that they have sufficient reserves for development and for protection should market forces adversely affect them. Thinking through the different claims on a co-operative's resources means that boards have to take a balanced and measured approach, not always easily done when a co-operative's membership is facing difficult economic times.

Equitable reward system and treatment of all employees

It is essential that employee performance and rewards be planned for and that all employees are treated equitably. Balancing employee performance rewards with member patronage rewards and with the need to retain capital to support growth must be done with great care and consideration.

Employee involvements in service delivery and in ensuring service quality

In successful co-operatives, employees are more than suppliers and deliverers of service; they are problem solvers and needs satisfiers, too. Often they have ideas, suggestions, and even proposals for how the enterprise might be run better. Ensuring that employees have practical opportunities to participate in the management functions of the co-operative can serve to increase their competence while also helping to strengthen and grow the organization.

Open and ongoing communication within the organization and externally

While organizations are relying more and more on electronic communications, face to face two way communication on urgent or pressing matters is always more effective. It is beneficial for spokespersons and for senior officials to remain prepared, visible, and approachable both internally and externally.

Ethical standards and behavior-/-social responsibility

Co-operatives as organizations, their elected officials, and their employees all must adhere to high ethical standards and to uncompromising codes of conduct. Conflict of interest, nepotism, and all forms of discrimination should be clearly and fairly dealt with in a responsible and timely fashion within board policy. Co-operatives do well when they ensure that their policies, positions, and practices reflect due consideration of their larger social, economic, and physical environments.

Self-help attitudes together with an appreciation of mutual interests

As much as seems practical, individual co-operatives must run their own show, but at the same time recognize that there is strength in numbers and in co-operating with other co-operatives (often through their second or third-tier co-operative organizations) when it comes to matters of mutual interest like risk management, relating to government, acquiring technologies, research and marketing, training and education, and so on.

Good governance and stewardship
In all co-operatives, the democratically elected representatives of the members must adopt and utilize policies and protocols that ensure the responsible operation of the co-operative. In some instances, larger co-operatives employ a delegate structure or other avenues as ways of ensuring equitable representation and two way communications between the co-operative and its membership. Good governance also involves aspects of what is sometimes referred to as enterprise risk management (ERM). ERM entails ensuring major risks are being identified and are well managed, and that the required capital needs of the organization are planned for and are being met.

Clear definition of board-management roles and responsibilities
In co-operative forms of enterprise, management is a shared responsibility. As co-operatives grow and mature, the roles and relationships between the board of directors, board committees, and senior management will likely evolve, but they must remain clearly defined. They must be reflected in the performance standards that are used as the basis for evaluating management's contribution to the success of the organization. Clarity in terms of roles and responsibilities and performance standards provides for greater teamwork and fewer surprises in all quarters.

Open memberships: non-partisan, non-racial, non-discriminating
These are all matters which if mismanaged have the potential to create dissention amongst the general membership. Ensuring that equitable policies are in place can help avert problems before they occur.

All of the above can help a co-operative to *pursue collective ideals*, and to *generate co-operative effort* amongst stakeholders, which in turn can serve to create strong communities of support for the work of the co-operative.

Building Financial Strength

In any enterprise, there are key performance indicators that tell one how well the business is performing. Looking at changes in key performance indicators will tell you if the enterprise is growing stronger or growing weaker. We will begin by looking at five key performance indicators. Trends over time in these indicators will show whether the enterprise is growing stronger or weaker financially.

Equity capital, as distinct from working capital, serves to strengthen the enterprise, provides risk mitigation, helps stabilize the co-operative in times of hardship, instills confidence among stakeholders, and provides a platform to justify investment in the development of future products, services, and markets Equity capital in its truest form, is either retained earnings or member-contributed share capital and is without conditions or obligations attached. It may be meagre in amount in the early stages, but it must be evident and it must grow as the scale and complexity of the enterprise grows. Loans, guarantees, grants, contributions in-kind, government relaxation of standards, non-compliance tolerances, all of these can play a supplemental-/-augmenting role; however, none can replace equity.

Liquidity (working capital) is needed to ensure that obligations are met on time and that creditors are not left wondering if the co-operative has the capacity to make good on its obligations. Internally generated cash flow through prudent management of the enterprise is very important. It includes: the timely sale of products and services; managing the collection of receivables and the processing of payables; co-ordinating inventories of inputs and materials with manufactured goods and services; as well as negotiating and receiving term loans; operating financing and repayment schedules appropriate to the amortization of assets; and realistic investment in the plant and equipment. "Sounds like pretty basic stuff" and we guess it is until you finance a grain handling facility with your operating line of credit and then find that you don't have enough cash available to purchase inventory necessary to meet production demand and processing capacity.

Profitability in non-formal accounting terms is the amount remaining after all enterprise expenses and planned or statutory allocations have been made, and any provisions required for taxes have been set aside. The generation of profit is necessary to create retained earnings, and creating retained earnings is a fundamental engine in building equity capital. We have already discussed how important equity capital is. In addition, profit can be distributed through a resolution of the Board in a manner that most equitably meets the needs of members, employees, and any other stakeholders in the co-operative. Generating profit in a co-operative is something that must be done on an ongoing basis and with as much care and precision as possible. The confidence instilled in members, staff, customers, suppliers, regulators, industry watchers, and so on through the maintenance of appropriate levels of profit is an essential part of being a successful co-operative over the long term.

Enterprise Growth is important in order to stay abreast of inflation and of competition. Growth in members, enterprise assets, enterprise capital, service offerings, business volume, and in facilities and employees normally can serve to create economies of scale. No growth, or even negative growth, unless carefully planned, can often be an indicator of some underlying problems or issues within the enterprise. Perhaps surprisingly, too much unplanned growth can be an indication that there will be problems coming in the future.

Risk Exposure is somewhat more difficult to gauge, but is an ongoing aspect of any enterprise. Risk exposure is measured in a number of different ways in different types of enterprises. In a financial co-operative, loan delinquency levels and loan write offs as a percentage of the total loan portfolio are good indications of risk. In a consumer co-operative, some examples might include internal controls risks, inventory turnover and aging risks, foreign exchange risk, reputational risk, faithful performance risk, facilities risk, and technology risk. In a producer co-operative, three major risks would be market demand variability, price variability, and production quality variability.

Each of the key performance indicators, as described above, contributes to the financial strength of the organization over time. Also, each of these key performance indicators and their relationship to the other indicators must be carefully understood and managed. Sound board-management policies within a broader legislative and regulatory framework help to ensure that the results achieved are those which are planned and desired.

In addition to managing the key financial elements mentioned, there are a great many strategies and tactics for building financial strength in a co-operative. The following list is not exhaustive or in any particular order of importance, but will provide examples of approaches that have proven successful.

- **Efficient delivery of quality member service while also ensuring sustainability of the co-operative** - Quality member service is one of the most important reasons why any co-operative in the world exists. The delicate part is for board and management to provide the best quality service possible while ensuring that the costs of doing so are offset by slightly greater revenues from within the organisation. A co-operative which grows too rapidly will find itself facing capital shortfalls if other forms of capital are not already planned for and available.

- **Taking a long term view and using an effective planning and budgeting framework** - Using a practical business planning framework complemented with a balanced and aligned financial budget can help a co-operative to strengthen its financial position over time.

- **Sound board management policies and procedure (a balanced approach)** – All facets of the co-operative's normal enterprise activities should be dealt with using board management policies and policy parameters. Policies and policy parameters (including variance to budget reporting parameters) assist both the board and management in ensuring that the organization is on track as planned. Specific policies will vary based on the type of co-operative that is being managed.

- **Clear risk management framework and business disruption preparedness** – No one likes surprises. One of the best ways of avoiding surprises is to identify and take measures to manage all of the major risks being faced by the co-operative. Many co-operatives go even further and actually simulate specific business interruptions (i.e., communications network failures or electrical outage) and then assess their ability to cope with events in a reasonable manner.

- **Capital access, capital planning and management** – While capital adequacy has and continues to be a challenge for many co-operatives, it is something which can and must be managed. Depending upon the regulatory environment, it is now possible for some co-operatives to gain specific forms of capital, including retained earnings, not only from members but from other forms of enterprise, based upon strict parameters, terms, and conditions. Co-operative organizations and systems around the world are continuing to explore innovative alternative mechanisms, such as public – co-operative partnerships, for accessing capital while remaining true to co-operative principles and values. Doing pilot projects or trial partnerships is one way of figuring out what might work and what may not!

- **Critical mass-/-industry involvement** – It is no surprise that today's co-operatives face stiff competition from other, often larger, private sector players, whether that is in the field of banking, production, or marketing. In order to compete, two conditions must be met. First, the co-operative, on its own or together with various other co-operatives, must attain a volume of business sufficient to ensure a reasonable degree of operational efficiency. Reaching critical mass for start-up co-operatives is often a challenge. Secondly, it is generally to the advantage of the co-operative to participate in events within the industry in which it is competing. Failing to do so can mean being left behind when new government legislation or regulations come into effect, or when new technology is replacing old.

- **Sound board management information system** – Even the most basic board management reporting system includes past performance to current performance; actual comparisons to a plan and to others, be they co-operative peers or other industry competitors; as well as, reporting of variances outside parameters or industry guidelines. Installing a sound board-management reporting system can be a major undertaking, but without it, the organization is much like a ship without a working compass, and as such may be forced to rely on other less accurate means of navigation. If a co-operative is not careful, board and management may find themselves well off course before they know it.

- **Professional, competent, and involved management and employees** – Today's co-operative senior managers and employees must not only be well acquainted with the unique facets of co-operative forms of enterprise, but also well versed and experienced in whatever function or functions (i.e., credit and finance, manufacturing, agricultural production, wholesaling, energy distribution, marketing) the co-operative needs to operate. Co-operative experience and education, coupled with broad industry knowledge, are essential. In many ways, managing human resources can be every bit as challenging as managing the financial resources of the enterprise. Educating and retaining qualified co-operative employees is often a challenge, particularly for many new co-operatives.

- **Business research, intelligence, and academic relationships** – Successful co-operative organizations require know-how, confidence, and understanding. In today's changing information-rich world, what worked five years ago may no longer be appropriate! Convincing decision-makers requires understanding and confidence. Investing in business research and business intelligence gathering are, for most co-operatives, no longer an option but a necessity if they wish to be confident in taking or recommending strategic business decisions. Fortunately, many co-operative systems are forging relationships with universities as well as with independent research bodies in order to strengthen their internal research and intelligence gathering activities. Others are using secondary sources of information, often times accessible via existing co-operative support organizations.

- **Product and service innovation and competitive benchmarking comparisons** – Finding ways to do it better has been the hallmark of many co-operatives around the world. In a competitive environment, finding creative ways of doing more with fewer resources remains the challenge to co-operatives everywhere. Many co-operatives are now finding it helpful to periodically (i.e., quarterly) compare their performance to other peer co-operatives and, in other cases, to commonly accepted industry bench-marks.

- **Professional management and director development programs** - We mentioned earlier that employee training and development were essential ingredients in the success of any co-operative. The necessity of training applies to new and existing boards of directors. Being an interested and honest director is only the beginning. Becoming a competent and confident director or board committee member is equally important to the success of the co-operative. While such development programs are increasingly available, finding ways of effectively and efficiently delivering them more broadly continues to be a limitation to be overcome.

- **Sound legislative and regulatory frameworks and environments** – In a number of countries around the world, governments appear (unconsciously or consciously) slow to develop even a basic functioning legislative framework, together with a reasonable level of resources for its maintenance. Thankfully, the attention and awareness raised by the United Nations and others during 2012 via the International Year of Co-operative is encouraging governments to seriously consider putting resources in place to update legislative and regulatory frameworks, usually in co-operation with co-operative movements and others.

- **Use of second-tier or other types of shared service support organizations for ancillary services** – Needless to say, most individual co-operative organizations recognize that there are limits to what they can do on their own. Forming second-tier co-operatives (sometimes called centrals or federations) can become an option. In some respects, the second-tiers can become effective internal forums for co-operatives to work their way through internal policy and operational matters. When the second-tier organization is owned and controlled by local co-operatives, it is well positioned to advocate for standard legislative and regulatory frameworks best suited to meet the needs of its member co-operatives, as well as to speak on behalf of the co-operatives with a unified voice. Of course, there are many variations and different structures involved, and in some cases two or even three competing second-tier organizations may end up serving the same co-operative. Moving towards a more integrated and simplified national co-operative structure clearly would serve to better satisfy member needs, and at the same time aid government in legislating and regulating co-operatives nationally and even internationally.

The reader is reminded that the items listed above tend to contribute to either *"satisfying member needs"* or *"ensuring operational efficiency"* of the co-operative, or to do both as described in Chapter Five. These two results in turn help to strengthen the financial base of the co-operative.

Successes Far Outweigh Failures

It is important for the reader to know that some co-operatives have failed in the past, and to appreciate that there will no doubt be failures in the future. It is true that co-operatives can and do fail just like other organizations because of poor leadership, mismanagement, and corruption. Others have failed by being at the wrong place in their development when an economic downturn occurred. While we do not have specific statistics on failures, we do know, based on the statistics available, that co-operatives tend to have a better survival record in comparison to those in the private sector. We will illustrate.

In Canada, in the province of Quebec, the success ratio for co-operatives is almost double, with 62 percent of co-ops surviving the first 5 years of operation compared to 35 percent of other businesses, and 44 percent surpassing the first 10 years, compared to 20 percent of other businesses![2] In Alberta, a recent study shows that more than 80% of co-operatives survived more than five years.[3] Overall, in Canada, which has over 9,000 co-operatives representing 8.8 million members, the survival rate of co-operatives is two times better than private companies over a period of ten years.[4]

In the UK, community-owned shops are those that are owned and run by the community itself.[5] They are viable and sustainable models of business, their 96% survival rate compares extremely favourably with the average small business's 5 year survival rate of 46.8%- this is thanks to their widespread engagement and ability to respond to customer needs.

In Portugal, while approximately three-quarters of co-operatives were still in existence ten years after their formation, less than 40% of capitalist firms had survived for the same time period.[6] The report was released in July 2012 but the comparisons were from 1996 through to 2006, which is a ten year period.

In Eastern Europe and in parts of Africa, the survival rates of co-operatives do not appear to be any better than conventional small enterprises. There appear to be two possible explanations. First, one can assume that in some instances the co-operatives, even in relatively recent times, were created in response to a government or other programs but failed to immediately grow and become sustainable. At the same time in countries like Kenya co-operatives were able to become very successful. Second, in Africa and parts of Asia, for example, it has been a common practice to maintain a manual registry of all co-operatives in the country and to count the number of co-operatives, but to not classify inactive co-operatives as failed co-operatives. Doing a one-time correction of this practice in record keeping may well explain the drop in the number of surviving co-operatives. Thankfully, improved statistical reporting systems are now being implemented in a number of countries around the world.

Beware Also Means Be Aware

Co-operatives and other user-owned businesses, present a rather unique problem as they become successful, large, and financially secure. They develop a large capital reserve. This reserve is owned by the user members - not the investors. Members often take the reserve for granted and as a sign of their co-operative's success. However, investors often watch the equity capital closely and feel it should be paid out as dividends or allocated as common shares as it is in investor-owned private corporations. The large reserves can become a target for greedy managers and leaders. For example, the USA Savings and Loans associations in the late 1980s were ruined as regulations were eliminated and the reserves were left exposed with no rules.[7] They were emptied for personal gain and the organizations collapsed.

Other examples in the 21st century include large agricultural co-operatives, some of which have been converted to investor-owned enterprises in order to access additional capital. This occurs when management and the board of directors decide, sometimes with members' unwitting approval, to take steps to convert the organization from a member-owned co-operative to a private sector corporation, and then by having investors buy up voting, common shares. These shares may then increase and later decrease in value depending upon when they are resold. The process is sometimes referred to as demutualisation. Further details are available in a thoroughly researched 324 page publication entitled *A Co-operative Dilemma: Converting Organizational Form*, edited by Jorge Sousa and Roger Herman, 2011 is available for purchase from the Centre for Co-operative Studies at: www.usaskstudies.coop .

We appreciate there may be instances where the conversion of a co-operative to a private sector corporation may be desired by an informed membership, or instances where government regulators see it as the only option short of bankruptcy. However, there are instances where the management and the leadership of the co-operative stand to benefit personally, and/or financially, if and when the co-operative converts to a private sector corporation. It is prior to this point that both the board of directors and the general membership would be wise to seek new and independent professional guidance before considering, or recommending any change in corporate form to the membership at large.

A Good Idea Until Properly Planted Can Not Produce

We have started this chapter by identifying why some co-operatives have failed in the past. Later in this chapter, we provided a buffet of approaches which have proven successful in co-operative enterprises from Europe to Africa and from Asia to the Americas. We are aware our lists and explanations are not exhaustive. They are drawn from various studies, reports, and personal experience of the authors and various other co-operative professionals. Of necessity many of these approaches are generic, with some perhaps being better suited to newly established co-operatives and others to larger co-operative organizations operating within a network of co-operative enterprises. Some examples are drawn from financial co-operatives, while others are drawn from other types of co-operatives. We have emphasized the importance of creating communities of support and of building financial strength.

We are aware that others within the International Co-operative Alliance are considering options for co-operatives to access equity capital and so we have not dealt with it at length as a success factor in this chapter. We will however include some further out-of-the-box thinking concerning equity capital in Chapter Eleven: *The Challenges and Opportunity Ahead*.

You are encouraged to look over the list of suggested approaches included above and to think seriously if one or more might contribute to the success of a co-operative you know, or of which you are a member. If the co-operative successfully implements the approach you bring forward, and is able to improve from doing so, perhaps you might ask to be reimbursed by the co-operative for what you may have spent personally to obtain this publication.

Take Aways

1. Starting co-operatives should be done with due care and diligence. Co-operatives have in many cases failed because they were not established, regardless of the rational or motives involved, as real co-operatives, but rather were established for purposes other than serving members' needs.

2. A great number of the factors that contribute to the success of a co-operative have to do with people and with relationships. It is through relationships that those in leadership and in management perform their roles. It is through the multitude of relationships that exist that communities of support develop in and around a co-operative.

3. A great number of factors that contribute to the success of a co-operative have to do with business functions and financial management. How satisfactorily business functions are performed and how prudently finances are managed ultimately determines the measure of financial strength that results.

4. Early evidence suggests co-operatives tend to have much higher five year and ten year start-up survival rates than other forms of enterprise.

5. The board of directors and the owner members need to be wary and also well informed, even to the extent of hiring and using independent qualified professional advisors, at such time as the elected or appointed leadership of their co-operative recommends changing the organization to some other private sector corporate form.

Chapter Ten - Towards a World Vision for Co-operatives

The Battle of Ideas: Taking Ideology to the Next Level

In the early part of this millennium, Daniel Yergin and Joseph Stanislaw published what was to become a world-wide bestselling book entitled *The Commanding Heights: The Battle for the World Economy*.[1] The same content was later produced as a video and was shown as part of the US Public Broadcasting Service as a 6 hour three part series. Their story begins in Doha, Qatar, at the World Trade Organization's summit on the Arabian Peninsula in November 2001. A total of 4,000 representatives from 142 nations were in attendance, including the two newest, economic powerhouse members of the World Trade Organization - China and Taiwan. This clearly was the recognition that the process of "globalization" had arrived. Supporting the globalization process was what Yergin and Stanislaw saw as three "moments of choice".[2] *First, there was following WWI the commitment by the nations of the West to a vision of interdependence in which trade was an engine of both growth and peace. Second, there was the push back in many western countries against Keynesianism, and the subsequent harmonizing of fiscal and monetary policies, resulting in a deeper economic integration than would have been possible through trade alone. Third, there was the failure of the closed economies and their re-integration into the global market economy. The Mexico's debt crisis because of its size, back in 1982 topped the list of South America national economic failures.*

The authors couch their opening claims about globalization by describing the economic dilemma created by it. Globalization, and the three moments of choice just mentioned that helped to create it, reflects the opening up of the world economy, the increasing integration of national economies, and the emergence of the global marketplace. Yergin and Stanislaw stated,[3] "It (globalization) can do much to reduce poverty worldwide and promote higher standards of living. At the same time, it creates broad anxieties and carries new risks that were not initially so evident."

Little were the authors able to foresee what was to unfold less than a dozen years later. The collapse of stock markets in the United States and around the globe. One of the greatest challenges for government they professed was in determining what will be the new role of government? After all, they explained:[4]

> ...there is no market without government to define the rules and the context. The state must create and maintain the parameters within which the market operates. And that is the new direction. The state accepts the discipline of the market; government moves away from being producer, controller, and intervener, whether through state ownership or heavy-handed regulation. The state as manager is an increasing laggard in the competitive, mobile, globalized economy.

It was Yergin and Stanislaw's view "... that instead, government had shifted toward becoming a referee, setting the rules of the game to ensure, among other things, competition—and working in collaboration with other states to establish the systems required to make the coming globality (sic) work well."[5]

What has transpired from 2002 until the present has indeed changed everything. In 2002, the prevailing economic logic claimed that less government, with more control left to the private sector (the invisible hand managing the marketplace) would create "new and improved" economic reality for people all around the world. This type of thinking in large measure was based on the work of the economist Friedrich August von Hayek.[6] Hayek, who was born in Austria-Hungary, became an economist and philosopher through the 1940s to the 1980s. His economic theory was that less government interference resulted in better economic performance. Credit for supporting this type of thinking must also go to two of Hayek's most avid proponents, British Prime Minister Margaret Thatcher, and just a little while afterwards, United States President Ronald Reagan.

As is well known, the financial crisis of 2008, which resulted in massive intervention in markets by the United States government, followed by continuing interventions by governments in the European Union, resulted in even deeper differences of view over what needs to be done, by whom, and under what theoretical framework. Systems, processes and ideologies that seemed according to many to be working were in fact failing. No one was more surprised at this fact than former Chairman of the United States Federal Reserve, Alan Greenspan. Senator Henry Waxman questioned Mr. Greenspan during a congressional hearing on Thursday October 23, 2008. The questioning went as follows: "In other words you found that your view of the world, your ideology was not right. It was not working." Mr. Greenspan replied: "That is -- precisely. No, that's precisely the reason I was shocked, because I had been going for 40 years or more with very considerable evidence that it was working exceptionally well".[7]

Thus begins our story of the battle of ideas – a story which initially appears to have little to do directly with co-operative enterprise. Yet, as you will see it has everything to do with the notion of co-operative enterprise.

To be clear, the economists and those in positions of power politically during the past century first proposed that the solution to the world's problems involved lessening the role of governments in local economies around the world. The heart of the ideology meant reducing government's oversight in corporate affairs. In the US, in particular, it meant lessening the control and regulation of those in the private sector and those especially in the financial services field. Alan Greenspan defended that ideology through most of his public career. Second, as we have seen in hindsight, in 2007 and onward government role shifted from "hands-off" to a more interventionist position. The US government under President Barak Obama deemed it necessary to intervene in a significant way by bailing out many of the "too big to fail" financial institutions and other private sector players as well, and further intervening with other measures,[8] including quantitative easing, while at the same time now pressing for greater regulation of the same institutions.

More recently, one country after another in Europe has gone through debt crisis brought about by mismanagement of public sectors funds and programs, and by weakness in banking intuitions. As in the US, many people in Europe are without work, significant personal savings have been lost and public debt is skyrocketing. The average person's confidence in their banking intuitions and in their political leadership has been severely shaken.

So in summary we have a globalized market economy – driven in the main by the activities of credit-granting financial institutions,[9] previously requesting less government oversight and being given it, then being forced to accept, because of mismanagement, massive amounts of money from governments to avoid bankruptcy. At the same time, those institutions were still able to find ways to pay enormous salaries and bonuses to many of the same managers who had mismanaged their institutions in the first instance. And at the same time, governments in many western countries were compiling public debt as if the capacity for borrowing was endless and the debt never required retirement.[10] In surveying the mess, it is difficult to ascertain who should have the greater accountability - those in the private sector or those in the public sector.

We referred to this section as the battle of ideas. In many ways, it has been a battle of ideas between the public sector and the private sector with most economists and most politicians positioning themselves and arguing for one or the other side. It has also been a battle between those who profess that globalization is the key and those who profess the necessity of putting up barriers and boundaries to prevent corporations from buying up their countries and their resources. In reality, both sides appear to be at a loss to explain exactly where their theories went wrong and more importantly where they might turn to remedy the situations going forward.

As John Raulston Saul forcefully argues in one of his latest book, *The Collapse of Globalization and the Reinvention of the World*, the thing that has failed us horribly is our faith in what universities and business schools generally, and economists particularly(like Friedrich Hayek, Milt Friedman, and John Maynard Keynes) tell our policy makers about what our problems are and how best to solve them.[11] Saul's view is that the far more serious problem that the West faces is that it remains stuck on outdated ideas of growth, wealth creation, and trade expansion.[12] Whereas public policy is still dominated by the people who created this crisis, Saul envisions a new sort of wealth creation, growth, and advocates new forms of action. While we may not accept everything which Saul argues, we do agree with his view that the most serious underlying problems are a failure to analyze and understand the situation, and a failure to recognize the kind of culture that has been created across much of the Western world.

At the same time, we appreciate that unraveling our messes may take some doing and may continue to cause some serious hardships for many along the way. The situation we are facing did not occur over night. It did not even occur over a decade. It has arisen in large measure over the past half century. It is unlikely it can or will be resolved in the near term. We appreciate there are at least some of those in positions of power and influence in the world today who, in spite of the daunting challenges and hardships facing most of the world's population, prefer to maintain the systems, structures and values (economic, social, political, and technical) as they are today. It is these same people who prefer to defend (and go to battle for) those ideas and experiences, frameworks, and theories which they feel will serve their best interests.

So What Is A Muddle?

As individuals, as groups, as businesses, and as governments we love to solve problems. In the past it was, and still is, how corporations and people can grow rich. It is how many of us get ahead in our careers. It is how governments get elected or fail to get elected. Unfortunately some of today's larger problems are different than in the past. And as we will illustrate, they are a lot harder to solve.

As we have shown, our wealth creation and wealth distributions systems, at least in the West, are in a bit of a mess. The mess is complex, and it is difficult to know what to expect when some elements (such as the rules) are changed to benefit certain players at one level of the system (i.e., major losses which normally should have gone to bank institutions and investors have now suddenly shifted to governments and eventually to tax payers). In essence, market losses were shifted from the private sector to the public sector; roughly translated market losses were shifted from shareholders to tax payers. A similar but slightly different shifting of wealth is occurring in a number of countries in Europe. Few feel that what is happening is fair to those concerned! The Occupy Movement has arisen worldwide as one response.[13]

We find we are no longer simply dealing with one particular problem, but rather a number of related circumstances all of which are interacting in real time. To illustrate, if Spain appears to be in financial difficulty, world markets tend to fall since investors conclude the Euro will be under pressure, and therefore they will wish to move funds elsewhere, and oil prices will rise or fall depending on whether or not funds move outside of the Eurozone. On the surface these may all appear to be economic problems but they are more involved. European pension fund managers are scratching their heads about what to do because many had invested in coastal retirement real estate in Spain. Those same pension funds are now left with thousands of properties which sit vacant and have little value. Spain's current unemployment rate is 25 percent; Greece's rate is 26 percent, and Cyprus and Ireland both have unemployment rates above 14 percent.[14] When such events occur social welfare costs (both direct and indirect) increase, as do levels of social unrest. European Central bankers, the IMF, and countries with stronger economies such as Germany and France end up having to provide monetary support. Again we are dealing with complexity and questions of what is fair.

Unfortunately, as a species we face more than money and banking problems, and problems based upon the way we govern ourselves. We will elaborate further with a couple of examples before presenting our conclusion.

We are now faced with a much greater degree of interdependence and interconnectedness because of advances in global trade and communications technology. For example, consider what happens around the world when US job growth statistics come out. If significant new jobs were created in the period, then world financial market indices usually climb. This means investors will guess US demand will be increasing, and thus sales will increase, and that factory production both in the US and in Asia will rise. Investor decisions, coupled with large value funds transfer facilities, can cause financial markets around the globe to swing wildly in just a few hours. When the news is bad, such as weaknesses in governments or in financial institutions, the effects can be devastating. A country's currency can plummet in just hours. In days, the cost of credit can rise dramatically; businesses fail and jobs are lost.

Let us look at some of our problems from a different perspective. Let's look at a couple of problems many would really rather ignore. For example, we now know that global warming is occurring at an even faster rate than we had expected. What does it really mean and how serious is it? Who is causing it? How might it be fixed? What will happen if it isn't addressed, and equally importantly who is going to pay for fixing it, assuming that it can be fixed? This is a complex global problem where there are many different interests and competing points of view. There may be solutions. Yet we do not hear of "agreed to" global solutions being implemented. The problems continue to exist. Look for example of corruption around the globe. There is considerable evidence that it is a real problem, and that it impedes social and economic development, yet few jurisdictions appear willing or able to tackle the problem.

Within one mess we often find the genesis of an even greater mess.[15] Political programs intended to protect one area of an economy (i.e., US, Canadian, and European agricultural subsidies) end up negatively affecting other economies elsewhere (i.e., African agricultural exports). Improved efficiency within a particular sector (auto production) may well increase unemployment within the same sector, which in turn can increase social welfare or other costs to tax payers. The same can be true technologically. Increased usage of carbon based fuels has allowed us to move people, goods, and services around the planet, yet has resulted in more pollution, which in turn results in more health issues and more medical costs, and contributes to the global warming problems described earlier.

In any particular setting when there are a series of messes happening at the same time, the problem might best be described by using a term Gregory Batson first employed. He used the term "muddle" to describe a situation when people who are involved in one or more forms of enterprises do not share the same understanding or the same perspectives. So we ask you, as we proceed, to recognize that in many ways, as a species, we are in a muddle or two; and that digging ourselves out will require some thought and some time, and most importantly some openness to new ways of thinking and acting.

We think most people in most if not all of the countries around the world would agree that today's techno-economic and human governance systems are clearly not functioning properly, and sooner or later they are going to require significant redesign if they are to serve the human race well. As Johan Rockström, Director of the Stockholm Resilience Centre, has explained, we are reaching and in many cases have reached tipping points where the planet can no longer sustain the demands human beings are placing upon it.[16] Anders Wijkman and Johan Rockström point out in their new book *Bankrupting Nature - Global Risks and Pathways to Global Sustainability* that we are very well along in a collision course with Nature.[17] We are already facing extreme water shortages, rapid rise in CO_2 N_2O and CH_4 concentrations, ozone depletions, and species extinctions. For a quick overview of facts and details please see www.slideshare.net/ and search for "Bankrupting Nature".[18] We encourage readers to take a moment to learn more about the work of this world famous advanced research centre by downloading their 2012 annual report.[19] You will see in the opening pages of their 2012 annual report that the Centre acknowledged the passing of Elinor Ostrom who was well known in many corners and around the world for her views respecting development, and in particular her views on co-operative forms of development.[20] Ostrom was the first woman to win the Nobel Prize in Economics for research which analysed the way in which people can co-operatively manage common resources without the implied need for government regulation or private ownership; her achievement was all the more remarkable as she was not an economist but a political scientist.

Therefore, it should not come as any surprise that interestingly, some of the more established co-operative organizations can and do serve as useful and successful mechanisms through which people (members) from the larger community have the opportunity to dialogue and to come to common understandings of complex issues, and even succeed in finding consensus of opinion on what might best be done about them. In the meantime, and also in the longer term, we believe that "co-operative enterprise" as we have described it throughout can provide "fertile middle ground", perhaps even "the seed" for people and organizations to actively engage in a process of building a better world, and perhaps, just perhaps, help to clean up some of the messes which the rest of the world seems unwilling, or unable, to address.

The Biggest Problem in the World

While one of our authors was working in Africa, he would often strike up a conversation with someone at the same meeting, or perhaps a taxi driver, or a church official, servers in restaurants, family members, business persons, government officials, and people waiting in queues. He asked the same question of friends and colleagues from North America and Europe. The question was also posed in a blog on the internet. The question was: "In your view, what is the biggest problem in the world?" The answers given and the discussions that followed were always interesting and personal. Everyone came up with an answer. Many people started by saying: "I'm not really sure, but this is just what I think…" or words to that effect. Over a five year period from 2006 through to 2011, as many as one thousand individuals gave their views and opinions. Many responses included statements such as the following:

People's greed.	Poverty locally and internationally.
Drug usage and all the behaviors (violence) associated with it.	The "rich people always get richer" economic system.
Inability to trust others in a competitive environment.	Corruption – people are always stealing someone else's money.
Laziness and people free loading on others and on the state.	Radicalism and extremists.
Terrorism.	Violence against women and children.
No plan or vision for the future.	No decent place to live plus unsanitary living conditions.
Global warming (more droughts and flooding).	The difficulties in getting educated.
Governments unaccountable for their actions.	Child mortality.
High interest rates and access to financing.	War and human conflict.
Man's inhumanity to his fellow man.	Bribery and corruption.
Civil war and what happens to refugees.	Inflation and fear of economic collapse.
Declining literacy and quality of education.	Too many people / over population.
Genocide.	Human trafficking.
Military dictatorships.	Rigged elections.
Family relationships and family violence.	Pollution across of the planet.
Addictions (cigarettes, drugs, and alcohol).	Cost of basic necessities like fuel and food.
Basic health care and disease (including HIV / Aids).	Increasing fear of everything from disease, to economic collapse, to personal security.
Gender inequality.	Cultural clashes.
Tribal and racial discrimination.	Child care for single parents.
Inflation.	Passable roads, reliable electricity, and communications.
Access to safe clean drinking water.	Loss of species and of bio-diversity.

These were some of the more common answers which different people gave. Most answers included a story as to why the person being asked saw that condition as the biggest problem. For example, the person who stated that trust was the biggest problem explained it this way: "When there is only so much to go around, you can't always trust that people will be willing to share what there is. Sometimes you can't even trust your own family members.[21] So you must try to take what you can before someone else takes it."

It was after sharing the question with a young university student from Uganda that a slightly new answer was given. The student's name was Aga Nkusi.[22] After she had heard some of the other answers she made this statement. She said: *"Yes those are all problems, but I think the biggest problem is that most people don't care for each other enough. It is true, they care for themselves, and they care for their family members and maybe some of their friends, but they really don't care for others enough."* It was a simple and to the point answer and she gave it without hesitation as she was in a hurry to leave for class. Although there had been attempts to categorize the various answers, there never had been groupings or categories that seemed fitting. That is because most of the problems which people described were already big problems – and many could even be considered embedded enough and complex enough to be messes or even muddles. However, in thinking about Aga Nkusi's answer, it became evident that if we all were able to care more for each other, then all of the other problems could, one way or another, over time, be made to disappear. All of the problems that had been mentioned in one way or another were caused by people not caring enough for each other, and could be solved by people caring more. For our colleague, after five years the question had been satisfactorily answered. However, it led him to yet another underlying question, and an equally important answer.

Our colleague explained to us that he had been reflecting for some time on what it was that gave co-operatives their special importance. He knew from experience all of the practical ways in which co-operatives benefit individuals, families, communities, and even entire nations. He knew full well that co-operatives were very much both social and economic enterprises. But he said he still wondered if there were any other reasons co-operatives were so popular and successful all around the world.

We will quote our colleague:

> **Suddenly it became clear to me. Although I had been involved in working in and with and for co-operatives throughout my life, I had not made the connection. It occurred to me that co-operative organizations were the ideal form of enterprise in and through which people could care more for each other ... and could do so as little or as much as they wished or were able. As I rolled the idea around for a time, I realized that co-operatives were, in thousand and perhaps millions of ways, already doing that very thing!**

The co-operative enterprise model provides a fair and equitable mechanism for creating mutual benefits while at the same time providing individual benefits. Co-operatives are a practical mechanism for people to consciously join together to help themselves and to help others like themselves. The co-operative model already exists in a whole variety of marketplace settings and successfully competes with and/or compliments both private and public sector entities. It is more than a financially successful business model because a co-operative enterprise fairly represents various interests in its affairs and is therefore, well suited to addressing complex issues and to creating consensus concerning solutions which can work. The co-operative model is not a welfare model, yet concern for the community is one of its principles, caring in various ways for those who may be less fortunate in the community is not uncommon, as is helping people in communities towards better control of their own destinies.

Building a Better World

As we look forward, it seems to us that co-operative forms of enterprise have today only begun to scratch the surface of their potential for building a better world. Here are a few of the possibilities that might be used globally:

- **creating sustainable industries with worker co-operatives,**

- **educating children, youth, and adults through co-operative schools and colleges,**

- **supporting good health through co-operative clinics, hospitals, and insurance services,**

- **serving communities with co-operative water, sewage, fire-fighting, recycling, and park services,**

- **quality assurance and marketing services provided by producer co-operatives,**

- **small business financing and support services through savings and credit co-operatives,**

- **funeral and burial services by funeral care co-operatives,**

- **energy production and distribution co-operatives,**

- **taxi, bus, ferry, and car sharing transportation co-operatives,**

- **international trade financing and marketing support services co-operative, and/or**

- **legal and other services through professional services co-operatives.**

All of these kinds of co-operatives already exist and the list is only a small sampling. A complete list would be almost endless. When people choose to work together to help themselves and their community through using the co-operative model almost anything that can be imagined, can become possible.

In the short term, in looking to help create a better world, there are a handful of co-operative options that active co-operators and co-operative leaders may wish to consider pursuing – not because they must, but because they consciously choose to do so. They include some broad-based concepts as well as some specifics:

- **Proactively look for new purposes and opportunities (from within some of the messes that have been created) within and outside of their normal business functions.**

- **Continuously reach out to, and actively involve, members, employees, and others in the day- to- day affairs of the co-operative or co-operatives to which they belong.**

- **Actively research and understand new growth and developmental opportunities and challenges intended to satisfy members' needs, without consuming more resources.**

- **Relentlessly look for practical ways to do more, much more, with less, and without harming people or the planet.**

Depending upon circumstances, each co-operative must consciously and carefully balance the demands of employees, the needs of members, the interests of its community, and the world's concerns for the broader environment, with the necessity to survive! A crucial and delicate task!

This is only a beginning – but a needed one. Let us put our energies and our ideas and our hearts together to create a shared future vision for co-operatives from around the world. To us, building a better world is about looking for purposeful possibilities, taking actions as possible along a variety of paths, balancing the resources available with the needs and interests involved, and working together to imagine a better and even brighter future for everyone.

Chapter 11 concludes with some of our thoughts on future paths, and some ideas on where to begin.

Take Aways

1. There are fundamental differences in how people believe the world should operate. There are various factions who believe "the market economy" should be allowed to dictate how things get decided. There are those who believe less government is the only way to go. There are those who would wish to throw out the socio-technical and political systems that we have today. There are those who are interested in maintaining stability and the status quo. We have described these differences as the battle of ideas.

2. In looking to the distant future, co-operative forms of enterprise, or some variation thereof, may well emerge as the primary enterprise of choice for those persons who are dissatisfied with what either the private or the public sector has to offer.

3. Many of today's problems and issues are highly complex and inter-connected with other problems and issues. Solving one problem often creates new problems and issues. We have

described this as a mess. When a number of messes are involved, we have said that we have a muddle. Co-operative forms of organization and enterprise have demonstrated their potential to address complex and inter-connected problems and issues.

4. Almost all of the world's problems involve "not caring enough for each other". Co-operatives provide an effective and proven mechanism to care more for each other, while at the same time providing the means for people to help themselves.

5. Co-operative Enterprises provide the means for building a better world. It really comes down to thinking and working together to imagine and to create a better future for all.

Chapter Eleven - The Opportunities and Challenges Ahead

Moving Forward

In continuing on with the idea of *Building a Better World* by co-operatively caring more for each other as described in chapter 10, we will now move forward by describing a series of world-wide opportunities as identified in the ICA 2020 Blueprint, and then proceed to present what we see as some of the key questions and challenges which will need to be addressed as co-operatives continue to move forward.

Blueprint for a Co-operative Decade

The recently released document *Blueprint for a Co-operative Decade*,[1] prepared under the guidance of Planning Work Group of the International Co-operative Alliance,[2] identifies five themes for the future: *participation, sustainability, co-operative identity, supportive legal frameworks, and co-operative capital.* These themes were presented before a Special 2012 General Assembly of the International Co-operative Alliance in October of that year. The Blueprint was considered and endorsed by delegates from around the world. We congratulate the ICA for this initiative. As the document states, the themes can only be realized if the worldwide co-operative movement embraces them and collectively seeks to achieve them.

In each of the five theme areas, the Blueprint document sets out a series of goals or as we see them a series of opportunities for co-operatives to embrace. We encourage interested readers to visit the ICA website (ICA.COOP) and to examine the Blueprint, its themes and its goals in greater detail.

Included with each of the themes and goals listed below are a series of possible or indicative actions to be taken. The following is an abbreviated version of the content included in the full *Blueprint* document as found on the ICA website.

1. PARTICIPATION - *The aim is to elevate participation within membership and governance to a new level, and to do this by focussing on the practical aspects of participation:*

- Finding new ways of "joining up" co-operators within the co-operative sector to create a more connected network of co-operators.

- Gathering and collating information about best practices; finding and sharing the best ideas, including in such areas as age and gender balance; identifying negative or damaging trends; helping to expose bad practices; and developing tools and techniques to improve them.

- Gathering and collating information which demonstrates how such examples of best practice are positively linked to strong performance across a broad range of indicators, including: financial success, employee engagement, social engagement, and environmental sustainability.

- Working with youth, young adults, and the social media industry to explore the motivation of younger generations in relation to collaborative activity and affinity; how communication and the forming of relationships have changed, and are changing, both on-line and off-line; and examining the practices which have evolved in recent movements.

- Examining and challenging existing practices of co-operative democracy, gathering evidence of innovative practice, encouraging trials of alternative approaches, and collating data.

- In relation to participation of non-user, funding members, gathering evidence of existing models and practice (more information below).

- Engage the Global 300 co-operatives to strengthen visibility of co-operative success and impact, and to amplify the co-operative voice, such as through a leadership roundtable.

2. SUSTAINABILITY - *The co-operative sector needs to demonstrate convincingly that sustainability is in the intrinsic nature of co-operatives, and that co-operative enterprise makes a positive contribution to sustainability in these areas:*

- Innovations in accounting: The co-operative sector needs to take the lead. There is already a large number of initiatives through which businesses, social enterprises, and charities are being encouraged to capture their non-financial performance; such as "triple bottom line accounting" (TBL), "balanced scorecard approach", "social return on investment" (SROI), "social impact reporting", and "well-being" measurements. Some of these indicators attempt to convert their various outputs back into monetary terms, as is the case with SROI (governments also do this when seeking to calculate the cost of environmental degradation). Others (such as TBL) simply present rival forms of valuation side-by-side.

- Case studies: The diversity of co-operative forms and goals is under-recognised. Case studies and first-hand stories showing the contributions of co-operatives to education, communities, health, and other public goals are important here and are needed. Consumer energy co-operatives are making a crucial contribution toward the shift to a low carbon economy, which needs recording, studying, and highlighting.

- Evidence gathering: In order to demonstrate their contribution to sustainability to public policy-makers, economic analysis of the "positive externalities" of co-operatives is valuable. A number of techniques exist (known as "contingent valuation") for capturing the value of non-market goods, such as health and a clean environment. Consideration should be given to the ICA facilitating the establishment of a virtual data bank.

- Public advocacy: The message about co-operatives can no longer be limited only to the language of democratic member control. It needs to be broadened, and needs consistently to include a reference to sustainability so as to attract interest from public policy-makers, the broader public, and young people.

- Technology: The co-operative sector should aim to become leaders in the development and use of technologies and social systems which specifically deliver human benefits, without despoiling the ecosystem.

- Management Practices: The co-operative sector needs to do more to develop and promote distinctive management practices that reflect the democratic values and long term horizon of the co-operative business model and which will fully exploit the potential co-operative advantage.

- Strengthen and Integrate the Co-operative Business Network: The co-operative sector should identify and remove barriers to inter-co-operation, including, where possible, integrating systems, such as procurement, using the principle of subsidiarity.

3. IDENTITY - *The goal is to build the co-operative message and secure the co-operative identity in order to secure moral economic authority and "better business" status for co-operatives.*

- There is no desire to undermine the Statement of Co-operative Identity, so the Statement should be celebrated. However, the Co-operative Principles (contained within the statement on the Co-operative Identity) could usefully be supplemented with "Guidance" for the purposes of translation into regulatory frameworks (this connects to theme four below). Developing Guidance involves establishing the irreducible core —e.g. what is the minimum requirement behind "controlled by their members" in the 2nd Co-operative Principle? Without such Guidance, it is difficult or even impossible for regulators to have a basis for accepting or rejecting a proposed constitution. It would also help to provide a clear basis for the ICA to work with national bodies and their governments where there are problems maintaining the irreducible core.

- Co-operatives need to think about how they are perceived by, and how they project themselves to, and communicate with young people. Securing their interest and positive engagement can only be achieved through an understanding of the changing ways in which they communicate and form relationships with each other using technology and social media. Human relationships are at the heart of a co-operative. Young people need to help shape the identity and the messages.

- Co-operatives also need to think about how they are perceived more widely by non-members and expert communities. The rise of terms such as "social enterprise", "corporate social responsibility", "employee ownership", and "social innovation" adds to the confusion surrounding the actual difference that a co-operative makes. Co-operatives are often not seen as sufficiently distinctive as to be dealt with separately on issues such as regulation. The message therefore, needs management if it is to function in the longer-term interests of co-operatives. Following development of Guidance, appropriate phraseology should be developed which is designed from the point of view of message projection.

- Consider permitting the allocation of ".coop" domain names only to those co-ops which meet the requirements of the irreducible core. Whilst this may take some time to establish, eventually it will provide the most visible evidence of what is denoted by "co-operative". This has the advantage of crossing jurisdictional boundaries. It would also provide the basis for the ICA to approach governments whose legislation has prevented compliance with the irreducible core, and result in their exclusion from use of ".coop" which might be a competitive disadvantage to their economy.

4. LEGAL FRAMEWORK - *Legislation both about the registration of co-operatives and about how they are treated in comparison with other entities is part of, and specific to, national jurisdictions and must be analysed as such. Therefore, specific improvements must be identified and lobbied for at the level of nations, and building directly on UN recommendations.*

- Assistance can be provided to national parliamentarians, legislators, and policy-makers through the comparative study of the way laws apply to co-operatives in different jurisdictions.

- Integrate the co-operative agenda into global development institutions, such as the World Bank, and with intergovernmental policy-setting bodies, such as the G8 and G20.

- Develop the capacity to respond to co-operative opportunities created by global and regional political events and changes.

- Evidence could be published for the social and public benefit of co-operatives. This evidence and the associated body of literature should be built up to support arguments for the appropriate treatment of co-operatives in different legal jurisdictions and in different stages of economic development.

- As referred to above under Identity, there is a need to establish an "irreducible core" of what it means to be a co-operative. This is clearly important as a basis for securing different treatment of co-operatives within national legal systems, because there needs to be a robust connection between the evidence of social and public benefit and the minimum criteria for being treated as a co-operative. This will be essential where, for example, different fiscal or regulatory treatment is afforded to co-operatives because otherwise there will be false claims of entitlement.

- A mechanism or tool should be developed to evaluate national legal frameworks and the extent to which they are enabling and supportive of co-operatives. A legal table of jurisdictions could be compiled to highlight the stronger and weaker ones. This would be a good way to highlight the poor performers and provide an opportunity to engage with them in political advocacy based on demonstrable factors.

- Establish a co-operative knowledge databank to measure and demonstrate impact and to facilitate knowledge transfer.

5. CAPITAL - *Secure reliable co-operative capital while guaranteeing member control. Essentially, this involves matching our needs as citizens for a safe place to keep the money we don't need right now but which we will need in the future, with the needs of businesses which require capital to develop and to meet changing needs.*

- Promoting and encouraging the funding of co-operatives by existing members.

- Ensuring that co-operatives have a clear proposition to make to providers of funds.

- Promoting the inter-change of ideas and experiences between jurisdictions in relation to capital and financial instruments.

- Developing a modern generic financial instrument which is classed as risk capital and meets the needs of co-operative businesses and co-operative funders.

- Developing a range of variations to the generic model to suit different sizes of co-operatives and sectors.

- Identifying institutions that can act as aggregators or intermediaries for businesses (large and small) needing capital.

- Utilising the Global Development Co-operative Fund to demonstrate establishment of the co-operative as an asset class (statistically).

- Undertaking research on changing attitudes and motivation for funding, and for new financial instruments.

- Reviewing risks and opportunities created by the use of subsidiary corporate entities, and other group structure arrangements, and the creation of co-operative groups or clusters to address capital accumulation.

While each of these five themes are vitally important for the future of co-operatives everywhere, we feel that the *Blueprint* needs to go farther in addressing larger, longer-term, underlying challenges which many co-operatives, both large and small, are facing today, and which many co-operatives will undoubtedly face in the future.

Three Key Questions

We know individuals and organizations are capable of achieving great results by working together and that there are now thousands of successful co-operatives around the world, including second-tier and third-tier co-operative entities and support organizations.

We will begin this section by asking three overarching questions. We feel each of these questions will need to be carefully and honestly considered if co-operatives are to successfully seize the opportunities described in the *Blueprint* document. These are fairly difficult and serious questions that are not easily considered or quickly answered. They cannot be answered once and then forgotten. They will need to be revisited by those within the co-operative system throughout the coming decade. Hard questions deserve honest answers.

Question One: *Why do co-operatives, in spite of their rhetoric and acknowledgement of the Principle of "Co-operation among Co-operatives," tend to resist sharing resources and working together to seize opportunities?*

Co-operatives and co-operative leaders may resist co-operating because they:

- have not looked for opportunities to co-operate beyond their front door,

- see too many other internal or external matters demanding their attention,

- fear putting their time and resources at risk, with little or no potential for return,

- feel they may be taken over by a stronger sister co-operative,

- may not feel there is anything new to be learned from others,

- see other co-operatives as competitors, and only share to a limited degree,

- leave it up to second-tier or support organizations to do so on their behalf,

- lack confidence,

- do not have a sense of where they might begin, and/or

- do not feel their membership is prepared to give them a mandate to do so.

Sadly, none of these are sound reasons for choosing not to co-operate with other co-operatives. In many respects, co-operatives are like family in that, while family members may be different from one another, they can still benefit from learning and supporting each other. Ignoring a parent, a brother or sister may not prove to be a wise course over the longer term. The same is true for co-operatives – ignoring others in the co-operative world may not prove to be the best strategy. To be successful, co-operatives must actively look for avenues by which to co-operate with other co-operatives.

We encourage every co-operative leader to seriously consider this question and to search out opportunities for your enterprise to co-operate with others. We expect you will be pleased that you did!

Question Two: *Why are there numerous local, national, and international co-operative organizations performing similar functions and not really co-ordinating their efforts or combining their resources?*

Co-operative organizations and co-operative leaders may duplicate efforts because they:

- receive local co-operative funding and support for the work they are doing,

- receive government funding which might not otherwise be available,

- feel what they are doing is more specialized than what others may be doing,

- are sometimes competing with other co-operatives for market share,

- may not be aware that they are duplicating the efforts of other co-operatives,

- are interested in maintaining the reputation and development capacity they have created,

- are interested in maintaining their positions, whether elected or employed,

- feel they are representing the interests of their membership and resist any change to the status quo, and/or

- believe their methods and expertise is superior to what other co-operative developers have to offer.

While each of these reasons may have some merit, the reality is that significant resources are being wasted by not sharing and learning from others, and by not looking for ways to do more together with less. In today's competitive world, co-operative enterprises must continually look for ways to become more efficient, while at the same time they improve the quality of what they produce. While bigger is not always better, we see cases where two or more co-operatives are performing the same or similar functions within the same market space. This does not make economic sense, since each organization is incurring significant overhead. Duplication of effort occurs in co-operatives at the local, national, regional, and international levels. We encourage every co-operative leader to ask if the larger co-operative world of which he or she is a part can be made stronger by reducing the duplication of effort, and by co-ordinating and sharing resources, and if so then seeking out options for doing so.

Question Three: *Why do many co-operatives place less and less emphasis on education, training, and information for members, elected representatives, managers, and employees?*

Co-operatives seem to place less and less emphasis on co-operative education, training, and information because they:

- feel people just do not have the time available to attend anything but short-term programs,

- feel spending only on training or education programs will negatively affect measurable performance and service,

- see people as more mobile, so investing in employees that are likely to leave may be a poor investment,

- have internal web-based sources of good information for officials and staff,

- feel knowledge depreciates so rapidly that many skills and abilities will be obsolete in five years,

- have already hired people who have education and experience so training is less important, and/or

- don't expect elected officials to be interested, as many are already professionals or business people.

We observe that co-operative education, training, and information-sharing have in many co-operatives become more and more technical as information and communications technologies have advanced. The education and training that is available is generally focused on business functions such as marketing, production, credit and finance, or ITC; and is less and less focused on the unique aspects of co-operative management and the nature of the co-operative system itself. In some cases, co-operative employees may not even know that they are working for a co-operative. The same may also be true when it comes to director education. New directors are taught what they need to know in terms of their roles. They learn about matters such as enterprise risk management, setting board policy, and how to gauge performance of the co-operative and of management. The co-operative movement touches on many more things than can be covered in one or two training sessions devoted to skills development. Members of the co-operative may receive a newsletter or an email, but receive very little information concerning the nature of the organization, its purposes, or how it operates. Sadly, annual reports are only intended to describe the organization, demonstrate how well it has performed, and sometimes to explain why results were less than expected but are projected to improve in the next period.

In an increasingly information-rich world, co-operatives are encouraged to look seriously at their members, elected officers, other volunteers, and their employees and to see them as vital parts of the organization. In today's fast paced, highly specialized world, we believe it is of vital importance that everyone receives an opportunity to learn the basics of co-operative enterprise. We feel it is vital that management and employees learn the basics of co-operative management. Co-operatives that rely solely on "importing knowledge and skills" from other sectors may find themselves operating less and less like co-operatives, and at some point may find themselves in difficulty for doing so. Hiring top or senior personnel out of the banking or retailing workforce must therefore be done with great care. Bringing in someone whose personal values don't mesh with those of the co-operative is a little like inviting the wolf into the chicken coop. We encourage all co-operatives and co-operators to make a commitment to "co-operative enterprise" training, education, and information.

Strategic Focus Areas

While the *Blueprint for a Co-operative Decade* is sound in terms of setting direction, we do not sense that it is sufficient for the longer-term success of co-operatives globally. Consideration of the *Blueprint* document and the questions above can be a good starting point.

In reviewing the *Blueprint* document and the possible and indicative actions, we believe there are five strategic focus areas which the ICA and co-operative organizations around the world will need to consider.[3] They are as follows:

- There will need to be a significant commitment of financial, technical, and human resources by co-operatives and others to help fund and support co-operative research and development efforts, as well as to support the implementation of such developments. It will be up to the ICA and co-operatives globally to identify and prioritize resources to be dedicated to the research and development work required, and in the end successfully manage a whole series of projects (some small, some large) while attending to day-to-day operations.

- There will need to be significant research and development focused on satisfying the diverse business, technical, and organizational needs of co-operatives globally. Research and development efforts must produce practical and applicable results. At least one stream of research should focus on the technology of participation. It will be up to the ICA and co-operatives globally to identify and to prioritize the research and development work required and to see that results are available for use by co-operatives everywhere.

- New business structures and mechanisms will need to be considered and then be put in place to help bridge the gap between major co-operative systems, and over time, to help reduce the duplication of efforts that exist globally. It will be up to the ICA and to co-operatives globally to explore ways of streamlining workflow and extending the way work is accomplished across the co-operative system.

- New participatory processes and mechanisms which support co-operative management, co-operative education, and co-operative planning and decision-making will need to be implemented. It will be up to the ICA and to co-operatives globally to seriously investigate and implement participatory methodologies and technologies. We refer to technologies in both face-to-face and electronically supported terms.

- Continued strong, informed, experienced and committed co-operative leadership will be critical. More than ever before, co-operative leaders everywhere will need to work together, to learn, to lead, and to support one another. Building a better world by co-operatively caring more for each other is not a small undertaking.

Thinking Outside of the Box

When we were considering the way forward we felt it was essential that we also think "more out of the box than in the box". We agreed that our thinking needed to extend beyond the coming decade and on into the next generation. The process of thinking about what we might like to see in future was not protracted nor intended to be synoptic. When we put our collective thoughts about the future together we found our ideas fell into the four areas illustrated in some detail below. Although at times, you may sense that some of our ideas may be a little too much out of the box, we make no apologies, since what we imagine is no more radical than what other co-operative leaders and innovators have suggested and implemented in times gone by. We would like to add that visualizing aspects of a desired or ideal future is part of an accepted enterprise and community planning process. We therefore, encourage you as a reader, or perhaps as a leader in your co-operative, to harness your own imagination and the imagination of your group and to see where it takes you.

Informing and Involving People

- We imagine new tools and mechanisms to link "member based" research to enterprise direction within co-operative organizations, for example,
    - Interest based planning sessions – as a means for involving members,
    - On-going invitations to members to discuss their needs, wants, and opinions,
    - Using crowd-sourcing in co-operatives to maintain active member inputs.

- We imagine an on-going series of internet-based videos on co-operative enterprises for members and potential members, as well as a series of customized educational workbooks and videos for specialized audiences such as educational institutions, government and regulators.

- We imagine an annual, formal, open, internet-based, Global Co-operative Week, including group discussions with leading co-operators, and showcasing different types of co-operatives as well as the diversity of governance approaches in use.

Money and Banking

- We imagine an international arrangement of cross guarantees (sharing capital) for financial co-operatives coupled with a scheme for dual controls to strengthen the capital base, and to enhance management performance.

- We imagine the creation of a joint venture "International Co-operative Financing Facility (ICFF)" with a minimum capitalization of $500 million US. This venture would focus: 20% on start-up of small co-op enterprises to alleviate "pain and suffering" through to self-sufficiency; 20% on venture capital financing to expand and accelerate the development of emerging co-operative enterprises; and 60% on financing business-to-business relations among co-operatives to enhance service levels and profitability which in turn creates and contributes to the first two objectives.

- We imagine the creation of an International Co-operative Development Bank (ICDB) with two divisions: finance and mutual aid. These two branches of the bank would operate in some aspects like a combination of the IMF and the World Bank, offering specialized forms of financing together with global co-operative regulatory compliance and development support. This bank's purpose would be to deliver a wide range of development services, as well as a range of specialized financial products and services to co-operatives. We imagine its operations to extend across the globe in developed and development settings and regions.

- We imagine finding avenues to expand altruistic and/or philanthropic endeavours within the system/movement, while at the same time we imagine moving away from an aid funding project model in international co-operative development to an enterprise partnership approach which looks for new business opportunities and which provides the potential for longer term mutual benefit.

Research Education and Demonstration

- We imagine forming a co-operative cluster of twelve or maybe even two dozen top quality universities around the world that would work jointly and specialize in the delivery of co-operative and human science studies, co-operative management studies, and co-operative policy studies. They would also offer recognizable graduate and post graduate programs focused on co-operative enterprise. We further imagine using a "contribution of resources model" to create a "joint venture" with a select number of these same institutions to provide for advanced study and research into co-operative enterprise, data gathering, and business intelligence and analysis.

- We imagine the creation of two to three venues per year where current global co-operative leaders and individuals of influence (including selected political leaders) are invited to engage in discussions focused on how "co-operative enterprises" can be used to greater advantage in building an even better world than they are doing today.

Governance, Structure, and Strategy

- We imagine, and after considerable research and dialogue, the creation of a small co-operatively sponsored body, structured as the International Co-operative Organization (ICO) and operating as a global agency but within the United Nations. Its purpose would be to represent the interests of all co-operatives globally to governments and to other UN agencies and bodies including the World Bank Group, and the International Monetary Fund. This agency could be staffed and managed by people seconded from co-operative enterprises around the world. This agency would work most closely with the International Co-operative Alliance and others players such as the World Council of Credit Unions, co-operative banking associations, major international co-operatives, as well as the International Labour Organization (ILO) in the development of global co-operative policy positions. We see this agency helping to offset the resource constraints faced by the ILO, while also working to address longer term co-operative policy concerns across the globe.

- We imagine creating a discussion process focusing on harmonization and eventual rationalization of existing non-primary support organisations. Specifically, we imagine stopping the creation of second and third-tier organizations unless there is compelling and strong evidence of need and sustainability. While there may initially be good rationale for local co-operatives to join together to create second-tier co-operatives, we feel today there may be instances where the number of second-tier (or even third-tier) co-operative organizations can be reduced.

- We imagine the formation of a global co-operative technology and communications service to supply ITC services to financial co-operatives, insurance co-operatives, and other co-operatives globally.

As we imagine the future, we do well to remind ourselves that all of the things that we imagine need to remain consistent with the notion of *building a better world by co-operatively caring more for each other.*

Some Next Steps

We all appreciate that good ideas without the means for employing them are of little value.

We believe that the *Blueprint for a Co-operative Decade* provides clear direction. Certainly, it contains many good goals and possible action ideas. As we have noted, consideration of some key questions, emphasis on strategic priorities, and some "longer term" and "out-of-the-box thinking" will be required.

One more ingredient will be required. It is the active support of co-operative enterprises and co-operators from around the world. Here are a few thoughts as to how you as a co-operator or your co-operative enterprise might become involved.

- **Start informing yourself and others by heading to the ICA.COOP website and gathering your facts.**

- **Initiate and lead a discussion group of other co-operators to see if you can answer one or more of the key questions presented earlier in the chapter. Be sure to post your answers on the Co-operative Enterprise website (www.cooperativeenterprise.coop), where you can ask for any further inputs or reactions from the co-operative community. Finally, apply what you have discovered in your co-operative.**

- **Volunteer to lead a major longer-term study group or research project or task force. Make sure to link up with others having similar interests or concerns. You can check out LinkedIn.com and look for credit union and co-operative discussion groups, or find similar discussion groups on Facebook.**

- **Maybe you are new to co-operatives. Why not look for a co-operative or credit union in your community? Approach them, find out how they are doing, and if you like what you hear and see, consider joining it as a way of getting involved.**

- **If you are an elected director or an employee of a co-operative or credit union, or a co-operative educator, researcher or developer, consider joining our co-operative (Global Co-operative Development Group Inc.). We are just getting started. To find out more, check out our site at: www.co-operativeenteprise.coop. Of course if you have ideas, stories, suggestions, questions, or criticisms by all means send them to us using our "Forums or Blog" menus on our website.**

- **Check through Chapter Twelve at the end of this publication for even more ideas and resources.**

Take Aways

1. Co-operatives, along with leadership provided by the International Co-operative Alliance, have created a *Blueprint for a Co-operative Decade*, complete with goals and associated ideas for action. The plan was endorsed by co-operative delegates from around the world at a special General Assembly held in Manchester, England, in November 2012.

2. There are at least three serious questions which many co-operatives around the world would do well to consider. They involve:
    a. The opportunities for greater co-operation among co-operatives.
    b. Reducing the duplication of effort and the waste of resources within co-operative structures.
    c. Expanding education, training and information possibilities across the co-operative system.

3. Success over the coming decade and beyond will require co-operative leaders and co-operative management to focus on five strategic areas: 1) research and development, 2) required resources, 3) business structures, 4) avenues for participation, and 5) strong leadership.

4. Success over the longer-term will require thinking outside -the-box and imagining the possibilities.

5. There can be lots of next steps; in this case the next step is up to you to the reader.

PART FIVE – EVERYTHING ELSE CO-OPERATIVE

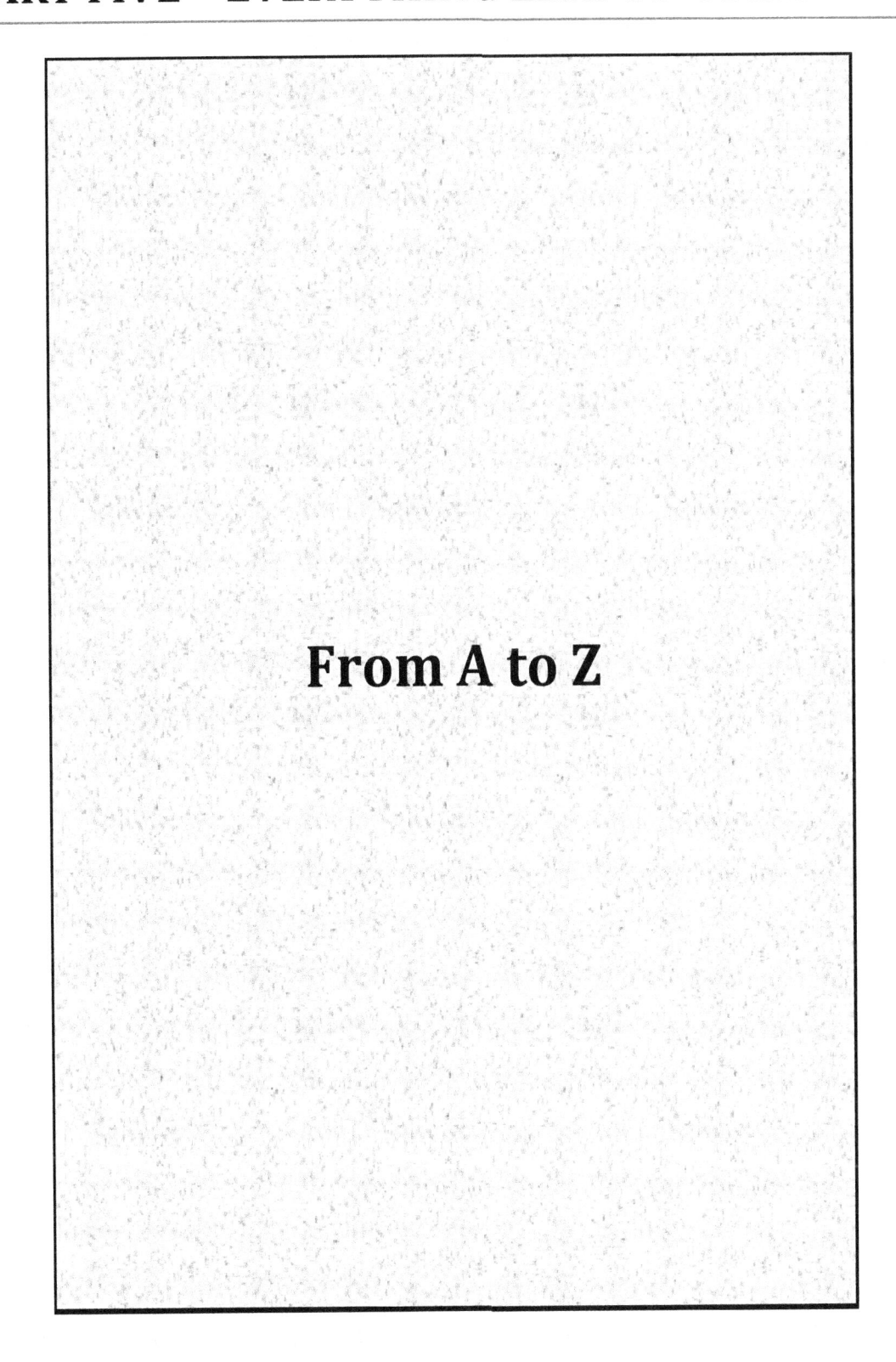

From A to Z

Chapter Twelve - Some Sources, Resources, and Postscripts

Sources and Resources

How to Start a Co-operative

The internet is one of your best research resource tools available.[1] We suggest you do a Google search for general materials and to familiarize yourself with what is available concerning co-operatives.

In Australia - Although a little dated, this manual is a good place to start if you are in Australia. Click here: www.australia.coop/ and type "start up" to locate the free download manual.

In Canada - Although the source is Canadian this site has an extensive list of publication and tools to help a person or a group manage their way through creation of a co-operative enterprise. Here is the link: www.coopscanada.coop/en/coopdev/StartCoop . All online materials on the site are free or if you are in Canada you may even call for help toll free @ 1-877-268-9588 and leave a message. If more extensive assistance is desired fee-for-services resources are also available. To learn more regarding services available use this link: www.coopscanada.coop/en/coopdev/Co-opAdvisory . Across Canada you will find provincial co-operative associations (check phone listings), as well as co-operative research centres located in some universities (University of Saskatchewan, Université de Québec á Montréal and University of Victoria). For worker co-operative expertise check: www.canadianworker.coop/. Also check: www.coopzone.coop/ to locate experienced co-operative developers, trainers and resources that are available across the country.

In the UK - For general help you can start here: www.uk.coop/start-co-op/ . For more details and to get support complete the query form at this link: www.uk.coop/publicservices/enquiry . If you are interested in starting a freelance and creative co-operative you can use this link to get help: www.creatives.uk.coop/ and download the guide. If you are interested in starting a food co-operative in the UK, then click here: www.conservativecoops.com/. Then use the search box near the bottom of the page to search for "nuts and bolts"

In US – There are a number of publications available. One that is well written but somewhat dated can be accessed here: www.rurdev.usda.gov/ . Click on the word "co-operative" on the left of your screen, and you will see "Starting A Co-operative" button appear on the right. It is provided by the US Department of Agriculture. You can access publications, resources, and assistance with development available across the country using this link: www.co-opsusa.coop/resources .

In South Africa click: www.westerncape.gov.za/eng/ and search for "starting a co-operative". You will find numerous publications and guidance is available. Alternatively you can click here:

www.southafrica.smetoolkit.org/sa/en/ and search for "a co-operative as a business entity". Both websites provide helpful details on what you need to know and how to begin.

In all cases you will do well to determine what legal framework exists to govern the creation of a formal co-operative enterprise. This is especially the case if you are considering the creation of a financial co-operative as there will be additional requirements depending upon the jurisdiction involved.. The above guidelines may not apply to your location but will still give you a good context to consider in your research. If you are new to co-operative enterprises we encourage you to search out and approach any existing co-operatives in your area for their experience and suggestions.

Popular Co-operative Magazines, Books, and e-Books

Magazines and eZines

- The USDA Rural Co-operative Magazine: www.rurdev.usda.gov/ .
- Co-operative Living (with electricity:) www.co-opliving.com/ .
- The Co-operative Grocer Network (North America) : www.cooperativegrocer.coop/ .
- The Co-operative Enterprise Hub: www.co-operative.coop/enterprisehub/ .
- Global Co-operative News Hub: www.thenews.coop/content/about-global-news-hub .
- Credit Union Journal: www.cujournal.com/ .
- The Credit Union Magazine: www.creditunionmagazine.com/ .
- CCA Cinema : www.ccacinema.coopscanada.coop/ .

CCA publications including Co-op News Briefs, International Dispatches, Internal Development Digest, and Governance Matters: www.coopscanada.coop/en/info_resources/Publications . Also from CCA: www.coopscanada.coop/en/international_dev/stories/year-in-review .

Printed and ePub Books

Capital and the Debt Trap: Learning from Cooperatives in the Global Crisis - Claudia by Sanchez Bajo and Bruno Roelants, Palgrave MacMillian, 2011.

The Enigma of Capital and the Crises of Capitalism - David Harvey, Oxford University Press, 2010.

Humanizing the Economy: Co-operatives in the Age of Capital - John Restakis, New Society Publishers, 2010.

The Nature of Co-operation - John G. Craig, Black Rose, 1993.

Integrating Diversities within a Complex Heritage: Essays in the Field of Co-operative Studies. (available as a free e-book from the Centre for Co-operative and Community Based Enterprise,

University of Victoria – look under "Ian MacPherson" in "Member Research" list) - Ian MacPherson and Erin McLaughlin-Jenkins, eds., Victoria: University of Victoria, 2008.

Mutual Aid: A Factor of Evolution - Peter Kropotkin, in paperback and epub from Amazon, 1902.

Co-operative Games and Exercises

- Co-opoly: The Game of Co-operatives. Good reviews: Details here: www.store.toolboxfored.org/co-opoly-the-game-of-co-operatives/ .
- If you would like to purchase a fun co-operative game such as Search and Rescue you may wish to check this seller's board game. Wares for all ages: www.ecochoices.com/ecotoytown/games/ .
- If you wish to experiment with co-operative games you can check out two free games from www.youngco-operatives.coop/Resources. The first is called Footfall is a Facebook and iOS game which teaches financial literacy to persons aged 14-19. The second is called Co-opville and teaches co-operative principles and values in a business setting and is intended for persons aged 10-16.

More Links to Co-operative Sources and Resources

- International Co-operative Alliance: www.ica.coop/ .
- Co-operative blogs: www.coopscanada.coop/en/info_resources/CoopBlogs .
- The Co-operative College in the UK: www.co-op.ac.uk/about/ .
- Canadian Co-operative Research Network (CCRN): www.ccrnrcrc.wordpress.com/ .
- Registering /searching a co-operative domain: www.domains.coop/whycoop/directory/ .
- Peter Davis on Co-operatives & Corporatism Parts 1, 2, 3 & 4: Use: www.youtube.com/ and search for "Peter Davis". We suggest watching all 4 parts.
- National Co-operative Union of India: www.ncui.coop/welcome.html and Indian Co-operative Movement at a glance: www.ncui.coop/profile.html.
- All-China Federation of Supply and Marketing Co-operatives (ACFSMC): www.chinacoop.coop/English/Focus%20on%20China%20Co-ops/ .
- Co-operatives and Mutuals in Argentina; three extensive publications of c-operative statistics are available here: www.inaes.gob.ar/es/ . You will need to search for "noticias.asp?id=851" to find all 3 reports plus an update.
- Uganda Co-operative Alliance: www.uca.co.ug/ .
- Tanzania's Moshi University College of Co-operative and Business Studies: www.muccobs.ac.tz/ .
- Malawi Union of Savings and Credit Cooperatives: www.muscco.org/ .

- Ghana Co-operative Credit Association: www.cuagh.com/ .
- Brazil and Co-operatives: www.thenews.coop/ and do a search for "brazil co-operatives".
- Japan's Co-operative Sector: www.jccu.coop/eng/aboutus/coopsjapan.php .

Social Media and Co-operatives

- Your Co-operative Needs Social Media: www.ect.coop/ and search for "Your co-op needs social media".
- What's Right for Your Co-op: www.store.toolboxfored.org/how-to-use-social-media-for-your-co-op/ .
- The Co-operative on Facebook: www.facebook.com/TheCooperative?v=info .
- Credit Unions and Social Media: www.cutimes.com and search for "credit unions ride social media".
- One of the best sources for numerous co-operative discussion groups on the web can be found at: www.linkedIn.com .

Another new initiative out of Ireland involves the creation of "ICCO" which is conceived and promoted by VoxWorld.Coop as an independent, member-controlled International Community Cooperative Organisation (ICCO) for operation under the new European Cooperative Society (SCE) format from its social innovation hub in Ireland. It aims to achieve this through harnessing the latent power of Third Sector Organisations worldwide through a collaborative initiative with Cooperatives organisations for the primary benefits of their coping classes. ICCO is an entity born of and for the digital era, whose ambitious goals include the co-creation of "Community VOX" social brands for distribution through a network of retail outlets to generate and sustain new livelihood opportunities among participating organisations and their memberships. These innovative social brands expect to play a pivotal role in the alleviation and ultimate elimination of poverty among participating communities. You can learn more at this link: www.voxworld.coop .

Say hello to www.cooperateUSA.coop/ your link to socially responsible living. At this site sponsored by the NCBA, you can download this powerful app which helps you find co-operatives anywhere, anytime—in your local community or across the US.

The Top Level Domain Name ".coop"

.coop is an email and web address sponsored top-level domain (TLD). It is intended for the use of cooperatives, wholly owned subsidiaries, and other organizations that exist to promote or support co-operatives. dotCoop is the sole registry responsible for the TLD operation, including the enforcement of registration requirements. Eligibility is verified through co-operatives references and verifiable materials provided by registrants. If you need further information about dotCoop, please contact the registry on support@nic.coop.

In order for any domain to be registered, the registration must be processed by a registrar. The largest registrar of .coop domains is Domains.coop. They deal primarily with the .coop domain and handle the major portion of all .coop domain name sales.

Global Co-operative Development Group Inc.

The Global Co-operative Development Group was created as a non-profit co-operative in the summer of 2011 to globally:

- Help create awareness, understanding, and appreciation of the unique aspects of the co-operative enterprise business model,

- Provide a space for co-operative practitioners, researchers, and educators to contribute their experience and expertise to advance the development of co-operative enterprise globally,

- Promote co-operative enterprise development through research, evaluation, and demonstration initiatives.

After slightly more than two years effort by three co-operators we are pleased to bring you this first edition of Co-operative Enterprise: Building a Better World publication. We welcome your responses via our website at: www.co-operativeenterprise.coop.

Co-operative Friends and Supporters

It is simply not possible to acknowledge all of the different people who in many different ways and from many different places helped to create this publication. There are too many. While three of us did much of the information gathering, drafting and organizing of content, the list of those supporting our effort is too long to include in full. Accordingly we apologize in advance because in acknowledging some we will unwittingly miss others. We will in any case do our best to include all who have provided suggestions, continuing interest, feedback, materials, moral support, editing, and even a few who actively supported the concept of this publication, but who were not otherwise in a position to be involved.

Andrea Levin – Argentina
David Sutherland - Canada
Emmauel Darko - Ghana

John (Jack) Craig – Canada (key contributor – see bio)
John Jordan – Canada (key contributor – see bio)
Joy Emmanuel – Canada (copy editor)

Gary Seveny – Canada
Greg O'Neill - Canada
Gretchen Hacquard - Switzerland
Hagen Henry - Finland
Hazel Corcoran - Canada
Jim Lowe- Canada
Joan MacDonald - Canada
Jo-Anne Ferguson - Canada

Leonard Msemakweli - Uganda
Lou Hammond Ketilson - Canada
Margaret Lund - USA
Murray Gardiner - Canada
Richard O'Farrel - Ireland
Sudha K - India
Suleman Chambo - Tanzania
Sylvester Kadzola – Malawi

Thanks to all for word and deed! Thank you too, to our many family members and friends who put up with our efforts over for what is now more than two years.

Post Script to Co-operative Enterprise

The three of us took on the task of creating this publication because we wanted more people to learn more about co-operative enterprises globally and to see the benefits they provide. We wanted to inform and to challenge co-operative leaders and thinkers concerning the opportunities before them. Plus we wanted people everywhere to see co-operative enterprise as something distinct from any other form of enterprise. It is up to readers like you to tell us if we have succeeded in achieving these goals.

Gathering and assembling the content and sorting out the concepts for this publication has taken the three of us more than two years. The project has been done entirely via numerous Skype calls and email exchanges. While it has required some serious effort, it has been a lot of fun. It certainly has been a privilege and a pleasure working with Ian MacPherson and Greg Wallace. Thank you both!

A number of other people have helped to make this publication possible. I wish to extend my thanks to all of those people who help by providing ideas and content. I also wish to thank those people who helped us with their encouragement and support for our efforts.

Terry MacDonald

For my part I have enjoyed the experience immensely and have learned much. After 40 or so years of being employed and otherwise involved with credit unions, I thought I had a fairly good understanding of the scope, depth, and breadth of the co-operative system and movement both locally and globally. Research for this book, however, allowed me a whole new insight into just how extensively co-operative forms of enterprise have developed. Co-operative Enterprise is without doubt a proven model of human organization. It is a model that is generating positive and sustainable outcomes (economically and socially) in communities around the globe.

While much has been done, there are still a variety of development challenges everywhere which co-operative enterprises may serve to address. Some argue that co-operatives are one of the few truly equitable and sustainable models of enterprise. I tend to agree.

Reading this book should help novice co-operators and veterans alike in developing perspective as to how significant co-operatives have become and how vital it is that we understand their unique dynamics if we are to leverage this success as a much needed means of moving forward. A safe and equitable world is not an entitlement; it is an opportunity. A strong and active co-operative sector has been and can continue to be a significant factor in realizing this opportunity. Our future truly is ours to create.

Greg Wallace

It is somewhat sobering (not to say frightening) to realize that the three people most responsible for this volume have, among them, some 150 years of experience with co-operatives of many kinds in many contexts. And yet, as we explored the issues we discuss here, we quickly appreciated that each of us still had much to learn from each other -- and from many others we have known, read and contacted.

The exchange of drafts and the frequent Skype conversations reminded me particularly of those conversations that went long into the night when the world was younger and the big issues were being discussed by fresh minds in a college town. The difference was that the understandings came not from what we imagined might be but rather from realistically appreciating how much more could yet come from what we think we have seen.

The best we can hope for our readers is that they can experience some of that same sense of enquiry, new insights, and increased understanding: the recognition that the co-operative world, in form, thought, and possibility, is truly a world without end, a point of vital importance for the times in which we live.

Ian MacPherson

Biographies

Biography of Terry MacDonald (co-author)

Terry MacDonald, currently a Managing Director of the Global Co-operative Development Group Inc., began his co-operative career in a credit union as a teller. Since that time he has held a variety of positions within the Canadian credit union system ranging from Head of Research for Credit Union Central of Saskatchewan, to General Manager of CULease Financial, a national Canadian credit union system leasing business which he helped to create, to Africa Region Director for the Canadian Co-operative Association. He has previously served as a director of ACE Credit Union and the chairperson of their credit committee. He is currently a member of five co-operative organizations. He has served on international co-operative development projects in China, Ecuador, Ghana, Malawi, Mongolia, Philippines, Rwanda, Sierra Leone, Tanzania and Uganda. His interests include general systems theory, flying (a former pilot), all forms of information technology including social media, theology, and co-operative management theory and practice. He completed a Master's Degree in Environmental Studies at York University in Toronto Canada where his research work focused on leadership and management effectiveness in co-operatives. Terry is an active Rotarian and has served as club administrator with his local club.

Biography of Gregory Wallace (co-author)

Gregory Wallace ("Greg") has served within and across the credit union and co-operative systems in Canada and internationally for more than 40 years. His career has taken him from managing a local credit union to serving as the Chief Financial Officer of a 15 billion dollar national financial co-operative. He has served on numerous second-tier co-operative boards and committees across Canada. Greg's co-operative management expertise and experience are both broad and deep. He has led and helped to lead various innovative co-operative start-up enterprises which have involved organizations such as Concentra Financial, CUCorp Financial, CULease Financial, and CUETS (Credit Union Electronic Transaction Services). Greg's career has included a position in enterprise risk management with the Credit Union Deposit Guarantee Corporation of Ontario, service as the Director of Public and Government Affairs with Credit Union Central of Saskatchewan, as well as Chief Financial Officer for the Credit Union Central of Saskatchewan, and later Chief Financial Officer and then Chief Operating Officer of Concentra Financial, which is a national co-operative services organization. Greg has served internationally in co-operative development technical project roles in Central America and in Africa. Whenever Greg is not working part-time on credit union projects, he is busy managing a small real estate development project, while at the same time building himself and his wife a new home.

Biography of Ian MacPherson (co-author)

Ian MacPherson, Professor Emeritus of History, is a former Department Chair, Dean of Humanities, and Director of the British Columbia Institute for Co-operative Studies at the University of Victoria. He has written, edited, and co-edited twenty books as well as some 150 articles. He has presented over 300 papers at numerous conferences in many countries. Most of his work has been concerned with the

Canadian and international co-operative movements and with Co-operative Studies as a distinct field of enquiry. An elected co-operative official for over forty years, he has received several awards from the provincial, national, and international co-operative movement. He chaired the process and wrote the documents whereby the International Co-operative Alliance developed an Identity Statement for the Twenty-First Century at its Manchester Congress, 1995. He served as Principle Investigator for the National Hub of the Canadian Social Economy Partnerships, a $13,000,000 eight year project funded by the Social Science and Humanities Research Council. He is currently director of the Co-operative Initiative for Peace and Social Inclusion at the University of Victoria.

Biography of John ("Jack") G. Craig (key contributor)

After the end of a brief farming career Jack was a Public Relations Officer with the Co-operative Union of Saskatchewan. Following this he then completed his BA at the University of Saskatchewan while working with the Co-operative College of Canada as an instructor. He completed an MA and PhD at the University of Washington in Seattle with theses on the democratic control systems of the Saskatchewan Wheat Pool and of The Credit Union Central of Saskatchewan. As a Professor at York University in Toronto teaching Sociology and Environment Studies from 1971 to 2001, Jack was involved in co-operative and environmental projects in Canada, Tanzania, Indonesia, Europe and Japan. He has authored numerous journal articles and books on Multinational Co-operatives, The Nature of Co-operation, and with others Making Membership Meaningful, and Patterns and Trends of Canadian Co-operative Development.

Biography of John E. Jordan (key contributor)

John E. Jordan's life-changing initial encounter with co-operatives was as a graduate student in Toronto in the mid-1960s. He spent the rest of his career in executive roles in housing, insurance, and worker co-operatives, including providing technical assistance to co-operatives in developing countries. For almost a decade he taught in a graduate program at York University in Toronto – an expression of his unresolved need to oscillate between the vita activa and the vita contemplativa. His publications have primarily been on co-operative organizational theory and innovation. Much of the second chapter in this publication is based upon the earlier work done by him. In his dotage, he returned to graduate school, this time in history, and is researching the distinctive legal dimensions of early modern co-operatives and similar enterprises.

Index

A Contingency Theory of Management Effectiveness in Co-operatives, 65
A Co-operative Dilemma: Converting Organizational Form, 151
A group of activities constitute a function, 73
Accountable to the members, 43
Adam Smith, 9
Adoption of co-operative principles and values, 38
Afghanistan, 126
African Confederation of Co-operatives Savings and Credit Associations (ACCOSCA), 127
Aga Nkusi, 162
Alan Greenspan, 156
Allocation of earnings, 37
Amul, 29
An Inquiry Into the Nature and Causes of the Wealth of Nations. See Adam Smith
and John Maynard Keynes, 157
Anders Wijkman, 159
Argentina, 108, 115
Automatic co-operation. See Types of Co-operation
Autonomous association of persons, 39
Autonomy and independence. See Principles
Avenues co-operative care for community, 111
Bangladesh, 108
Bankrupting Nature - Global Risks and Pathways to Global Sustainability, 159
Barak Obama, 156
Barriers to entry, 104
Battle of Ideas, 155
Belgium, 105
Benkler's Boost. See Yochai Benkler
Beware Also Means Be Aware, 151
Bicycle and car sharing co-operatives, 38
Biggest problem in the world, 160
Biofuels co-operatives, 38
Blueprint for a Co-operative Decade, 167
Board, management, employee and member education, 142
Bolivia, 105, 114, 115
Branding and brand promise, 142
Brazil, 105
Broader purposes or on the interests of the members, 25
Building a better world, 163
Building Financial Strength, 145
Business factors comparison, 37
Business functions and metrics, 38
Business school logic, 65
Canada, 114, 150
Canadian farmers, 41
Canadian International Development Agency (CIDA), 120
Carbon based fuels, 159
Caring for others. See values
Change agents locally and nationally, 116
Characteristics of social movements, 19
Charles Darwin, 3
Clear definition of board-management roles and responsibilities, 145
Clear roles and responsibilities, 66
Collective good thinking of the board and management, 78
Collision course with nature, 159
Colombia, 105, 108, 115
COMAPI, 32
Communities of support, 76
Community development defined, 111
Competition, 9
Competition as the opposite of co-operation. See flawed analysis
Competition of ideas, 9
Concern for community. See Principles, See Principles
Concern for community principle, 111
Concerns can easily be raised, 43
Conditions for contractual co-operation, 14
Confidentiality respecting a particular member's dealings, 43
Conflict, 9, 10
Conflict defined, 10
Consider joining our co-operative, 179
Consumer Co-operatives Worldwide (CCW), 90
Consumer-owned co-operatives, 86
Continued strong, informed, experienced and committed co-operative leadership, 176
Continuity, 78
Contractual co-operation. See Types of co-operation
Control structure, 37

INDEX

Converted to investor owned enterprises, 151
Cookie cutter legislative frameworks and regulations, 126
Co-operation. *See* Co-operation defined
Co-operation among co-operatives, 172, *See* Principles
Co-operation amongst co-operatives, 72
Co-operation as a social movement, 19
Co-operation defined, 3
Co-operation Triumphs Over Self-Interest. *See* Yochai Benkler
Co-operativa de Servicios Publicos Santa Cruz Limitada, 114
Co-operativa Obrera Ltda. de Consumo y Vivienda, 108
Co-operative agents, 117
Co-operative and collaborative examples, 11
Cooperative Bank of Kenya, 28
Co-operative College, 119
Co-operative development, 85
Co-operative development defined, 111
co-operative education functions, 71
Co-operative enterprise, 160
Co-operative enterprise business model, 35
Co-operative enterprise sustainability, 75
Co-operative Identity. *See* Statement on the Co-operative Identity
Co-operative law in development settings, 126
Co-operative leadership, 65, 80
Co-operative leadership is a shared responsibility, 66
Co-operative legislators, administrators or regulators, 133
Co-operative movement, 17
Co-operative News, 92
Co-operative or collective ownership. *See* ownership and control of assets
Co-operative organizations and co-operative leaders may duplicate efforts, 173
Co-operative ownership and control of financial resources, 109
Co-operative principles and values, 38
Co-operative relations, 7
Co-operative sector compared to other sectors, 53
Co-operative spirit, 6
Co-operative structures, 87
Co-operative system, 17
Co-operative systems are guided by ideals, 22
Co-operative systems of enterprise, 21
Co-operative taxation considerations, 133
Co-operative Trust Schools, 114
Co-operatives and community development, 111
Co-operatives and Poverty Reduction, 116
Co-operatives and the global economy, 99
Co-operatives and wealth creation, 104
Co-operatives are not a quick fix, 121
Co-operatives are significant economic actors, 105
Co-operatives can and do fail, 141
Co-operatives can create particular benefits, 43
Co-operatives create and maintain employment, 115
Co-operatives for everyone, 87
Co-operatives in Western Settings, 129
Co-operatives remain non-partisan, 131
Corruption, 159
Cost of credit disclosure, 43
Create and retain local jobs, 44
Creating communities of support, 142
Crédit Agricole, 30
Credit union system, 21
Cuba, 126
Cyprus, 105, 158
Dairy Co-operatives of Gujarat. AMUL, 107
DamDam Haiti- Women's Handicraft Cooperative in Léogâne, Haiti. *See* Womens co-operatives
Daniel Yergin, 155
Decision-making, 37
Declares 2012 the International Year of Co-operatives, 46
Definition. *See* Statement on the Co-operative Identity
Deir Bzei Women's Cooperative of Deir Bzei, Palestine. *See* Womens co-operatives
Democracy. *See* Statement on the Co-operative Identity
democratic control and governance functions, 71
Democratic dimension of co-operatives, 43
Democratic governance / transparency, 143
Democratic member control. *See* Principles
Democratically-controlled enterprise, 39
Demutualization, 42, 151

Denmark, 105, 130
Department for International Development (DFID), 120
Designing for co-operation. *See* Yochai Benkler
Desjardins Group, 28
Desmond Morris, 5
Deutsche Gesellschaft für Technische Zusammenarbeit (GTZ), 120
Développement international Desjardins(DID), 118
Different allocation of earnings, 36
Different control structure, 36
Different Purpose, 35
Dimensions of reality, 25
Directed co-operation. *See* Types of co-operation
Discontinuity, 78
Distribution of profits after reserves (surplus). *See* Organizational dynamics
Distribution of profits after reserves (Surplus), 53
Durbar Mahila Samanwaya Collective. *See* Womens co-operatives
Eastern Europe and in parts of Africa, the survival rates, 150
Education, training and information. *See* Principles
Elevate participation, 167
Elinor Ostrom, 160
Emmauel Darko, 116
Employee involvements in service delivery and in ensuring service quality, 144
Employees provide service to, 53
Employees provide services to. *See* Organizational dynamics
Ensure operational efficiency, 73
Ensure supportive legal frameworks for co-operative growth, 170
Ensuring operational efficiency, 78, 150
Enterprise Growth, 146
Equality. *See* Statement on the Co-operative Identity
Equality and empowerment, 44
Equitable reward system and treatment of all employees, 144
Equity. *See* Statement on the Co-operative Identity
Equity capital, 146

Ethical standards and behavior / social responsibility, 144
Euro - under pressure, 158
European Association of Co-operative Banks (EACB), 92
European Research Institute on Co-operative and Social Enterprises (Euricse), 91
European Union, 156
Evergreen Co-operatives of Cleveland, Ohio, 113
Examples of business functions, 71
Extreme water shortages, 159
Factors needed for contractual co-operation. *See* Contractual co-operation
factors that contribute to co-operation, 12
Factors that contribute to co-operation, 12, *See* Yochai Benkler
Fairtrade, 116
Federated Co-operatives, 104
Fighting poverty, 116
Fighting poverty and creating wealth, 116
Financial Liability, 37
Financial strength, 76
Finland, 105
First arena is the private sector. *See* Ownership and control of assets
First list of principles in 1937, 38
Flawed analysis, 9
Fledgling co-operative movement, 127
Focus, 37
Four domains of co-operative management, 78
France, 105, 115, 158
Friedrich August von Hayek, 156
Friedrich Hayek, 157
Fundamentally different, 65
Futures orientation of movements, 23
Gender diversity, 45
Generate co-operative effort, 71
Generating co-operative effort, 78
Germany, 108, 115, 158
Ghana, 127
Global Co-operative Development Group, 93
Global ownership and the control of assets, 50
Global warming, 159
Globalization, 155
Good governance and stewardship, 145
Good legislation is important to co-operatives, 134

INDEX

Governance and control. *See* Organizational dynamics
Governance and control, 53
Governance, structure, and strategy, 178
Governments legitimize certain behaviors and beliefs, 123
Greece, 158
Greedy managers and leaders, 151
Green energy, 38
Gregory Batson, 159
Groups or Agencies Supporting Co-operative Development, 120
Gujarat Co-operative Milk Marketing Federation Ltd. *See* Amul
Hagen Henry, 124
Harmonizing co-operative legal frameworks, 130
Herbert Spencer, 3
Holding a love in or a group hug, 38
Honesty. *See* values
How co-operatives create value, 42
Human governance systems, 159
Hungary, 105
Hybrid cooperatives and multi-stakeholder co-operatives, 87
ICA Blueprint for the Coming Decade, 136
ICA Housing, 91
Ideal form of enterprise, 162
Ideas for building a better world, 163
Ideas for co-operative for building a better world, 163
Importance of purpose in a co-operative, 40
Improved efficiency, 159
In Canada, 115
In India, 108
In Ireland, the Irish Credit Union League Foundation (ICUL Foundation), 119
Income Tax, 37
Indian Farmers Fertiliser Cooperative Limited (IFFCO), 101
Indian Farmers Fertilizer Co-operative (IFFCO), 107
Individual or personal ownership. *See* Ownership and control of assets
Individuals wanting insurance services in Kenya, Canada and in the Philippines, 41
Indonesia, 115
Informing and Involving people, 176
Initiate and lead a discussion group, 179
Inspiring to visiting co-operators, 26
Institute for the Promotion of Peace and Social Cohesion, 46
Intangible or difficult to quantify benefits, 42
Integrated systems of enterprise, 26
International Co-operative Alliance,, 21
International Cooperative and Mutual Insurance Federation (ICMIF), 89
International Co-operative Fisheries Organisation (IFCO), 91
International co-operatives, 88
International Credit Union Regulators Network, 127
International Health Co-operative Organisation (IHCO), 90
International Labor Organization (ILO) Recommendation No. 193, 124
International Labour Organization (ILO), 120
International Organisation of Industrial, Artisanal and Service Producers' Cooperatives (CICOPA), 90
International Raiffeisen Union (IRU), 92
Investor orientation, 35
Investors, 158
Invisible hand, 156
Iran, 105, 115, 126
Ireland, 158
Issues or concerns addressed, 43
Italy, 115
Japan, 106, 108, 115
Job growth statistics, 158
Johan Rockström, 159
John G. Craig (Also known as Jack Craig), 7
John Jordan, 18
John Raulston Saul, 124, 157
Joining together, 104
Jorge Sousa, 151
Joseph Stanislaw, 155
Kenya, 106, 115, 127
Keys to co-operative success, 117
Korea, 106
Kuwait, 106
La Riojana Co-operative, 108
Land O' Lakes, 28
Large capital reserve, 151
Large value funds transfer facilities, 159
Latvia, 106

INDEX

Lead a major longer term study group or research project or task force, 179
Leadership and Management Effectiveness, 65
Leadership and management of co-operatives. *See* Women's Co-operatives
Learning from other co-operatives, 142
Legislation for second / third tier co-operatives, 130
Likeable business, 76
Liquidity (working capital), 146
Local co-operatives, 87
Malawi, 127
Managed community, government and political relationships, 142
Management effectiveness, 80
Management of aspirations, 54, *See* Organizational dynamics
Management of assets, 54, *See* Organizational dynamics
Management of decision making, 53
Management of decision making. *See* Organizational Dynamics
Management of information, 54, *See* Organizational dynamics
Managing the co-operative difference, 65
Many different types of co-operative structures, 132
Margaret Thatcher, 156
Market behavior (competition), 123
Market losses shifted from shareholders to tax payers, 158
Mauritius, 106
Member economic participation. *See* Principles
Member ownership, involvement and education / use of social media, 143
Member participation functions, 71
Member- versus- investor orientation, 35
Members versus memberships, 99
Microfinance services, 116
Might there be a good fit... for You. *See* Might there be good fit?
Might there be a good fit?, 66
Milt Friedman, 157
Mind the Gap, 67
Moldova, 106
Moments of choice', 155
Mondragon Co-operative Group, 101
Mondragon Corporation, 29, 113
Money and banking, 177
Money remains in the community, 44
Moral compass, 12
Movements and systems, 23
Movements defined, 18
Mozilla's FireFox internet browser, 11
Muddle, 159
Multi-stakeholder co-operatives, 26
Mutual Aid
   A Factor of Evolution. *See* Peter Kropotkin
Mutual Aid: A Factor of Evolution. *See* Peter Kropotkin
Mutual goals. *See* Superordinate goal
Mutual-aid, 4
Mutuals and co-operatives, 87
myth of self-interest. *See* Yochai Benkler
National parliamentarians, legislators and policy-makers, 136
Natural tension, 76
nature of co-operatives and of their requirements, 116
Nature of human needs, 24
Needs and wants, 67
Negative effects of globalization, 124
New business structures and mechanisms, 175
New participative processes and mechanisms, 176
New Zealand, 106
Next decade, 136
Non-aligned politically, 131
Norway, 106
Occupy Movement, 158
Open and ongoing communication within the organization and externally, 144
Open memberships: non-partisan, non-racial, non-discriminating, 145
Openness. *See* values
Openness and transparency, 43
Operating philosophies, 35
Operational efficiency, 13
Orange growers, 68
Organization for Economic Co-operation and Development (OECD), 124
Organizational dynamics, 49, 53
Outcomes every co-operative enterprise needs, 76, *See* Financial Strength; Communities of Support

INDEX

Outdated ideas of growth, wealth creation and trade expansion, 157
Overseas Cooperative Development Council (OCDC), 118
Ownership, 37, 53
Ownership and the control of assets' does indeed make the world go around, 50
Ownership \t, 54
Ozone depletions, 159
Part of the mainstream, 25
Partnerships have developed between co-operatives, 116
Patronage rewards and community support projects when practical, 144
Pay various taxes, 44
Peace making process, 46
People's movements, 17
Personal and party political dynamics, 124
Personal commitment and leadership by elected officials and management, 142
Peter Kropotkin, 4
Planning and participation, 54, *See* Organizational dynamics
Poland, 106
Portugal, 106, 150
Preliminary indicators of the extent of interdependence, 22
Principles, 39
Priority of the co-operative, 35
Producer-owned co-operatives, 86
Profitability, 146
Pro-party practices or positions, 130
Pseudo cooperatives, 141
Public debt, 157
Public ownership and control.. *See* Ownership and control of assets
Public sector and the private sector, 157
Public, private, and co-operative sectors, 49
Purchasing/Shared services co-operatives, 86
Purpose, 37
Pursue collective ideals, 74
Pursuing collective ideals, 78
Pursuit of peace, 45
Quality of life, 35
Rabobank, 104
RaboBank Group, 26
Rapid rise in CO_2 N_2O and CH_4 concentrations, 159

Rationale for decision making, 53, *See* Organizational dynamics
Reasons co-operative fail, 141
Reasons why people still co-operate, 12
Research education and demonstration, 177
Resilience of the Co-operative Business Model in Times of Crisis, 60
Return on Investment, 37
Risk Exposure, 146
Roger Herman, 151
Ronald Reagan, 156
Royal Norwegian Society for Development (Norges Vel), 120
Saskatchewan Wheat Pool, 41
Satisfy member needs, 70
Satisfying member need, 150
Satisfying member needs, 78
Satisfying member's needs, 35
Scotland, 107
Second and third tier co-operatives, 52
Second tier co-operatives, 88
Secure reliable co-operative capital while guaranteeing member control, 171
self-help. *See* Statement on the Co-operative Identity
Self-help attitudes together with an appreciation of mutual interests, 144
Self-help', 68
Selfishness of mankind, 10
Selfishness of the individual, 10
Self-responsibility. *See* Statement on the Co-operative Identity
Sex Trade Workers Co-operative, 45
Shared future vision for co-operatives, 164
Significant commitment of financial, technical, and human resources, 175
Significant research and development, 175
Singapore, 107
Slovakia, 115
Slovenia, 107
Small traders in the Philippines and in Ecuador, 41
So What Is A Muddle?, 158
Social and power relations, 6
Social responsibility. *See* values
Solidarity. *See* Statement on the Co-operative Identity

Solution to the world's problems involved lessening the role of governments, 156
Some Intangible Benefits, 47
Some next steps, 179
Some reasons co-operative fail, 150
Some tangible benefits, 47
Songtaab-Yalgré Association in Ouagadougou, Burkina Faso. *See* Womens co-operatives
Sources of funds. *See* Organizational dynamics
Spain, 158
Species extinctions, 159
Specific circumstances or approaches can invite failure:, 128
Spontaneous co-operation. *See* Types of co-operation
Starting Co-operatives for the Right Reasons, 141
Statement of identity in many languages, 40
Statement on the Co-operative Identity, 39
Stock companisation of co-operatives, 124
Strategic focus areas, 175
Strategies and tactics for building financial strength, 147
Strategies and tactics for success, 141
Strengthening the local economy, 44
Success ratio for co-operatives, 150
Successes Far Outweigh Failures, 150
Successful co-operatives need, 116
Sunkis, 69
Support across the system for ongoing co-operative development, 143
Survival rates of co-operatives, 41
sustainability. *See* Co-operative enterprise sustainability
Sweden, 107
Switzerland, 109
Systems are composed of interdependent parts, 22
Systems defined, 18
Systems forward orientation, 23
Systems of enterprise, 26
Take Aways, 15, 32, 48, 81, 102, 121, 137, 152, 164, 180
Taking an "interest" in "member interests" to better understand unsatisfied needs, 143
the Canadian Co-operative Association (CCA), 118
The Collapse of Globalism, 124
The Collapse of Globalization), 157
The Commanding Heights: The Battle for the World Economy., 155
The Co-operative Commonwealth Federation or CCF party, 130
The Co-operative Group, 28
The Co-operative Party, 130
The co-operative value proposition, 35
The International Association of Co-operative Banks (CIBP), 92
The International Co-operative Alliance (ICA), 89
The International Co-operative Banking Association (ICBA), 89
the International Monetary Fund (IMF), 124
The Naked Ape. *See* Desmond Morris
The National Co-operative Business Association (NCBA), 118
The need for co-operative leaders to be knoweldgeable, 70
The Penguin and the Leviathan: How Co-operation Triumphs Over Self-Interest. *See* Yochai Benkler
The Swedish Cooperative Centre (SCC), 121
The Theory of Moral Sentiments. *See* Adam Smith
The World Council of Credit Unions (WOCCU), 92
Theories of management, 71
Theory of Natural Selection, 4
Theory of Natural Selection, 3
Thinking Outside of the Box, 176
Third sector, 41
Third tier co-operatives, 88
Three key questions, 172
Tipping points, 159
To Tax or Not to Tax, 132
Too big to fail, 156
Traditional co-operation. *See* Types of co-operation
Types of conflict. *See* Conflict defined
Types of co-operation, 7
Types of co-operatives, 85
Uganda, 126
UK's Co-operative College, 114
United Kingdom, 107, 150
United Nations website on co-operatives, 46
United States, 107, 108

INDEX

United States Agency for International Development (USAID), 120
United States Federal Reserve, 156
United voluntarily, 39
Universal selfishness. *See* Yochai Benkler
Unreported wealth'. *See* Ownership and control of assets
Unwillingness of banks, 41
Uruguay, 107
US National Co-operative Bank, 101
Values, 37, 39, *See* Statement on the Co-operative Identity
Vietnam, 107, 126
Voluntary and open membership. *See* principles
Weakness in banking intuitions, 157
Wealth creation and wealth distributions systems, 158
Wealth, capital or assets, 50
What co-operative leaders must do, 70
What is best for the members and for the co-operative, 78
Why less emphasis on education, training and information, 174
Women's Co-operative Bank in Goa, India. *See* Womens co-operatives
Women's Co-operative Guild in Sheffield, England. *See* Womens co-operatives
Women's co-operatives, 44
Womens Co-operative Bank in Larnaka, Cyprus. *See* Womens co-operatives
Worker-owned co-operatives, 86
Workers in Argentina, 41
Working together within defined communities towards a shared vision, 142
World Bank, 124
World Council of Credit Unions, 21
World Trade Organization, 155
World-wide opportunities, 167
Yochai Benkler, 11
Your ideology was not right, 156
ZEN-NOH, 31
Zimbabwe, 126

Notes

Interviews with selected contributors and supporters are generally not included in notes.

Spelling of the word "co-operative" is always hyphenated, unless it is part of a corporate name. We endeavor not to use the word 'co-op' or 'coop' and again as a matter of style have chosen to use the full English spelling of 'co-operative' as is used in Canada. Other spelling is Canadian as well. In some cases we may deliberately omit the hyphen as might be the case when including a direct quotation. All dollar amounts in the book unless otherwise noted are in US currency. In some cases when there are multiple sources in a paragraph, we use one super-script note number at the end of the paragraph instead of numbering each source. In this notes section, sources are listed in the same order in which content appears in the paragraph. We have for simplicity and ease of reading deliberately avoided including page footnotes. Instead we have on occasion directed the reader to refer to these notes for further details.

Web addresses for online sources are included in the notes area. Since many web sources are transient should the link fail we direct the reader to the home page of the source. We have done our utmost to ensure all home pages used are available at time of publication. Web links and access to additional reference material can be found at www.co-operativeenterprise.coop .

Chapter 1

[1] *On the Origin of Species*, Charles Darwin by Down, Bromley, Kent, public domain, 1859, p:7.

[2] *The Principles of Biology Volume I*, Herbert Spencer by Williams and Nobgate, public domain 1864 p: 748-796.

[3] See note 1, Chapter 4 which describes the adaptiveness of a species as its basis for survival. This is emphasized in the 1859 edition but in the later five revisions this point receives less attention. These changes tend to obscure the original argument and the first edition is thus by far the clearest expression of Darwin's insight.

[4] "The individual chapters had originally been published in 1890–96 as a series of essays in the British monthly literary magazine, Nineteenth Century." You may use www.en.wikipedia.org/wiki/ and search for "A Factor of Evolution".

[5] *Mutual Aid: A Factor of Evolution*, kniaz' Petr Alekseevich Kropotkin by William Heinemann Ltd., public domain 1902.

[6] See note 5, p:196.

[7] See note 5, p:177.

[8] The book Mutual aid: A Factor of Evolution still is offered for sale at www.amazon.com and may be located at that site using the search terms "mutual aid a factor of evolution".

[9] See note 5, p:176-189.

[10] See note 5, p:3.

[11] *The Naked Ape*, Desmond Morris by McGraw Hill, 1967.

[12] See note 11, p: Preface.

[13] See note 11, p:31.

[14] See note 11, p:27-28.

[15] See note 11, p:182.

[16] See note 11, p:182.

[17] See note 11, p:5.

[18] John G. (Jack) Craig, while not an author of this publication has been an active contributor and supporter of this work.

ENDNOTES

[19] *The Nature of Co-operation*, John G Craig by Black Rose Books, 1993, p: 11.
[20] See note 19, p: 15-16.
[21] Credit unions across Canada often compete with each other for member business. At the same time, those same credit unions through their provincial and national Centrals actively work together in areas such as liquidity management, marketing, technology, and enterprise risk management.
[22] *An Inquiry Into the Nature and Causes of the Wealth of Nations*, Adam Smith by W. Strahan and T. Cadell, public domain 1776 p:364.
[23] To learn more click www.investopedia.com/ and search for "Smith invisible hand".
[24] *The Theory of Moral Sentiments*, Adam Smith by A. Millar, A. Kincaid &J. Bett, public domain 1759 p:147
[25] See note 5, p: 4-5.
[26] See note 19, p: 15.
[27] The four types of conflict as described were included in class reading materials used by John G. Craig at co-operative study classes conducted as elements of a Master program at York University 1980.
[28] *The Penguin and the Leviathan: How Cooperation Triumphs Over Self-Interest*, Yochai Benkler by Crown Business 2011.
[29] See note 28, p: 13-14.
[30] See note 28, p: 15.
[31] See note 28, p: 32-43 for a more detailed explanation.
[32] See note 28, p: 21 plus all of Chapter 6 starting at p: 119.
[33] See note 28, plus all of Chapter 9 starting at p: 202.
[34] See note 28, p: 238.
[35] See note 19, p: 116-125.

Chapter 2

[1] You can learn about the Canadian Federated Co-operative System here: www.coopconnection.ca/.
[2] To learn more about social movements click on www.en.wikipedia.org the search for "List_of_social_movements" being sure to include the three underscores as shown.
[3] Discussion Paper *Co-operative Movement, System, and Futures*, John Jordan by The Co-operative College of Canada, 1980. Various portions of this chapter have been drawn from this paper with the author's permission.
[4] See note 3, p: 5-7.
[5] See note 3, p: 6.
[6] *Each for All: A History of the Co-operative Movement in Canada 1900-1945*, with a quote from November 1910, p: 34 reported by Ian MacPherson and published by Macmillan, 1979.
[7] See note 3, p: 6.
[8] See note 3, p: 7.
[9] CUNA is the Credit Union National Association of America. The statement was made as part of a CUNA appointed committee submission to government; document is no longer accessible except upon request, and was available from www.cuna.org/. September 2012
[10] This example is from France and is of a milk producing co-operative. To learn about their co-operative please click www.laita.com/en/societe/index.php.
[11] This example is from Uganda. To read about marketing reforms and the systematic organization of marketing activities in a paper prepared by Leonard Msemakweli, General Secretary, of the Uganada Co-operative Alliance please click here www.uca.co.ug/ and from the menu click on publications and using the 2008-09 time period you will see a downloadable file called Co-operative marketing reforms in Uganda.
[12] The AMUL site describes the world's largest (in terms of members) dairy co-operative in the world. Cool site. Check it out www.amul.com/. June 2013
[13] See note 3, p: 9.
[14] See note 3, p: 10.
[15] See note 3, p: 10-11.
[16] See note 3, p: 11-12.
[17] See note 3, adapted from figure on p: 14.

[18] See note 3, p: 14.
[19] See note 3, adapted from figure on p: 15.
[20] The publication El cooperativismo de trabajo en la Argentina: contribuciones para el diálogo social, by Mirta Vuotto published in 2011 by the International Labour Organization can be found on this website www.ilo.org and elsewhere if you used Google search. The report, number 217, although it is written in Spanish, can also be ordered in print form.
[21] There is some excellent material on multi stakeholder co-operatives in Canada at this site: www.coopscanada.coops but use the search terms "Multi-Stakeholder-Co-ops" and scroll thru the list until you find the heading "Multi-Stakeholder Co-ops", then click on that link.
[22] For a quick overview of Rabobank you may use www.en.wikipedia.org/ and search for "Rabobank".
[23] For a quick overview of Desjardins you may use www.en.wikipedia.org/ and search for "Desjardins Group".
[24] For a quick overview of the Co-operative Group you may use www.en.wikipedia.org/ and search for "Co-operative Group".
[25] For a quick overview of Land of Lakes Co-operative you may use their main website which is www.landolakesinc.com/company/default.aspx .
[26] For a quick overview of the Co-operative Bank of Kenya you may use www.en.wikipedia.org/ and search for "Cooperative Bank of Kenya".
[27] For a quick overview of Amul you may use www.en.wikipedia.org/ and search for "AMUL".
[28] For a quick overview of Mondragon you may use www.en.wikipedia.org/wiki/Mondragon_Corporation and search for "Mondragon Corporation".
[29] For a quick overview of Crédit Agricole you may use www.en.wikipedia.org/ and search for "Credit Agricole".
[30] This organizational structure illustrates the extensive complexity involved in large co-operative organizations. It is included as a pdf download file taken from 'Update of the 2011 Registration document - A01 Crédit Agricole Group financial statements 2011' and was found at: www.credit-agricole.com/en/.
[31] For a quick overview of Zen-Noh you may use www.en.wikipedia.org/ and search for "Zen-Noh".
[32] For a not so quick overview of Compai you may use www.naterraworld.com/PDF/comapi.pdf . The report we refer to is entitled "The Experience of a Honey Cooperative in Northeast Brazil" and was written by Claudia Chaves and released October 2009.

Chapter 3

[1] The source from which this content has been adapted (see note 2) by us is Module #1, an instructional booklet called Basics of the Co-operative Model" and which is distributed by the Newfoundland-Labrador Federation of Co-operatives, in Canada. You can download it from this site: www.ibrd.gov.nl.ca/ and search for "basics of co-operatives model guide".
[2] See note 1, the table as shown here is an adapted version of the table as shown in Appendix A.
[3] Please see the news piece at www.worldbank.org/en/news/feature/2012/10/26/argentina-urban-solid-waste-management-best-practices and also if you have time please see this news piece although it is in Spanish www.youtube.com/watch?v=fS1ztlaPYGU&feature=plcp . It is worthwhile without language.
[4] *Third Sector: The Contribution of Nonprofit and Co-operative Enterprises in Australia*, Mark Lyons by PMI Corporation, 2001.
[5] A report by Richard Stringham and Celia Lee of the Alberta Community and Co-operative Association with the BC-Alberta Social Economy Research Alliance reported their research finding in August 2011. To see details click on www.auspace.athabascau.ca then search for "co-operative survival" to locate study results from 2011. See the survival rates of co-operatives in the province of Quebec Canada www.cultivatingfoodcoops.net/ by using the search terms "survival rate Quebec".
[6] *Cooperative Conversions, Failures and Restructurings: Case Studies from Canadian and US Agriculture*, editors Murray Fulton and Brent Hueth by Knowledge Impact in Society et al 2009, p: 1-18.
[7] Perhaps the very first conference ever held on the subject of "co-operatives and peace" was help in Canada in 2006. The conference was attended by 38 participants from Nepal, Sri Lanka, Indonesia, Japan, India, Kenya, Israel, Colombia, the UK, Finland, Germany, Italy, the US, and Canada. Learn more by clicking at www.uvic.ca and searching for "co-operatives and peace" Also see note 8 below.

[8] *Co-operatives and the Pursuit of Peace*, Joy Emmanuel and Ian MacPherson by New Rochdale Press, 2007.
[9] This was part of the message delivered in the closing address by Dr. Yehudah Paz at the Co-operatives and the Pursuit of Peace conference, held in Victoria, British Columbia, Canada, June 2006. See note 7 & 8 above.
[10] The head of the United Nations Ban Ki-moon's message to the International Co-operative Alliance Congress held in Cancun Mexico in November 2011. You can click on the www.youtube.com/ link and search for "Ban Ki-moon co-operatives".

Chapter 4

[1] *Global Wealth Report 2011* by Credit Suisse Research Institute October 2011. This report may or may not be accessible depending upon where you live. You may need to contact Credit Suisse Research Institute for a copy. The link we used is: www.infocus.credit-suisse.com/ and we used "global" and "wealth" report in our search. We obtained the report in June 2013. The report is proprietary and may not be available in all regions.
[2] To see some details of 'offshore banking' you may use this link www.shelteroffshore.com and use the search terms "Offshore Jurisdictions in Europe" for a comprehensive report on the topic. June 2013
[3] Table 7 "Organizational Dynamics – Co-operative Sector Compared to Others" and the explanations which followed have been adapted and updated from York University study notes prepared by John G. Craig 1980.
[4] To learn more about multi-stakeholder co-operatives you may wish to download a user manual entitled *Solidarity as a Business Model: A Multi-stakeholder Cooperatives Manual:* by the Cooperative Development Center @Kent State University, a program of the Ohio Employee Ownership Center. The link is: www.uwcc.wisc.edu/ and the search terms are "multistakeholder co-operatives".
[5] *Resilience of the Co-operative Business Model in Times of Crisis*, Johnston Birchall and Lou Hammond Ketilson, by International Labour Office, 2009 p: 3.
[6] See note 4, p: 23.
[7] See note 4, p: 24.
[8] See note 4, p: 24.
[9] *European Co-operative Banks in the Financial and Economic Turmoil – First Assessments*, January 2010 Research Paper by European Association of Co-operative Banks. To download it go to www.eacb.coop/ and search for the title.
[10] See note 9, p: 2.
[11] *Resilience in a Downturn: The Power of Financial Cooperatives*, Johnston Birchall, International Labour Office 2013, p:32 June 2013.
[12] See note 11 p: 32.
[13] It is difficult to obtain consistent statistics concerning co-operatives globally. They are constantly being updated. These statics some of which were antidotal were obtained from the ICA website in June of 2012 from the following link: www.ica.coop/. Since 2006 ICA has been gathering statistics on co-operatives from across the globe. In 2012 the ICA partnered with the European Research Institute on Cooperative and Social Enterprises (Euricse) to re-launch what had be the Global300 as the World co-operative Monitor. You may read or download a copy either via the ICA website as shown or www.euricse.eu/ and use the search terms "world monitor".
[14] *Global Business Ownership 2012: Members and Shareholders Across the World*, Ed Mayo, by Co-operatives UK, 2012. To obtain your copy click on www.uk.coop/ and then use the search terms "global business ownership".

Chapter 5

[1] *A Contingency Model of Management Effectiveness in Cooperatives*, Terry W MacDonald, Thesis/dissertation, York University 1982 and *Management Effectiveness in Co-operatives :A Contingency Model*, Terry W MacDonald by Co-operative College of Canada 1982. These two publications provided the foundation for a further 25 years of validation of the theoretical framework developed during the initial research project.
[2] Michel Chevalier, a professor at the Université de Montreal in the Institute d'urbanisme, and for much of the same time, a member of the faculty at Toronto's York University where he taught Environmental Studies with a focus on advancing co-operative management. His lectures and theoretical frameworks provided the foundation

upon which the contingency model of management effectiveness in co-operatives was developed. Michel Chevalier passed in 2006.

[3] There are many different groups concerned with the environment. To see the various groups who are working in various regions you may (see note following in this sentence) use this link www.econurse.org/ plus add without quotes "links1.html" after the "/". Otherwise the list we refer to is a little difficult to locate.

[4] Bill and Melinda Gates are working with Rotary International to help eradicate polio. Read all about it at www.rotary.org/en/ and search for "Time to ramp up the fight against polio "which is a June 14, 2011 story from Rotary International.

[5] Here is the Sunkist website: www.sunkist.com/about/cooperative.aspx .

[6] Story of LaFleche Credit Union, Saskatchewan can accessed by clicking on www.youtube.com/ and using the search terms "LaFleche Anniversary".

[7] To learn more about the Bihu Co-operative in China click on: www.ica.coop/en/ , then select Co-op Stories, and select China for more details.

[8] To learn more about Argentine worker co-operatives click on: www.ica.coop/en/ , then Co-op Stories, select Argentina, and then see "Argentinean workers take destiny in the own hands".

[9] For a quick overview of traditional management theory you may click on: www.cmguide.org/ and use the search terms "Management Theories: History and Practice". You will find an excellent online article written in 2008 by Samer H. Skaik.

[10] Rabobank mentions their need and the need of co-operative banks to re-invent themselves in their publication *Co-operative Banks in the New Financial system* by Rabobank Group 2009. p: 3,16,29.

[11] See note 2.

[12] To learn more about Peter Davis you may click on www2.le.ac.uk/ and use the search phrases "Peter Davis" plus "co-operative management".

[13] To learn more about John G. Craig you may use www.zoominfo.com and using their search facility enter name "John G. Craig" and title "Board Member".

[14] To read more about the Co-operative Group and their vision you may click on www.co-operative.coop/corporate/ then click the About Us menu item.

[15] To learn more about the co-operative Women's Guild you can click on www.cooperativewomensguild.coop/ then click the About menu item and select purpose.

[16] To learn more about the mission statement of the SEMO Electric Co-operative's mission statement click here: www.semoelectric.coop/ then click on Your Coop menu item and select Mission. August2013

[17] This article challenges co-operatives to consider pursuing social as well as economic purposes. *Cooperatives as the "enfants terribles" of economics: Some implications for the social economy*, first published in *The Journal of Socio-Economics* Volume 37, Issue 6, authors Yair Levi and Peter Davis by Elsevier, December 2008, Pages 2178–2188.

[18] Use www.uwcc.wisc.edu/ and search for "Co-operative Identity and Co-operative Management", for a paper by Peter Davis as part of a Report of the Special Workshop on ICA Co-operative Identity Statement - From Theory to Practice, 17-21 August, 1997 which was used in Jaipur, India, pp.32-41.

[19] *Likeable Business: Why Today's Consumers Demand More and How Leaders Can Deliver*, Dave Kerpen by McGraw Hill, 2013, p: 7-10.

[20] See note 1, p: 40.

Chapter 6

[1] To learn more about the 2012 International Year of Co-operatives click: www.un.org/en/ and search for co-operative year.

[2] To learn more about the Global Co-operative Development Group click here: www.co-operativeenteprise.coop .

[3] The ownership used by mutuals affiliated to the co-operative sector is for the mutual to be controlled by other co-operatives or member-based organizations. In Sweden, for example, Folksam, a leading insurer, is controlled jointly by the consumer cooperatives and the trade union federation. In the US, CUNA Mutual is controlled by credit unions. In France, the mutuals in GEMA (Groupement des entreprises mutuelles d'assurance) provide about half of all life, auto, and home insurance policies, and have a vibrant participatory culture. See: www.gema.fr.

ENDNOTES

[4] National Cooperative Business Association's new website is located here: www.ncba.coop/ see "About Co-ops".

[5] International Co-operative alliance web site: www.ica.coop/.

[6] The European Research Institute on Co-operative and Social Enterprises (Euricse) is located in Italy. You may access their English language website at: www.euricse.eu/en/about .

[7] The World Council of Credit Unions (WOCCU) is located in the United States. You may access their website at: www.woccu.org/ .

[8] The European Association of Co-operative Banks (EACB) website: www.cibp.eu .

[9] The European Association of Co-operative Banks (EACB) website: www.eacb.eu .

[10] The International Raiffeisen Union (IRU): www.iru.de/index.php/iru/was-ist-die-iru?lang=en .

[11] Co-operative News website: www.thenews.coop .

[12] Home of the Global Co-operative Development Group: www.co-operativeenterprise.coop .

[13] The World Co-operative Monitor- Exploring the Co-operative Economy Explorative Report 2012 can be downloaded from this website: www.monitor.coop/doc/2012/Explorative_Report_2012.pdf.

[14] See note 13, p: 7.

[15] See note 13, p: 8.

[16] See note 13, p: 9.

[17] This graphic was published by ICA as part of International Year of Co-operatives (2012 IYC) website. Various acts and figures were provided at: www.2012.coop/en/.

as of June 2012. This site is no longer accessible, and using it redirects the users address to www.ica.coop . The ICA is in an ongoing process of updating data concerning co-operatives around the world. Please see note 13 above.

[18] For further details see: www.ica.coop/en/ and click on "What's a co-op", then on Facts and Figures.

[19] *It's Our Time - Celebrating the Insurance Social Enterprise Movement Around the World* presentation materials by Edward L. Potter, CAE Executive Director, International Cooperative and Mutual Insurance Federation, American Fraternal Alliance Annual Meeting, New Orleans, Louisiana, September 8, 2012.

[20] The World Council of Credit Unions maintains and publishes historical data on credit unions across the world. You may use this site to review or download aggregated historical statistics. www.woccu.org/.

[21] See note 20.

[22] See note 20.

[23] *Global Business Ownership 2012 New Insight 9,* Ed Mayo, research report, Co-operatives UK. 2012.

[24] This website was published for the 2012 International Year of Co-operatives and may not be available in future. www.usa2012.coop/about-co-ops/cooperatives-around-world.

[25] You can read about a number of national and international co-operative expositions at this blog. To see the Manchester story look for Nov 8: www.icaexpo.blogspot.mx/ .

[26] Learn more about this one of a kind worker co-operative here: www.essential-trading.coop.

[27] *Workers United* winners story including Mondragon published by the Financial Time March 21, 2013 special report "Boldness in Business www.ft.com/intl/reports/boldness-2013.

[28] To learn more about this successful co-operative click on: www.en.wikipedia.org/ and use the search terms "Indian Farmers Fertiliser Cooperative".

[29] *NCB Coop 100 - The Secret is Out* by National Co-operative Bank 2012. Available on their website for download by clicking here: www.ncb.coop/ or from: www.coop100.coop/.

Chapter 7

[1] Mega Projects Sustain Growth By Nadine Olson, The Leader-Post August 13, 2013 Regina Saskatchewan Canada This story describes the recent 2.6 billion dollar expansion of the world's first co-operatively owned oil refinery. You may search for news using: www.leaderpost.com and searching for "Federated Co-operatives Limited" or "co-operative refinery".

[2] Rabobank has been expanding rapidly in California since 2002, growing rapidly through acquisitions and internal growth. In January 2006, Rabobank acquired Community Bank of Central California. In January 2007 it acquired Mid-State Bank & Trust. In 2010, the bank acquired Napa Community Bank. Also in 2010 it acquired the failed Butte Community Bank and Pacific State Bank.

ENDNOTES

[3] The details provided were taken from the ICA Americas website at: www.aciamericas.coop/ . Some statistics have since been updated and we suggest you click on the above link, select English language, then on COOPERATIVES and click on Facts and Figures.

[4] Source for IFFCO detail: 2011-2012 Annual Report 44, Indian Farmers Fertiliser Cooperative Limited, Oanda FX was used to estimate USD currency values. To learn more visit the website: www.iffco.nic.in/ .

[5] To learn more about India's largest dairy co-operative use: www.amul.com/m/about-us .

[6] To learn more about Argentina's consumer co-operative used: www.cooperativaobrera.coop .

[7] Learn about Argentinian wine production here: www.lariojanawines.com/english/lariojana_history.html . June 2013

[8] An Argentinian producer co-operative: www.acacoop.com.ar/acai/Index.asp .

[9] To learn about US co-operatives use: www.usa2012.coop/co-ops-in-usa/quick-facts .

[10] To learn about rural electrification in Bangladesh use: www.nrecainternational.coop/ and search for "Bangladesh".

[11] See note 9.

[12] Health care in Columbia is provided by Saludcoop. To visit their website in Spanish use: www.saludcoop.coop/ .

[13] Remarks by Mr José Manuel Salazar-Xirinachs, Executive Director, Employment Sector, ILO, at the Ministerial Breakfast on "Promoting productive capacity for sustainable livelihoods: the role of cooperatives" at ECOSOC, New York, 5 July 2012.

[14] See note 13.

[15] See note 13.

[16] See note 13.

[17] DFID Briefing Notes UKAid 2010/08, p: 9 2013. To see full report use: www.co-op.ac.uk/.

[18] Detail provided by Canadain Co-operative Association www.canada2012.coop/ .

[19] The person was Ms. Betty Bauhuis. Ms. Bauhuis still is an active credit union and co-operative leader in Saskatchewan, Canada.

[20] Cooperatives in the African American Experience, by Jessica Gordon Nembhard provided as course notes as part of a cooperative curriculum on wikispaces. p: 3. See: www.cooperative-curriculum.wikispaces.com/ .

[21] To learn more about Evergreen Co-operatives innovations see: www.evergreencooperatives.com/ June 2013

[22] Mondragon is famous. See: www.mondragon-corporation.com/language/en-US/ENG.aspx June 2013

[23] An excellent Youtube video on Mondragon and Evergreen Cooperatives. Use www.youtube.com/ and search for "shift change - putting democracy to work". The video is about 7 minutes long.

[24] To learn about a successful water co-operative in Bolivia use: www.stories.coop/ and use the search term "saguapac".

[25] For a credit union example from Saskatchewan Canada of giving back to communities you can use: www.saskcu.com/pages/Sponsorships.aspx .

[26] An innovative and co-operative approach to education: www.co-operativeschools.coop/ .

[27] ICA in the Americas www.aciamericas.coop/Co-operative-Movement-in-the-World .

[28] *The Reality of Life: How to Get Yourself Out of Poverty*, Emmanuel O. Darko by Wesley Printing 2006 p: 24, 80. Mr. Darko is the General Manager of the Ghana Co-operative Credit Unions Association (CUA) and has been involved in co-operative development in Africa for more than 30 years.

[29] Fairtrade from Co-operatives UK. Click here: www.youtube.com/ and search for "Tackling Global Poverty - The Co-operative".

[30] United Nations Economic and Social Council Distr: General submission by the International Co-operative Alliance referred to as 11 April 2012, Substantive session of 2012 New York, 2-27 July 2012
High-level segment: annual ministerial review. See P 3. You can search www.un.org/en/documents/ods/ and search for E/2012/NGO/24 in English. Note the file date shown in the site appears incorrect.

[31] See Chapter 4, notes 5 and 11.

Chapter 8

ENDNOTES

[1] *The Collapse of Globalism and the Reinvention of the World*, John Ralston Saul by Penguin Canada; 1st edition 2006 together with a 27 minute YouTube video: www.youtube.com/ which you can search for using the search terms "John Ralston Saul: The Collapse of Globalism".

[2] *Basics and New Features of Cooperative Law – The Case of Public International Cooperative Law and the Harmonisation of Cooperative Law – Uniform Law Review* Volume 17, Issue 1-2 P: 197-233 2012, Hagen Henry.

[3] *Guidelines for Cooperative Legislation*, Hagen Henry by International Labour Office, 2012 p: 1.

[4] See note 3, p: 200.

[5] To obtain a copy of this report click on: www.accosca.org/ and look under the Downloads as the Regulatory Framework Workshop 2012 report.

[6] Working Paper Number 24, 12 *New Study Group on European Cooperative Law "Principles Project"*, Euricse, Fajardo G., Fici A., Henrÿ H., Hiez D., Münkner H.-H., Snaith I. 2012.

[7] To see this news story use: www.thenews.coop/ and use search terms "Bill to bring UK legislation up to date".

[8] To learn more about the Co-operative Commonwealth Federation (CCF) you may use: www.en.wikipedia.org/ and search for the expression "Co-operative Commonwealth Federation".

[9] The Cooperative Party: Politics for the People can be accessed by clicking: www.party.coop/ .

[10] To see and download a complete copy of the *Blueprint for a Co-operative Decade - February 2013* click here: www.ica.coop/en/ and search for the title as shown.

[11] See note 10, p: 28.

Chapter 9

[1] Official Office of the President of Uganda statement announcing the program. See: www.mediacentre.go.ug/ and search for "Bonabagagawale Official Launch".

[2] Report on the Co-operative Model of Business Enterprise in Ontario: Applications, Successes and Challenges Prepared for the Ministry of Economic Development and Trade by Ontario Co-operative Association September 2008, p: 11.

[3] To see more details on co-operative survival rates in Albert and British Columbia Canada you may use: www.auspace.athabascau.ca/ and use the terms "co-operative survival".

[4] This website provides details on the survival rates of co-operatives in Canada. To see the details click: www.2012.coop/en/ and use the search expression "cooperatives build a better world for international day".

[5] You can download a full report of Plunkett's experiences in the UK by using this link: www.plunkett.co.uk/ and use the search expressions "Community owned Shops" and "A Better Form of Business".

[6] To learn about co-operatives survival in Portugal click here: *Scale, Scope and Survival: A Comparison of Cooperative and Capitalist Modes of Production* a preliminary research paper Natália Pimenta Monteiro and Geoff Stewart. July 2012. You can download a copy of the article using this link: www.econpapers.repec.org/ and the search expression "Scale, Scope and Survival: A Comparison of Cooperative and Capitalist Modes of Production".

[7] To learn about the failure of savings and loan associations you can use www.en.wikipedia.org/ and use the search terms "savings and loans crisis".

Chapter 10

[1] *The Commanding Heights: The Battle for the World Economy*, Daniel Yergin and Joseph Stanislaw by Simon & Schuster, 2002.

[2] See note 1, p: 377.

[3] See note 1, p: 382.

[4] See note 1, p: 397.

[5] See note 1, p: 397.

[6] To learn more about Friedrich Hayek and his life you can click on: www.en.wikipedia.org/ and use his name as your search expression.

[7] Alan Greenspan's testimony is quoted here by George Packer in an article entitled *End of an Era(2): Greenspan's World View Fails Him*, October 23, 2008. www.newyorker.com/ .

[8] To learn more about the financial meltdown in the United States starting in 2008 use: www.en.wikipedia.org/wiki/ and the search terms "Financial crisis of 2007–08".
[9] See the global world debt here: www.economist.com/content/global_debt_clock and in particular see Public Debt as % of GDP and Public Debt Per Person. June 2013 See also: *Capital and the Debt Trap: Learning from Cooperatives in the Global Crisis*, Claudia Sanchez Bajo and Bruno Roelants by Palgrave MacMillian, 2011 p: 77-78.
[10] See note 9 for up to date global debt levels along a variety of dimension.
[11] See Chapter 8 note 1; *The Collapse of Globalism and the Re-invention of the World.* Penguin Group 2009 P: 36-51.
[12] See note 11 for quotation from back cover of the publication.
[13] To learn more about the Occupy Wall street movement click here: www.occupywallst.org/ .
[14] To learn about the unemployment rates in Europe you can use the Guardian site located here: www.guardian.co.uk/ and then use the search expression "Unemployment in Europe".
[15] A mess may also be called a meta-problem or a problematique. Use this link to download a paper with more detail by Eric Trist www.moderntimesworkplace.com/ and first search for "Eric Trist", then select Volume 3, called The Socio-Ecological Perspective, and below look specifically for a paper entitled "Referent Organizations and the Development of Inter-Organizational Domains". The paper is from a distinguished lecture to the Academy of Management (Organization and Management Theory Division) 39th Annual Convention, Atlanta, Georgia, 1979. This paper was also published in Human Relations, 36:269-84, 1983.
[16] From an interview by Mary Hoff with Johan Rockstrom entitled "What would it take to protect the Earth's systems from catastrophic failure?" See the full interview at www.environment.umn.edu/ by searching for "Johan Rockstrom".
[17] You may need to search for *Bankrupting Nature - Global Risks and Pathways to Global Sustainability*, by Anders Wijkman and Johan Rockstrom, is described in considerable detail here: www.wijkman.se/book/. There is an excellent overview presentation by the authors which is downloadable from: www.ebookbrowsee.net if you use the search terms "bankrupting nature".
[18] To see an overview presentation titled "Bankrupting Nature" by the authors Wijkman and Rockstrom use: www.ebookbrowsee.net and the search terms "bankrupting nature". You can download a copy.
[19] We encourage you to download the 2012 annual report of the Stockholm Resilience Centre from this link: www.stockholmresilience.org/21/about.html . You will also see in the opening pages of their 2012 annual report that the Centre acknowledged the passing of Elinor Ostrom. See also note 20 below.
[20] Elinor Ostrom was a world recognized scientist. Her work was associated with the new institutional economics and the resurgence of political economy. Learn more hear: www.en.wikipedia.org/ and search for "Elinor Ostrom"
[21] An unknown taxi driver who engaged one of the author of this publication in a 20 minute conversation while travelling from central Nairobi to the Jomo Kenyatta International airport in early 2008.
[22] Aga Nkusi worked full time as an administrative assistant for the Uganda Co-operative Alliance while attending university in Kampala Uganda.

Chapter 11
[1] See chapter 8, note 10.
[2] See note 1.

Chapter 12
[1] The internet can also be overwhelming in terms of co-operative related content. If you are so inclined here are a couple of things you can try. In Google try "site:.coop" without the quotes. Or try this search in Google to bring up thousands of images. In your browser go to Google, click Images, and enter "~co-operative" or even "~cooperative". You will get to see co-operatives images from around the world!

CPSIA information can be obtained
at www.ICGtesting.com
Printed in the USA
BVOW04s1404280917
496215BV00011B/42/P